OVERCOMING STUDENT LEARNING BOTTLENECKS

Define
a bottleneck
1

Uncover the
mental task
2

Model tasks
3

Give practice
and feedback
4

Motivate and
lessen resistance
5

Assess
student mastery
6

Share
7

Decoding the Disciplines Wheel

OVERCOMING STUDENT LEARNING BOTTLENECKS

Decode the Critical Thinking of Your Discipline

Joan Middendorf and Leah Shopkow

Foreword by Dan Bernstein

STERLING, VIRGINIA

Published by Stylus Publishing, LLC.
22883 Quicksilver Drive
Sterling, Virginia 20166-2102

Library of Congress Cataloging-in-Publication Data

Names: Middendorf, Joan K., author. |
Shopkow, Leah, author.
Title: Overcoming student learning bottlenecks : decode the critical
thinking of your discipline/Joan Middendorf and Leah Shopkow.
Description: First edition. |
Sterling, Virginia : Stylus Publishing, LLC, 2017. |
Includes bibliographical references and index.
Identifiers: LCCN 2017017026 (print) |
LCCN 2017035756 (ebook) |
ISBN 9781620366646 (cloth : alk. paper) |
ISBN 9781620366653 (pbk. : alk. paper) |
ISBN 9781620366660 (Library networkable e-edition) |
ISBN 9781620366677 (consumer e-edition)
Subjects: LCSH: Critical thinking--Study and teaching. |
Learning, Psychology of. | Group work in education.
Classification: LCC LB2395.35 (ebook) |
LCC LB2395.35 .M53 2017 (print) |
DDC 378.1/662--dc23
LC record available at https://lccn.loc.gov/2017017026

13-digit ISBN: 978-1-62036-664-6 (cloth)
13-digit ISBN: 978-1-62036-665-3 (paperback)
13-digit ISBN: 978-1-62036-666-0 (library networkable e-edition)
13-digit ISBN: 978-1-62036-667-7 (consumer e-edition)

Bulk Purchases

Quantity discounts are available for use in workshops and for
staff development.
Call 1-800-232-0223

First Edition, 2018

10   9   8   7   6   5   4   3   2   1

Contents

FIGURES

TABLES

FOREWORD

*O*vercoming *Student Learning Bottlenecks* captures an important body of work, and it appears at an opportune time for higher education. Joan Middendorf and Leah Shopkow have created a readable and engaging guide to addressing one of the central teaching challenges we all recognize. Many students do not go beyond a novice understanding of the intellectual skills in academic fields, resulting in rote knowledge of our work. In this book the authors explore the skills that differentiate novices from experts and demonstrate how careful course design enables novices to learn expert analysis and thinking. The results they report feel like the holy grail of postsecondary education, helping student go beyond learning the vocabulary of a disciplinary language by mastering the habits of mind characteristic of a field of study. What constitutes evidence? How is the evidence examined, interrogated, and analyzed? What are the conventions for connecting evidence, ideas, and concepts in the field? How do scholars construct an argument? I have been impressed with this work as it unfolded in conference sessions led by the authors, as I saw it in our collaborative projects, and as it has appeared in publications. Now there is an organized guide to the practices and rationale for decoding disciplinary intellectual skills, filled with many well-chosen and well annotated examples.

American higher education is navigating a period of rising national expectations of postsecondary education for virtually everyone. Critics and supporters alike urge more accessible and more successful education, while faculty members must find ways to achieve those goals while maintaining a high quality learning environment and appropriate levels of intellectual achievement. Meeting the demands of retention, completion, and assessment is an important mission of contemporary higher education, and the work richly described in this volume will be a great help. When faculty members ask students to understand intellectual work in more than a rote way, many students feel that academic discourse and analytic skills are an impenetrable barrier to continued or deeper study of a discipline. The discourse and the habits of mind convey important insights, but our descriptions often condense terms used for frequently discussed phenomena, and we mention methods and conceptual analyses only by name without revealing their substance. It is essential that we find ways to bridge that gap between novice and expert language and thinking, so that fewer students are left out of our disciplinary conversations and more will successfully pursue our fields of study.

This book is nicely organized around a series of steps that the authors have found very useful in working with colleagues who want to decode the implicit meanings and methods of academic thinking. The approach focuses on the mental moves characteristic of and necessary in a field, not just on the content of evidence or the resulting concepts derived by practitioners of the discipline. The metaphor of bottlenecks refers to those places in a course or curriculum where the content jumps ahead without explicit description of the mental moves that support, for example, a leap from evidence to conclusion. The redesign methods follow in the tradition of work that breaks complex skills into component parts and starts with assuring recognition of and skill at those initial tasks. The authors take pains to assure readers that they take disciplinary ways of knowing seriously, not as barriers to comprehension but as important structures to be understood.

Overcoming Student Learning Bottlenecks is also a how-to book, filled with hands-on and useful ways to proceed in your analysis of the gaps in your learning plan; the book often addresses "you," the reader, in providing opportunities for exploration of your own courses. Each chapter contains rich examples of how to approach one aspect of course redesign, including stepwise procedures to explore and implement the work of decoding. The examples include useful strategies for engaging students and learning about their challenges, and there are helpful invitations to try out your own examples in a blank template. The chapters constitute an impressive product of the authors' experiences in working with colleagues on the challenge of identifying and filling in gaps in analytic skill. The bottlenecks become places where novices are asked to make expert moves and are provided practice and feedback to learn how to make them.

I feel this book is critically important as a tool to engage a wide range of faculty members. Instead of criticizing the habits of mind of disciplines, it offers dedicated faculty a way to share those valuable skills with a wider range of learners. Our implicit intellectual skills are deeply honored in academic life; people often take pride in making analytic leaps that others (even some colleagues) cannot follow. Even students buy into the status of advanced understanding. I once explained to a class how my course design had helped the vast majority of them to succeed on the most challenging problems. The top student in the class spoke up and said that was "cheating, because you are helping them do what I already learned on my own." Another student responded that it was about time that faculty made learning targets and paths to learning more clear to students. And so I feel this book is a very powerful tool for making a substantial change in academic culture, a change away from expecting deep understanding and simply selecting for it. Middendorf and Shopkow are showing us ways toward teaching and learning.

Overcoming Student Learning Bottlenecks can be used with many audiences. It is an excellent selection for faculty book club conversations or teaching center seminars, as it comes complete with activities groups can adapt to their own purposes. Individual faculty members will also find it useful for individual study, though I expect there would be an enormous urge to share insights and ideas with colleagues. I also think there is a lot of good work in this volume that can be shared with students. Many of us find very good results from being transparent with our students about the nature of our instructional designs. There is less resistance to change and some shared interest in the results of our inquiry into learning. No matter who reads it, however, the fundamental idea driving the work is that people with great academic skills and understanding are not born that way. There are ways that people learn about the implicit habits of mind, assumptions, and conventions of academic and intellectual work. Without claiming universal equality, this book argues that successful teaching can bring many more people into a disciplinary community with expert forms of analysis and discourse. In the final chapter, the authors urge everyone to make their work visible in academic forums so more people can share in the benefits. That chapter also has some excellent conceptual analysis that should not be skipped over. In the best spirit of inductive teaching, those insights come last, not first.

Dan Bernstein
Emeritus Professor of Psychology
University of Kansas

ACKNOWLEDGMENTS

The Freshman Learning Project, out of which Decoding the Disciplines emerged, was devised in 1996 as a result of David Pace and Joan Middendorf's participation in the Indiana University Leadership Institute. Institute leaders Pat Hutchings, Sue Sciame-Gisecke, Barbara Cambridge, and Eileen Bender won a well-deserved John L. Blackburn Award for the Outstanding Administrative Model. Debbie Freund had the foresight to encourage Joan to form a team to participate in that institute.

Decoding the Disciplines could not have come about without the championship of W. Ray Smith, former assistant vice provost for academic affairs at Indiana University Bloomington. He trusted our efforts in the Freshman Learning Project and in the History Learning Project, consistently supporting our experiments and bearing with our failures. To give a few examples, early on in our experimentation with the Freshman Learning Project we realized the significance of bottlenecks to student learning (J. A. Anderson, 1996). Anyone who knows David and Joan could understand our determination not to leave teachers and students stranded at the bottlenecks. There were several unsuccessful exercises, such as giving Ray Smith a knitting lesson (he begged us not to make anyone else do that!) and critiques of the lecture method (which put professors off). The breakthrough that led to decoding came when we interviewed Bob Orsi (a former associate dean) about his students' difficulties in reading. In this first decoding interview, we found that his religious studies students needed to do five kinds of reading within the one course. It was an "aha" moment for him and for us, the first of many decoding interviews that led to more explicit teaching. David Pace modeled gratitude in all the work we did.

Since Joan and David published their model (Middendorf & Pace, 2004), the theoretical aspect of decoding has matured, especially with the collaboration of Arlene Díaz and Leah Shopkow. Arlene has the vision of a natural leader—seeing the possibilities of Decoding the Disciplines for curriculum development and for recognizing the understanding of diversity as a cognitive move. Leah Shopkow's genius lies in making connections between theories, such as her groundbreaking work connecting bottlenecks to epistemology (Shopkow, Díaz, Middendorf, & Pace, 2013a) and defining way stations on the path toward learning threshold concepts (Shopkow & Díaz, forthcoming).

Joan owes a debt of gratitude to all of the Indiana University faculty who participated in learning communities where we developed the model and theory of Decoding the Disciplines—the Freshman Learning Project, the History Learning Project, the Affective Learning Project, the Engaging Differences Faculty Learning Community (FLC), the Inclusion FLC, the School of Informatics and Computing Collegium, the Latino Studies FLC, the Media School Collegium, and the Transformative Learning Collegium. Diane Dormant (2011) has mentored Joan about planned change and diffusion of innovations, because she loves the challenge of a difficult change project. Michael Heinz introduced her to systems thinking. But more importantly, both believed in her. She wants to thank the students in her many pedagogy courses, especially Drew Clark-Huckstep, for his insightful comments on an earlier draft of the book, and Kate Altizer, who articulated expertise in music. She also thanks her colleagues at the Center for Innovative Teaching and Learning.

Every time Joan tried Decoding the Disciplines in a new context, she learned as much as the faculty with whom she worked. She appreciates the colleagues who collaborated with her on overcoming bottlenecks at their universities in every corner of the United States and all over the globe. She offers a special thanks to faculty who allowed us to use their materials— they will be acknowledged in the text. And to all the faculty who let me "decode" their critical thinking—thanks for letting me walk around in your heads.

Leah came to this project from a somewhat different direction. Her first exposure to the scholarship of teaching and learning (SoTL) came through the Peer Review of Teaching Project, which Jennifer Robinson asked her to join in 1998. Jen needs no introduction to SoTLites, who will find in her a tireless champion of SoTL work. While creating her teaching portfolio, Leah encountered Dan Bernstein, whose encouragement has been important and sustaining. She was asked to be a fellow in the Freshman Learning Project in 2002 by David and Joan, and she became one of the founding directors of the History Learning Project, with David, Joan, and Arlene Díaz. Arlene's expertise with social science methodology and her theoretical acumen helped develop that project in too many ways to enumerate. That project also could not have been as successful as it was without the support of Bob Thompson of Duke University, the principal investigator of a Spencer and Teagle Project that helped finance our further research.

Thanks to all the teachers from all the many universities who have participated in Decoding the Disciplines workshops. We have learned from your examples and built on them in this book. And to all the teachers who have joined in decoding research—too many to name here—thanks for inspiring us.

Finally, we would like to thank Erika Biga Lee for the lovely cover design of this book. We hope it will be as great a pleasure to use this book as to look at it!

Happy decoding!

INTRODUCTION

Why Decoding?

Why do you need another book on teaching and learning?

You may be asking yourself this question, whether you are an individual college instructor or an educational developer. So many books have been published purporting to show the one true path to improve student learning or satisfy teaching. What does this book add to that store?

Teachers want their students to do better work but don't know how to get them to do better work without giving them the answers. Teachers are aware that they want to teach students more than a bunch of content, but they aren't really sure what the more is, although they know it when they see it in their own work and in the work of others. In other words, this is a how-to book about the gap between the ways experts and novices think in any discipline (or across fields).

Where this book differs from other approaches to teaching and learning is that it puts a powerful methodology that respects disciplinary difference into the hands of individual instructors. It does not dictate to instructors what paths they should follow toward improving student learning, but shows them how to find the path that works for them and their disciplines. It provides them with tools for evaluating other teaching innovations to find the ones that fit into their own teaching frameworks. For educational developers, it provides a tool for guiding faculty without experiencing pushback against "alien" knowledge (i.e., knowledge from the field of education). And finally, for those who wish it, this methodology provides guidance for creating a teaching commons and for systematic change at the departmental and institutional level.

These are big claims! However, they are based on our experiences working with faculty from a variety of institutions for more than a decade. In the chapters that follow, we will demonstrate the methodology, provide evidence of its efficacy, and explain the pedagogical theory behind it. In this introduction, however, we want to provide an overview of the decoding paradigm and suggest some of the reasons for its power.

What makes the decoding approach different from many other approaches to educational improvement is that it takes disciplines seriously.

By taking disciplines seriously, we do not mean that we think of them as having an objective or eternal existence, that we see them as unchanging, or that we do not recognize that practitioners frequently know or borrow from methods in related disciplines. Nor are we accepting that disciplines are "academic tribes" occupying "territories" (Becher & Trowler, 2001). We are aware of the arguments theorists have had over disciplines and interdisciplinarity, and yet we start from what is: Many scholars who work across disciplines have a "home" or primary discipline that shapes their initial approaches, even if they read widely across disciplines. Most academics teach in departments defined by disciplines and most students take courses in departments defined by disciplines. We would define *disciplines*, then, as epistemic communities, communities of knowing, that produce knowledge through certain tacitly agreed-on rules governing mental moves. We expect our students to be able to make the moves of the disciplines in our classrooms and to understand the rules. Educators have come up with generic models of critical thinking (Paul & Binker, 1990), but our work indicates that critical thinking is specific to each field, differing from discipline to discipline. Educational specialists cannot teach disciplinary experts how to teach—it takes the involvement from within the discipline to define teaching in that field.

Faculty as practitioners may understand their disciplines in this way, as approaches, techniques, and applications. However, they tend to organize their courses around specific contents rather than around the mental moves they want students to make. As a result, their efforts to change what students learn may focus on looking for more engaging or effective content or choosing new classroom "activities" in the hopes of promoting student learning. In contrast, decoding focuses on the mental moves students must learn to make to produce high-quality work, spelling out what "critical thinking" means in a specific disciplinary context. These moves are usually unarticulated within a discipline and may even be so completely internalized by practitioners that they are not aware of them. Not surprisingly, instructors do not teach these moves explicitly, and students, who have experienced many years of schooling in which they were not instructed in disciplinary modes of thought, may not even realize that particular kinds of thinking are called for in a discipline. For instance, students in physics may be used to plugging numbers into a formula to find the answer, rather than thinking about the problem the way a physicist would. Geology students may think that an earthquake can be summed up in a single number, because they do not understand all the components that seismographers consider when studying earthquakes. History students may think that their job is to memorize facts, because they do not understand how historians construct narratives about the past.

Decoding the Disciplines is a methodology that starts at this gap between novice and expert thinking. It shows how to identify places where students get stuck mentally, termed *bottlenecks*, and how to analyze the critical thinking or define specific mental actions that can get them through the bottlenecks. Through "decoding," *implicit* or *tacit* expert modes of thought can be turned into *explicit* mental tasks. These tasks can then be modeled for students, and they can be given the opportunity to practice them. Assessments of the mental actions can then check student performance and reveal where further modeling or practice is needed. The bottleneck and assessment perspective can help teachers in any field become learning centered and vested in the learner's journey.

When, instead of getting annoyed when students don't "get it," teachers look for the bottleneck in which students are getting stuck, their view of what is happening in the classroom shifts. The bottlenecks become helpful indicators. Students are holding up red flags showing where they don't know how to do the critical thinking specific to our disciplines, showing us what needs to be prioritized in the classroom and where to dig in. Learning to recognize bottlenecks is a way of recognizing patterns in student difficulties.

In the process of recognizing bottleneck patterns, decoding reveals the tacit knowledge of expert practitioners. This is the revolutionary kernel of Decoding the Disciplines. Although instructors are very good at judging when a student performance does not meet their expectations, they are often not particularly good at identifying why a performance is substandard, or what the student *should* or *might have done* to produce better work. An instructor might conclude, for instance, that a student didn't understand the reading—which might certainly be true—but not realize, for instance, that the student read for facts without looking for an argument or didn't understand the purpose of a data section in an article. The instructor might tell the students, "Read more carefully!"—advice that under the circumstances wouldn't really address the problem. If instructors are not aware of what reading consists of in their disciplines, they can't make that explicit to students.

Another reason experts may be unconscious of what they do is because they chunk and process information in larger and more complex units than novices (Chase & Simon, 1973; Glaser, Chi, & Farr, 1988). They may very rapidly consider a number of possible words before choosing the right word for a poem or a number of features when identifying an artist's style or a number of possibilities for how DNA is expressed. In the previous example, for instance, a historian might consider the argument of an article at the same time as taking in quite a lot of factual information, while a geologist might skip to the data section of an article first and then look to the end for the conclusions, all without being conscious of doing so. Thus, it takes some practice to learn to decode, but those who do find that mental actions under-lie much of what we do in teaching because they reveal where disciplinary critical thinking occurs—the mental muscles we want students to develop.

At this point, you may be wondering about our emphasis on the disciplinary nature of thinking. Don't we want students to be able to do many kinds of critical thinking? Of course we do! We would make two points about this, however. First, students often believe that there is only one way to think, just as they often believe that there is only one way to read. But how a scientist reads a scientific paper is probably different from how an English scholar reads a literary article, and even within disciplines there are different ways to read depending on one's purpose. To clarify the differences for our students makes their overall learning—whatever disciplines they study—better.

In addition, making the kinds of thinking done in different disciplines explicit actually puts an important intellectual tool in the hands of students. When they know different sorts of mental moves, they get to decide which moves they will apply in a given situation. For instance, they may understand how economists think about concepts such as replacement cost, but they may decide in a given situation that they do not want to think as economists. They may decide to think like historians in their day-to-day lives, but not in their faith communities. They may want to worry about germs and contamination in their labs and not so much in their homes. The same is the case in writing. Helping students become aware of different forms of discourse helps them develop a metacognitive skill—the strategic considerations about writing that differ from discipline to discipline. By deciding on the audience, purpose, and discourse for a writing task, students can use the appropriate moves for the task at hand (Bean, 2011).

The bottlenecks students experience in the classroom frequently arise because students see all sorts of concepts and all sources of information as being more or less the same. Moreover, emotions and learning are completely intertwined (Dragon et al., 2008). To learn, one has to physically change, break old habits, and foster new connections in the brain (Timmermans, 2010). Students tend to use the same mental patterns they have always used; it's more comfortable than trying something new. Decoding the Disciplines shows teachers how to help students differentiate conceptions arising from outside of disciplinary thought from those originating within it, by making the contrast between external conceptions and the disciplinary ways of operating clear.

For example, media encourage students to associate immigration with "illegals" violating American borders in a great uncontrolled flood. In a history class, however, students might instead examine historical patterns showing emigration as well as immigration. They have to understand that this media image is not a historical one. They might, however, consider historically how this media image came to be. Similarly, in an ethnic studies class, students might look at immigration through the lens of administration. They might look at the government agencies controlling immigration and how these have shifted toward a more militarized and criminalized treatment of illegal immigrants. Just like the history students, the students in ethnic studies would have to come to understand that the media image of complete lack of control is not supported by disciplinary thought, and the ethnic studies students might similarly apply disciplinary thought to consider why this might be so.

Other concepts students may bring in from outside of a given discipline similarly impede their learning. For example, students in a service-learning class may understand their efforts in terms of volunteerism, instead of reciprocity (all participants, including community partners, as cogenerators of knowledge). And in a geology class, students may think of the age of the earth in terms of their religious beliefs (6,000 years) rather than in terms of science (4.6 billion years from fossil record and isotopic analysis). In a history class, they may judge historical "winners" and "losers" rather than see events from the viewpoint of a person living in that earlier time. To overcome student resistance to new ways of thinking, we show their conceptual category compared to the expert or disciplinary way of thinking (Middendorf, Mickut, Saunders, Najar, Clark-Huckstep, & Pace, 2015). We can further help students recognize the difference between the way people think about these issues outside of the discipline and inside of the discipline, contrasting analogies for the two, taking the similarities and differences into account (Jones, Ross, Lynam, Perez, & Leitch, 2011). In other words, decoding can show students the exact mental action (or "mental muscles") to use to operate in a field, while allowing students to recognize that different situations may call for different sorts of thinking.

The Decoding Process in Brief

In the chapters that follow we will write at length about each of the seven steps (see Figure I.1) of the Decoding the Disciplines model, but we will present them briefly here:

- Step 1—Identify bottlenecks to learning.
  Using student work, we identify a place or places where many students get "stuck" in their learning.
- Step 2—Decode what experts do.

Figure I.1. The Decoding the Disciplines wheel.

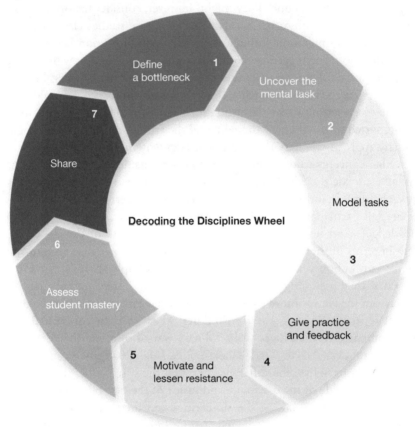

We define the *mental action* a specialist would take to avoid getting stuck in the way the students have gotten stuck.

- Step 3—Model the mental actions.
  We explicitly model the mental actions we want students to do to negotiate the bottleneck.
- Step 4—Give practice and feedback.
  We design a classroom practice or assignment in which students are required to perform the mental action. We give them feedback about where they need to make improvements.
- Step 5—Motivate students to use the mental action.
  We hold students accountable for practicing the mental actions they need to master. We design courses to disrupt old learning habits that impede learning. We provide additional modeling and practice as needed.

- Step 6—Assess student performance on the mental action.
  We ask students to apply the thinking they have learned to an authentic disciplinary task to see how well they are able to do this.
- Step 7—Share findings with others.
  We share what we've found with others, through informal conversations, through discussion in learning communities, through more formal presentations, through the scholarship of teaching and learning (SoTL), and through strategic decoding and planned change.

The first two steps of decoding—the bottlenecks and the tacit thinking of the expert—drive the later teaching and assessment steps, because they clarify what students need to learn. They uncover the epistemology of the discipline and are the intellectual core of the methodology. The next four steps are the application part of the methodology, in which the instructor teaches the students the requisite thinking and measures how effective the instruction has been. These steps are inherently less distinct from each other; for example, one form of modeling might be to walk students through a practice assignment, while practice assignments can also be used as assessments. The iterative nature of the decoding process tends to blur the distinctions between these steps. We will speak at length about the seventh step, which individual instructors working alone may not choose to take, but which we have found to be enormously powerful.

It may seem from the previous model that decoding is very focused on one specific mental action in one specific discipline and that it is consequently narrow. There are a number of reasons why this isn't the case. Just because our theory is called "Decoding the Disciplines," some assume it means we are limited to working only within disciplinary boundaries. Disciplines are silos holding a set of mental actions that make up one way of creating knowledge. By uncovering disciplinary tacit knowledge we can make it available to students. But decoding also works well in cross-disciplinary fields, whose silos comprise a different cross section of mental actions. Our work with cross-disciplinary groupings revealed early on the value of many perspectives, which participants found very helpful and which identified unexpected insights into the similarities and differences among disciplines. For example, close reading can appear in literature, history, and informatics, just as evidence has to be deployed in geology, accounting, and history. When an accountant and a geologist compare their notions of evidence with each other, the similarities and differences help each of them see the epistemologies of their disciplines more clearly; in other words, it is easier to see the shapes of disciplines in comparison to each other. The cross-disciplinary process creates a transformative community. As one participant reported, "This cross pollination of ideas is incredibly deep and is fully shaping my work and professional and personal identities. . . . I am getting increasingly aware of my own thinking and approaches" (Pettit, Calvert, Dean, Gleeson, Lexier, Rathburn, & Understood, 2017, p. 79).

The other misconception is that faculty members, when they use the decoding process, are concentrating on just one skill and that this may be too narrow, as students need many skills. When we look at one significant bottleneck, such as in history, where we made our original breakthrough, we realized that the places students got stuck were often connected to the underlying epistemology of history. When an instructor focused on one of these significant bottlenecks, student understanding increased in many areas, not just in the one the instructor focused on. Defining the epistemology can keep instructors focused on the most essential learning in a field, and we found it can increase student learning (Shopkow, Díaz, Middendorf, & Pace, 2013b). As we have worked with teachers on individual classes and lessons, we have increasingly realized that we are clarifying the underlying epistemologies of different fields. This emerges very clearly from cross-disciplinary discussions. Perhaps we can't (in the beginning) describe the kinds of knowing in our fields, but when we see yours across the room, which might be very different from ours, perhaps somewhat similar, or maybe even largely the same, our own ways of operating and the epistemology our fields (the mechanisms of thought that produce the characteristic knowledge and meaning within a discipline) become clearer to us. These also emerge when we look at significant bottlenecks.

Individuals or Teams? Sharing or Not?

From what we have said, it should be clear that we have found collaborative work to be a forceful way to apply the decoding model to improve student learning. In our workshops, we tend to form teams of three individuals from different disciplines, keeping the same teams for most of the exercises, because team members familiar with one another's bottlenecks are in a good position to generate appropriate analogies, practice exercises, and assessments that fit the mental actions.

We have run such groups for half days over two weeks, for 3 eight-hour days, for a year (or two) with once monthly meetings, and for as little as half a day or a couple of hours. When we are working within a short time frame, we focus on Steps 1 through 3 (bottlenecks, decoding, and modeling, usually in the form of analogies). When we have a little more time we will add in Step 6. When we have longer periods of time, we are able to have faculty fully develop their bottleneck lessons and assessment plans. When we meet over longer time frames, faculty collect iterative assessments and review them with their teams, making adjustments to the bottleneck lessons along the way.

Still, we recognize that to have this kind of time is a luxury. Many faculty will have time for only one workshop, in which case the rest of the process may have to be pursued individually. In addition, many faculty members would prefer to work alone, and it is possible to use decoding successfully on one's own. We also recognize that faculty may wish to work in informal groups, without an educational developer or facilitator present. Finally, some faculty will choose to join a more formal faculty learning community led by a facilitator. Throughout this book, therefore, we have provided guidance for all three circumstances.

In the same way, we think that sharing what one has learned is an excellent way to clarify for oneself what one has learned and to master it fully. Not for nothing did the medical profession used to say, "Watch one, do one, teach one!" Sharing is the logical extension of our role as teachers. This kind of sharing can be very informal. In fact, if you are working in a group, whether formal or informal, you are probably already sharing what you are learning. But sharing in a more formal way closes the gap between teaching and research, clarifying that these are indeed related activities. One of the reasons for founding SoTL was to serve as a base in the disciplines and to bridge the gap between teaching and research (Boyer, 1997).

However, many faculty members will want to apply decoding without sharing, wishing only to become scholarly teachers. This too is an excellent thing, and we intend this book to provide many ideas about how to apply one's classroom research short of sharing it.

Decoding Beyond the Disciplines

While decoding is a highly effective methodology for improving student learning, we do not see it as standing alone. There is a large body of literature about teaching and learning available at all of our fingertips these days. The problem for teachers is figuring out what applies. Teachers often adopt a teaching tip or approach and then are disappointed that it doesn't work well for them. While the problem may be that the teacher has not fully understood how to implement the technique, it may also be that the technique was ill suited to what the teacher was trying to do. When teachers have a clear notion of what kind of thinking they want their students to do, they are better able to sort through all of the possible assessments and techniques written about in the literature.

However, the other reality of teaching is that teachers are not artisanal workers. They do not teach any given student everything from the introductory course through the capstone. This teaching is done across departments. Similarly, in American education a student's disciplinary work is likely to be no more than one-third of his or her course work. Departments and universities are systems. Decoding can be very useful in promoting effective curriculum design within departments and discussions of student learning across institutions. This book is also intended to offer a sense of where decoding can fit into larger structures.

The Chapters

Each of the chapters in this book includes exercises to show teachers how to bring students into the critical thinking that comprises their discipline. We have provided at least one exercise that can be done individually and one that can be done in a group (whether formal or informal). We have provided examples from many disciplines. You may find examples from your own discipline useful, but examples from disciplines different from your own may help you learn the Decoding the Disciplines processes by seeing the methods without being drawn into the content. In addition, seeing how someone else's discipline thinks is very helpful in clarifying what is specific to your own. Finally, we offer two examples of a bottleneck lesson, one for a scientific discipline and one for a humanities discipline, to model how one might create such a plan for oneself. These two lesson plans appear as Appendix A. In Appendix B we provide a blank template for readers to use themselves.

The *bottleneck*, the term the decoding methodology uses for the places where students get stuck, is the subject of chapter 1. In this chapter we show how to identify significant bottlenecks in your students' work and how to select a good bottleneck on which to focus. Experts can do many things quickly and at once. Bottlenecks show us where the expert thinking needs to be decoded so that the novice can be brought into that kind of thinking. The goal of this chapter is for you to identify a good bottleneck to decode.

In chapter 2 we turn to the actual decoding step, figuring out what experts do or what students might do to avoid getting caught in the bottleneck. Here we provide several different methods for decoding, depending on whether you are working alone or in a group. We show how individuals can use modeling of objects, rubrics, a reflective writing process, and analogies to decode and explain how to conduct a decoding interview for people working in groups. The goal of this chapter is for you to have clarified the mental actions—the components of critical thinking in your field—that your students need to master in order to progress through your bottleneck.

Simply being told about a mental action isn't enough for most students to learn to do it. In chapter 3, we discuss how to model the mental actions for the students, rendering the actions clearer to them. We pay particular attention to how to develop and use analogies, which we have found help students see which "mental muscles" this mental action takes.

Once students have seen a demonstration of the kind of thinking they need to do, they need to practice it. Chapter 4 explains the process for matching the mental action to teaching methods for different types of mental moves. We will also discuss the feedback students need to direct their improvement efforts and the value of iterative practice with that feedback in mind.

When students are asked to use new (to them) disciplinary forms of reasoning, they can resist and revert to methods they are used to. In addition, some of the material and even some of the subjects we teach have an emotional resonance that gets in the way of student learning. Chapter 5 explores two different issues. First, we discuss emotional bottlenecks, which often point to areas where the categories students bring into the classroom conflict violently with disciplinary constructs. Second, we discuss methods to hold students accountable for doing the work in the modeling and practice steps that will ensure that the students get used to new mental habits. By designing final assignments that make use of social pedagogies, teachers can organize their courses in ways that undercut students' earlier habits (e.g., regurgitation of content, just going through the motions, or not doing the work) and reduce the likelihood of their reverting to ineffective learning behaviors.

Chapter 6 explains how to assess student mastery on the mental action. While in many ways the assessments faculty do to determine how well their students have negotiated the bottleneck look a lot like the practice the students have done, we have further suggestions about what faculty can do with their results.

Chapter 7 addresses the issue of what teachers can do with their results if they choose to share them. Faculty may wish to apply their results only to their own classroom as a form of action research, but we suggest some ways of reflecting on that experience. They may also wish to present their findings informally or formally, orally or in writing, and we discuss the ways of benefiting from the feedback and support of belonging to a teaching community. In this chapter, we also explore systems thinking and planned change to bring about educational transformation beyond the individual classroom, including for curriculum design and program assessment.

Although the research on teaching and learning is embedded in every chapter, chapter 8 situates Decoding the Disciplines in relation to the larger field of SoTL and its relation to specific research and theories—cognitive science, troublesome knowledge, epistemology, threshold concepts, backward course design, and signature pedagogies. We also show decoding as a natural partner for SoTL and demonstrate its function vis-à-vis teaching innovations and pedagogy courses.

Decoding the Disciplines is a pedagogical theory about how to bridge the gap between novice and expert thinking and a seven-step methodology for teaching to bottlenecks—the places where students get stuck on their way to expert thinking. Together the bottleneck and assessment perspective can help teachers in any field become learning centered and invested in the learner's journey. By helping students get through even one bottleneck, we can help them better understand the nature of a discipline. Beyond the individual classroom, decoding can be applied to curricula, departments, institutions, and fields. While decoding is not a cure-all, if it has to do with learning, decoding can usually provide a useful frame.

STEP 1

Identifying Bottlenecks To Learning

Some teachers complain about their students' work: "Students can't write; students have not mastered high school math; they lack basic scientific skills; they want me to provide the answers; they don't know where things are on a map of the world." It is probably true that students don't know how to do many of these things, but they are the students we have in front of us. We can complain about this, or we can take a more productive approach.

We prefer to view the places where students encounter difficulty and get stuck in the learning process as bottlenecks. They can serve as the starting point for much useful work. When we view these places where students get stuck as bottlenecks, instead of contenting ourselves with criticizing the students, we shift our attention to the places where they legitimately struggle to perform the mental moves that make up the critical thinking of a field. Identifying a bottleneck provides teachers with a sense of ownership of the issue and often a sense of commitment to working on it. Furthermore, identifying the bottlenecks is crucial to provide a basis for connecting critical thinking with teaching (Shopkow, Díaz, Middendorf, & Pace, 2013a).

This chapter will focus on the first step in the Decoding the Disciplines process: identifying bottlenecks to student learning. We will define *bottlenecks*, describe their relation to critical thinking, and explain the value of seeing patterns in student bottlenecks. Because some bottlenecks are more significant to a given instructor and more central to disciplinary thinking than others, we will describe how to select and refine them. When teachers have completed Step 1, they will be able to see student difficulty in a new way that challenges pervasive assumptions about teaching and learning. More importantly, this step prepares teachers to follow their bottleneck through the rest of the Decoding the Disciplines process and to uncover expert thinking that helps students develop new competencies.

Bottlenecks and Patterns of Bottlenecks

In Step 1 of "decoding," teachers identify places where large numbers of students have difficulty mastering essential tasks—that is, bottlenecks—in their courses. Bottlenecks are places where students get stuck, even when the teacher has carefully presented the disciplinary concepts and when students have been attempting to do the preparatory work. For example, students may struggle with the following:

- Analyzing a text and inferring an author's intent in writing it
- Making sense of geologic and evolutionary processes that occur across vast timescales
- Generating hypotheses in science or arguments in history

There are always a few students who have little trouble with these bottlenecks (often seen as students who are "naturally" talented). This may divert attention from a large group that legitimately struggles with them. Teachers may conclude that these students simply haven't worked hard enough.

Instead of blaming students for learning difficulties, expert teachers learn to value bottlenecks and teach to them, because when students get caught in a bottleneck, they are showing us where our own critical thinking is not clear to students. The direct connection between bottlenecks and ways of operating is one of the key ideas of Decoding the Disciplines, first pointed out by Arlene Díaz (Shopkow et al., 2013a). Learning to spot the bottlenecks— getting the bottleneck perspective—is a way of identifying where students need additional or different instruction.

Teachers who want to address these critical thinking moves switch from thinking about the content as the organizing principle of the course to what students will *do* with the content. To put it another way, they consider what type of thinking the students need to learn. The difference can be quite striking. For example, when a course on personal finance (see Figure 1.1) is organized by its content, the instructor might spend a class on each topic: "If this is Tuesday, the topic is 'Compound Interest'; Wednesday the topic is 'Building a Financial Vocabulary.'" Topics with more content may be given more time, even if students don't find them particularly difficult. But when the course is organized around important bottlenecks in the material, topics that students struggle with get priority. Time is better spent guiding students through the difficult process of thinking differently rather than covering material. Thus, compound interest, risk/return trade-off, and inflation may be allotted more time and effort, while less difficult topics, such as building a financial vocabulary, which students simply need to memorize,

Figure 1.1. Personal finance course organization (Kimberly Fatten, Indiana University), showing organization by coverage (left) and by conceptual difficulty (right).

Equal time for all topics	Bottlenecks prioritized
1. Compound interest 2. Building a financial Vocabulary 3. Budget, savings, & debt 4. Anatomy of a paycheck 5. Saving prioritizations 6. Investment horizons 7. Risk adversity 8. Risk/return trade-off 9. Investment vehicles 10. Retirement projection 11. Balancing liquidity and risk With savings goals 12. Inflation	1. **Compound interest** (Building a financial vocabulary) 3. **Budget, savings, & debt** (Anatomy of a paycheck) 5. **Saving prioritizations** (Investment horizons) 7. **Risk adversity** 8. **Risk/return Trade-off** 9. Investment vehicles 10. Retirement projection 11. Balancing liquidity and risk with savings goals 12. **Inflation**

or analyzing a paycheck, may be de-emphasized or assigned as a homework reading. By giving priority to the bottlenecks rather than equal time to every course topic, teachers allocate precious course effort where the students need it most.

Bottlenecks, while varying in scope and scale and types of thinking required to overcome them, are nonetheless the impediments that students encounter in our courses. Across many different disciplines, students can encounter similar bottlenecks. The good news is that all of these different types of thinking can be taught and learned. Take "reading," for example. Students habitually read any text—a book, a play, an article—to find out "what happened." They have been taught to look for the plot, whether that text is a historical source, a dramatic play, or even a scientific report. Students may not know that there are different ways to read and that these differ depending on the field of study (see Figure 1.2). Yet each of the disciplines has its own ways of reading that instructors practice without thinking about them. Students don't know about these methods because they are never told about them; consequently, they make mistakes.

That students don't read the way a discipline requires, therefore, isn't a sign that they are lazy but that they've hit a bottleneck. For instructors,

Figure 1.2. Bottlenecks in reading.

Students may not know that in

Literature—they need to bring other texts to bear on the text at hand or that multiple interpretations are possible. They may not realize that they need to invent a backstory for a character.

History—there is a difference between reading a primary source and a secondary source. They may read an argument as evidence, if they do not know that arguments are being made.

Geology—scientific papers have distinct parts, each with its own function. They may not know what the parts are or what role they play in the paper as a whole.

---

then, the important thing is to learn to recognize when students have hit a bottleneck. We begin working with bottlenecks by noticing where students experience one.

Identifying and Refining Bottlenecks (Working Solo)

Identifying a Bottleneck

There are several approaches to identifying bottlenecks where students get stuck. When a teacher has taught a course before, he or she is probably aware of places where students have gotten stuck. When a teacher has not yet taught the target course and thus has not run into the bottlenecks, experienced teachers can be a resource on this topic. A literature search is another way to locate common bottlenecks in a particular subject. You can use one of the exercises at the end of the chapter to identify bottlenecks in your class.

Most experienced teachers can readily identify the mistakes students make over and over again. Teacher reflection on where students have repeatedly struggled to learn is the fastest way to identify bottlenecks. Looking through past student work can also clarify places where students frequently get stuck, particularly when the teacher concentrates on categories of errors rather than individual mistakes (see Exercise 1.1).

When teachers have never taught a particular course or topic, however, they may not know where the bottlenecks lie. In this case, experienced teachers who have taught the course can help uncover the bottlenecks because they are likely to know where they appear. If these teachers are not familiar with the term *bottleneck*, you can ask questions to get at the concept without using the term (see Exercise 1.2).

At least initially, the answers a teacher gives may seem somewhat vague, such as, "The students can't interpret texts." You will need to probe for more specific answers ("What do they do when they're trying to interpret a text?" "When they write down their interpretations, what do they say?" "What aren't the students doing with their textual interpretations that you usually do?") until you arrive at a very specific picture of where the struggle lies and you can restate the bottleneck in detail. It may be useful to ask several teachers who have taught the target course to name some bottlenecks. If several teachers report the same bottlenecks, these bottlenecks are probably worth your efforts.

As an example, Joan asked an experienced teacher (Gordon Rowland, Department of Strategic Communication, Ithaca College) about where the bottlenecks lie in a course on systems thinking. He was readily able to describe four bottlenecks:

1. Systems modeling. Students often have difficulty using systems modeling as a tool to gain new insights rather than simply express what they already know. In other words, they tend to produce simplified graphics for an audience, as they've been taught in communication design classes, rather than use modeling as a means to explore the complexity of a system to further their own understanding.

2. Systems ontology. It takes a while for them to get their heads around the notion that systems are artificial constructions—our representations of the world, not the world itself. (The system is the integrated set of elements *we* designate as comprising the system.)

3. Emergence. It can take some pushing to get them to explore deep enough to recognize emergent properties and to distinguish such properties from characteristics of parts.

4. Boundary setting. In systems modeling students will distinguish a system from its systemic environment, but then create other types of models of the same system that cross the boundary they just established (i.e., they model different systems rather than create multiple models of the same system). I need to revisit this bottleneck multiple times. (G. Rowland, personal e-mail communication, March 11, 2017)

It's no wonder students struggle to learn systems thinking (and teachers struggle to teach it): These are challenging mental moves, and students might find it difficult to move away from simple model-based reasoning.

Another way to determine bottlenecks is to turn to the research literature. Bottlenecks can be cognitive, procedural, or affective, and thus may include both persistent science misconceptions and threshold concepts, bottlenecks being the overarching category. Failure to understand the reasoning behind bottlenecks, misconceptions, and threshold concepts can block student understanding. Because these are common difficulties for students, chances are the work of identifying bottlenecks has already been done in some fields and will appear in the scholarly literature.

There is a growing literature on bottlenecks. Abbott (2015) describes the bottleneck of making and documenting objective observations in music therapy. In history, students misunderstand the interpretive nature of the historical discipline; they also get caught in bottlenecks in generating arguments and analyzing primary sources, operate from a presentist rather than disciplinary perspective, find it difficult to tolerate ambiguity, and have difficulty maintaining an appropriate emotional distance (Middendorf, Pace, Shopkow, & Díaz, 2007; Shopkow, Díaz, Middendorf, & Pace, 2013b). In political science, students face the emotional bottlenecks of discomfort in dealing with conflict and minority rights (Bernstein, 2013). In mathematics, students tend to read mathematical expressions sequentially rather than holistically and focus on the operational character (rather than the explanatory role) of mathematical definitions, both mathematical literacy-related bottlenecks (Riegler, 2016). In psychology, students are overconfident and also encounter difficulty with introductory concepts (Gurung & Landrum, 2013). Some of the literature not only identifies bottlenecks but also offers some analysis of them or ways to address them, as in the math case, where some remedies are proposed that a teacher might further test, or in the psychology case, where the troublesome concepts are organized in a hierarchy for teachers to concentrate on.

There is a well-developed literature on science misconceptions (Chi, 2005), on such topics as electricity, heat and temperature, and evolution—proven bottlenecks. To come up with a bottleneck, especially for science, technology, engineering, and math (STEM) courses, teachers can search this literature for persistent misconceptions along with their course topic.

The literature in threshold concepts can also reveal important bottlenecks in many fields. Threshold concepts is a theory of difficulty that posits that certain concepts are crucial to the understanding of a discipline, that many students have great difficulty with these concepts, but that they are necessary for students to move forward. (For more discussion on threshold concepts and other theories related to Decoding the Disciplines, see chapter 8.) For example, Ross and colleagues (2010) describe the importance of variation and change over large timescales as fundamental for biology and evolution. Davies and Mangan (2007) describe opportunity cost (the opportunities an individual foregoes when choosing a particular course of action) as a threshold concept in economics.

The key to a successful literature search for bottlenecks is the use of appropriate key words. We recommend that you do Boolean searches using the name of your discipline, alternating with the terms *bottlenecks, misconceptions,* or *threshold concepts.* We recommend that you try them all, as, for instance, the term *bottlenecks* can be used in different contexts (e.g., to talk about population bottlenecks in biology). You may also search using the name of your discipline and "concept inventory." Concept inventories are lists of basic concepts particular to a discipline. Invariably, some of these concepts cause problems for many students. While not all disciplines have concept inventories, those that do (physics, statistics, engineering, biology, chemistry) sometimes have tests to evaluate student mastery of these concepts.

Once you have found the bottlenecks in the literature, you will need to make sure that the bottlenecks you've identified are issues that particularly concern you or are crucial to your course. If you are not particularly concerned about whether students master the concept of replacement cost in economics because your course is on the economics of philanthropy, you wouldn't choose that to work on. If you are teaching about modern ecosystems, you might want students to understand geological timescale, but it might be less pertinent to your course. And if you are teaching a course on nonfiction writing, selecting the exact right word would be a useful skill for students to have but might be less important to concentrate on than in a course on writing poetry.

Why does identifying a worthwhile bottleneck matter? For one thing, you will be using it for the rest of the book as we uncover the tacit knowledge that experts automatically use to avoid bottlenecks, which are often complex, multistepped mental moves. And because bottlenecks are related to our field or discipline, they tell us something about our field, which again may be invisible to the expert.

Using one of the three methods—a problem observed by a teacher in his or her own class, suggestions from an experienced teacher, or a literature search—you can generate a list of bottlenecks for the course. Before we move on to what you will do with the bottleneck (Steps 2–7), it is worth spending some time refining the bottlenecks and deciding which one to focus on. We usually recommend that a teacher focus on one bottleneck at a time, because given the need for students to practice the mental operations, it is not possible to focus on multiple bottlenecks within the time frame of a course. This means the instructor has to narrow down the list to one significant bottleneck and refine that bottleneck to make as clear as possible what that bottleneck entails.

Refining the Bottleneck

There are two parts to refining a bottleneck. The first is to select one bottle-neck from among the possibilities to focus on in your course. The second is to make the contours of the bottleneck as clear as possible to yourself and to make sure that you are dealing with a single bottleneck, rather than a complex bottleneck with a number of components.

Selecting a Bottleneck to Work on From Among Several

Often a course has more than one bottleneck. That is, even when the course is well designed and uses active learning methods, several concepts still tend to trip up students. It is advisable to select a *crucial* bottleneck that inhibits student learning (e.g., providing evidence for an argument) to work on initially even though some faculty are quite bothered by procedural errors such as students not using the proper citation format or getting dates wrong. Note, however, that some bottlenecks may be too trivial to merit the amount of effort involved in teaching students to negotiate it. For example, students in English frequently shift tenses improperly or fail to make their verbs and nouns agree. While there are concepts about good writing and correct grammar that underlie errors of this kind and these errors are not trivial in the sense that they mark one as a poor writer, the errors are not produced by larger epistemological blockages. Students can relatively swiftly be taught to check their writing for this sort of error and given (or helped to develop) checklists for doing so.

What do you do if you have more than one bottleneck? You should choose the one that bothers you the most, because your frustration suggests that this bottleneck is closely connected to what you are trying to teach that the students are not learning. The centrality of the bottleneck to your course will make it worth the time to invest in it, and it probably also means that the bottleneck is very important to your discipline.

This doesn't mean that in a given course there is one "right" bottleneck on which to focus. Different teachers tend to focus on different aspects of disciplinary thinking and to take different approaches to the material that get students stuck in different ways. Our job as teachers is to expand student understanding of the elements we are trying to teach them, but we cannot possibly teach them everything they ought to know. This observation should alleviate some of the fears teachers often have that when they concentrate on one element of learning they are letting students down by neglecting others. As teachers, we are always prioritizing some things over others. But because significant bottlenecks are connected through the larger epistemologies of the disciplines (Shopkow et al., 2013a), when a teacher concentrates on one and improves understanding, a student's general understanding is likely to be improved. We also have to trust our colleagues to be concentrating on aspects of learning that are crucial to our disciplines. This is why it is important to focus on aspects that are central to the ways practitioners in our discipline think, not just things students often do wrong, such as using the wrong citation style.

To help choose among several bottlenecks, you can apply the following criteria:

- *Common and frequent*: Do many students get stuck on this one? Does it trip students up every time you teach the course?
- *Foundational*: Is it needed for later course work, something the work builds on, such as force concepts in physics?
- *Central*: Is it critical to operating in the field, such as the concept of bias in data for any field involving statistics (not superficial like calculation errors)?
- *Aggravating*: Does the students' inability to "get" this concept frustrate either the teacher or the students a great deal?

You should not be too concerned about picking the "perfect" bottleneck. There may be two (or more) perfectly good bottlenecks in a course. Choosing the right bottleneck will not solve all the problems your students experience in the course, and if you wait until you have a perfect understanding of each bottleneck, you won't be able to get started. The good news is that teachers can switch to a different bottleneck or refine the bottleneck at any time. This highlights one of the important ways in which research of this kind differs from classical educational research, where interventions are planned and carried out and then the results of the experiment are assessed. In our context, given our responsibilities for our students and their learning, it would be irresponsible not to respond to what we learn about their understanding as we learn it. The bottleneck perspective actually provides you with tools to change course as needed.

Still, the more specific a teacher is about the nature of the bottleneck, the easier it will be to decode it (see chapter 2). The examples in Figure 1.3 show the difference between less and more fruitful descriptions of bottlenecks.

The observations in the useful cases are specific and provide enough information to serve as a starting place for the analysis of the bottlenecks.

Identifying Bottlenecks Within Bottlenecks
Once a bottleneck has been selected from the few that were identified, you may find that, on further analysis, the bottlenecks contain sub-bottlenecks—multilayered tasks within a bottleneck that are in effect bottlenecks within

Figure 1.3. Clarifying the bottlenecks.

1. English
Vague: Students cannot interpret texts.
Useful: Students in literature classes have a particular problem in the basic approach to textual interpretation. Students forever want to go directly to interpreting a text without first getting a good grasp of a text's content. They need to observe before they interpret, but they are constantly skipping a thoughtful observation stage. Skipping this stage leads to poor interpretations. (P. Gutjahr, personal communication, May 12, 2001)
2. Biology
Vague: Students have difficulty moving from fact learning to a deeper understanding of biological processes.
Useful: Students have difficulty visualizing chromosomes, appreciating the distinction between similar and identical chromosomes (i.e., homologs and sister chromatids), and predicting their segregation patterns during mitosis and meiosis. (Zolan, Strome, & Innes, 2004, p. 26)

bottlenecks, like the layers of an onion that when peeled back reveal more layers. For example, a teacher may find that students cannot write, but writing includes more than the mechanics of grammar and sentence-level construction. Students may not understand that different fields have different forms of discourse, as well as different writing conventions. We give examples of some of these differences in Figure 1.4, recognizing that many fields use more than one kind of writing and that each sort of writing might involve strategies and conventions peculiar to it.

For students to write in the discipline, they need to know that different forms of discourse exist and which one they are operating in. When instructors assume that students intuitively know what they mean by "writing," they are actually assuming that students have a whole set of skills and understandings, each of which can constitute a sub-bottleneck. For example, in history, what *is* evidence? What kinds of arguments or interpretations can historians make and not make? What does using evidence to support an interpretation entail? In English, a literary textual analysis begins with multiple readings of the text; situating the text in its social and historical contexts; deconstructing the text using a variety of critical strategies (e.g., Marxism, feminism,

Figure 1.4. Disciplinary functions of writing.

In . . .	Writing may mean . . .
History	Making an argument backed by primary and secondary source evidence
Literature	Providing textual analysis and/or bringing other texts to bear on the one the writer is working on
Geology	Asking a question, collecting data, analyzing the evidence, and drawing conclusions
Journalism	Collecting information and presenting news in a highly specific narrative form for a public audience
Education	Describing or testing the application of a model based on an educational theory
Accounting	Collecting, analyzing, and judging key financial documents in order to make recommendations to clients

structuralism, poststructuralism, postmodernism, reception theory, psychoanalysis); bringing to bear what, if anything, everyone else has said about that text; and comparing other texts to this text. In journalism, as traditionally practiced, students need to be able to encapsulate a story in their first paragraph, meaning that they have to distill the essence of the story and then create a hierarchy of details, obviously connected but distinctive protocols. Narrowing down the bottleneck to the sub-bottleneck, the component of the larger but less focused bottleneck, makes it more likely that you will be able to get students through the bottleneck. In creative writing, starting with the recognition that students don't know how to interpret a poem, and choosing a particularly challenging step from the many steps of interpretation, such as that students tend to avoid the most difficult, seemingly daunting features of a poem, makes it more likely to successfully get them through this part of the bottleneck. And when we can get them through one specific bottleneck well, they tend to get a better idea of the larger bottleneck. The job of the teacher is to decide which layer of a bottleneck will be the focus—and students help with this because they show us which layers of the bottlenecks give them the most trouble. What we think is a single bottleneck often turns out to have many sub-bottlenecks.

Refining Bottlenecks Through Assessment of Student Work
Once we have a bottleneck in mind, it is useful to find out more specifically where the students are getting stuck. The bottleneck is our best guess, but we can actually collect evidence, either through brief assessments or through interviewing students.

In the example in Figure 1.5, the teacher has noticed that students in a course on personal finance struggle with compound interest. The teacher can ask students to answer a question (in class or for homework) that will help pin down their preconceptions or get more information about where they may deploy nondisciplinary concepts instead of the disciplinary way of operating. Figure 1.5 shows possible questions and prompts to uncover student bottlenecks about compounding interest (see Angelo & Cross, 1993, and chapter 6 for similar assessments).

We ask, "Why do you say that?" in the first and fifth questions to get students to think metacognitively—that is, to reflect strategically on their own learning. It is most useful in situations when students may have rote answers that don't necessarily involve reflection (e.g., if we asked students why scientific modes of thought were important, they might say that without it our gadgets couldn't be relied on to work, which is true, but not profound). When we ask the second question, we are asking the students to move beyond course material to their own thinking. This sometimes reveals thought processes that have gone unnoticed and that do not align with critical thinking within a discipline, which may block their learning in it, and which may help you refine the bottleneck.

The concept map is an especially powerful assessment because it reveals students' conceptual grasp; it shows the taxonomy the students are using and what elements they bring to bear on the subject. For instance, when we ask students to use a map to show a process or to sort different elements into

Figure 1.5. Getting more evidence about the compounding interest bottleneck.

1. What is compounding interest? Why do you say that?

2. Compounding interest is like . . . ? (Analogy Classroom Assessment Technique [CAT]).

3. Assign a simple compounding interest problem. Ask students to answer the problem down one column of a page and in the second column describe in words what they did at each step to solve it (Documented Problem Solution CAT).

4. Write a letter to a roommate or friend describing what he or she needs to *do* to perform well in a class on compounding interest.

5. How will we study compounding interest? Why do you say that?

6. Make a concept map of the time value of money.

categories, we can see how they are understanding processes and what categories they are using. When we get such feedback, we can see the patterns of their mistakes. This is one of the most important themes of this book: Decoding the Disciplines assessments help teachers to view critical ways of operating in the disciplines from the students' viewpoint.

Refining Bottlenecks Through Partnerships With Students
One of the newest approaches to decoding encourages student–teacher partnerships so that students may better identify the bottlenecks and the gaps between the expert and novice ways of operating (Rouse, Phillips, Mehaffey, McGowan, & Felten, 2017; see chapter 8). The burgeoning practice of undergraduate research encourages the inclusion of students in teaching and learning development efforts. Undergraduates can be taught what bottlenecks are and can, in partnership with the teacher, interview other students about the bottlenecks they are experiencing. In interviews, they can ask their peers, "What do you find most difficult in this course?" and then probe at their replies. In this way, students can learn to be aware of the bottlenecks in a course and benefit from becoming aware of different disciplinary ways of operating in different courses. For example, they might interview other students about bottlenecks in writing. Being engaged in this work can help the undergraduate researchers become aware of the different forms of writing discourse and the strategic considerations about writing that differ from discipline to discipline.

Comparing Bottlenecks Across Disciplines

Now that you have refined your bottleneck, it can help to consider it in light of the bottlenecks in other fields. Why do we do this? The tacit nature of expertise makes it hard to see what makes a bottleneck difficult and to even find the words to describe it. We will make this comparative move often throughout this book because it is hard to work on a bottleneck in disciplinary isolation. Three ways we can make comparisons with our bottlenecks are to read lists of bottlenecks, read in the literature for a fuller description of a bottleneck from a similar or distant field, or talk to a colleague in a different field. Figure 1.6 provides some short descriptions of bottlenecks that you can compare to your bottleneck. Which ones are written at a more specific level than your bottleneck? Less specific? Do any of these bottleneck descriptions make you want to refine the wording of your bottleneck? Do any of these bottlenecks seem similar in kind to yours? And finally, because you are probably considering bottlenecks in at least one discipline quite different from your own, would you also get stuck where the students get stuck? One of the most humbling experiences we've had when working across disciplines is recognizing that we are often novice thinkers in relation to other disciplines, but as you will see in chapter 2, our ignorance, when coupled with our proven ability to learn, is an asset when we work with others. Considering the bottlenecks students encounter in disciplines alien to our own can give us a greater appreciation of the challenges our students face in our disciplines.

When faculty reflect on bottlenecks and explain them in detail, it helps them to see and appreciate what is difficult to learn in their discipline and to take the view of the student. Being able to readily spot bottlenecks where students struggle with disciplinary mental moves—the bottleneck perspective—helps us see things from the student perspective and is one of the transformative aspects of Decoding the Disciplines. The detailed descriptions of bottlenecks in Figures 1.7 through 1.9 give a much better idea of where the difficulties lie for students than the short descriptions we have provided in Figure 1.6.

In the example in Figure 1.7, the students are showing several things: They do not know what to draw on for textual analysis nor do they know how to generate double and triple meanings. The students seem to suspect that there is a secret formula to follow (and, indeed, there are probably some unarticulated heuristics involved, words that would set off bells for a scholar in English or structures in the writing that a scholar would routinely look for). And some students seem to expect to receive answers, which indicates they are treating literary analysis as dualists—looking for black-and-white answers, not complexity (Perry, 1999).

There are several layers in the bottleneck described in Figure 1.8. One is theory versus application, in which theoretical individuals are all the same, whereas real people vary from one another, while another is that students in their classroom practice don't encounter a broad variety of humanity, so that they struggle to learn to sense an injury when none exists, which seems like a legitimate learning difficulty.

By uncovering what students are not able to do (Figure 1.9), we can begin to see what students need to learn to do to negotiate the bottlenecks in developing good news stories. For this teacher these would include developing sensitivity to current topics of interest, learning to see through one person the impact of larger issues, and becoming more aware of and representing the underrepresented.

These fuller descriptions of the bottlenecks are quite rich and point to what critical thinking consists of for the field that needs to be decoded.

Finally, instead of thinking about your bottleneck as an idea in your head, you can bring it out into the open by discussing it with a colleague

Figure 1.6. Short descriptions of bottlenecks from many disciplines.

Second Languages
> Students struggle to communicate and speak because they have weak grammar skills. For example, they confuse the subject and direct and indirect objects when trying to speak a sentence in Spanish.

Physics
> Students expect graphs (abstract representations of phenomena) to mimic the physical, "real" world, and therefore have difficulty making sense of the "abstract world" symbolically represented in equations and graphs.

Chemistry
> Students have difficulty identifying which substances are acids and which are bases from their chemical formulae and structures.

Composition
> Students struggle to write for an audience that wants to learn something, rather than an audience that is merely an evaluator of their learning (the teacher).

Nursing
> Students may score well on a test of principles of osmosis, yet struggle to apply the principles to what is causing an individual patient's cells to swell.

Economics
> Students confuse everyday language with the more precise (and sometimes counterintuitive) economics terminology, which interferes with their learning about the price and quantity relationship in firms' and consumers' decision-making processes.

Accounting
> Students understand the mechanics of bond pricing, but they don't see its connection with the underlying business activity of raising capital by borrowing money and eventually paying it back.

and hear that person describe his or her own bottleneck. Try to pair up with someone from outside your department in a field different from your own. Where can you find a colleague for a bottleneck discussion? Do you know a faculty member who has children at your child's school? Goes to your church? Plays racquetball with you? Belongs to a club you belong to? Ask this person if he or she would be interested in exploring an aspect of teaching over lunch. You can start by asking this person the bottleneck prompt in Exercise 1.2. The bottleneck discussion provides us with terminology to discuss the unique and difficult aspects of reasoning in our fields.

Figure 1.7. Bottleneck: Double and triple meanings in literary analysis (Paul Gutjahr).

Often in my introductory freshman literature courses, I take a moment to have students speak about what they do not like about the study of literature. Two complaints seem to always rise to the surface. First, they are bothered by the subjective nature of the enterprise. Unlike science and mathematics, there are no "right" answers, and this bothers them. It seems to outrage their sense of justice and fair play. Second, they have become convinced somewhere along the line that the study of literature is much like the process of solving an incredibly obscure code or puzzle whose answer is known only to the teacher, who frequently takes sadistic pleasure in making them guess an author's intent or a text's true meaning. These complaints are interesting because, on the one hand, students are complaining that they hate the fact that there is no right answer when it comes to literary analysis while, on the other hand, they are complaining that there is a hidden right answer for which they are forced into a fruitless and painful search to discover. (Ardizzone, Breithaupt, & Gutjahr, 2004, p. 50)

Figure 1.8. Bottleneck: Link between theory and application in athletic therapy.

Because the events in the clinical or field placements are entirely unpredictable, students are often unlikely to encounter practical learning in a way that neatly synchronizes with their classroom learning. In class, they are often practicing feeling for anatomical structures on one another. However, a common problem in athletic therapy (and indeed in many clinically based programs) is that there is a challenge in providing a practical example at the moment where it would support theoretical learning. Julie explains:

> The problem in class many times is if someone in the class doesn't have something wrong with them we are feeling a whole bunch of normal, and it is not until you feel abnormal that you go, "Ohhh!" like, "I get the difference." We can only hope for people to come in with injuries that we can . . . people can find that stuff on.

(Yeo et al., 2017, p. 90)

Now that you have identified your bottleneck, refined it, and compared it to other bottlenecks (again with an eye to refining it), we can move on to Step 2 Decoding, where we will learn how to uncover what an expert does to avoid the bottlenecks (which he or she may not experience as bottlenecks and may be unaware of).

Figure 1.9. Bottleneck: Developing ideas for good news stories in journalism.

The ability to develop ideas for interesting, topical news stories is fundamental to success as a journalist. The ability has names in journalism practice: a nose for news, gut instinct; and it is a subject of theorizing in journalism scholarship (Schultz, 2007; Kronstad, 2014). In a decoding interview done at Mount Royal university, a journalist called "Bonnie" was asked why, in her view, students lacked the nose for news.

"They don't seem to hear and see the things that I think as a journalist I hear and see. When I have a conversation with someone over the years I have realized—it is really tough on my friends and my circle of acquaintances—but everything you say is potential fodder for a story idea."

Who did students not talk to?

"Often what they miss is a face of the story, or people who are marginalized or disenfranchised, and that is often a big missing piece for me." (MacDonald, 2017, p. 67)

Finding the Bottlenecks in Teams

Up until this point, we've discussed how you might work as an individual to identify and refine a bottleneck in your course. However, we have found that working in teams enhances this process considerably. Teams do not need to be formal entities; you could create your own bottleneck "pickup" group. Here we will talk about what we do in more formal settings, but these are activities that can be done more informally. When we are working in formal teams, we often use icebreakers to get people talking.

Before the first team exercise, we introduce the concept of bottlenecks and provide some examples using the sections in this chapter in which we define and look for patterns in the bottlenecks (see p. 14, this volume). We ask participants to come up with some ideas about where students get stuck in their classes and perhaps with student work illustrating the bottlenecks. In the first team exercise faculty members describe their bottlenecks to each other. Sometimes this discussion is preceded by three minutes of silent writing about their bottlenecks if the idea is new to them. When time is short teams start immediately working with the discussion prompt in Exercise 1.3 (see the end of the chapter).

In this process, everyone takes turns stating his or her bottlenecks, then his or her teammates question the speakers about the bottlenecks and restate them. Having teammates restate the bottleneck back to the speaker prompts the speakers to clarify the bottleneck, because as novices to the field, the teammates probably will not be able to explain it well. This exercise might not seem very difficult—faculty often assume that when they are starting out their ideas will be clear to those in another discipline—but faculty often find it so. They are probably not used to doing this and they are often siloed in their own fields. The listeners also find it difficult. When we first started doing this work, when we were listening to a point on a topic very different from our expertise, we would glaze over and stop following the flow of ideas. This often indicated that we were not really understanding (and we responded just the way students do—we tuned out). We have found, however, that with encouragement and modeling, the participants (who are generally highly accomplished learners) can learn to notice where they can no longer follow along and when they are tuning out as a result. Unlike students, their job is then to seek clarification of what they have not understood. Faculty are then proxy novices for each other, providing an outsider's view on the critical thinking of an alien field.

We follow that with a debriefing discussion that helps the participants pull back from their content and see the *patterns* in the thinking that underlies the bottlenecks. In their team discussions of bottlenecks, teachers will sometimes find—to their surprise and despite differences in their fields—that they have similar bottlenecks (e.g., "My students are not able to generate a hypothesis or cannot write well"). Or they may find that their bottlenecks are very different ("My students struggle to visualize, while your students struggle to explain in words"), which is equally useful. In either case, they are beginning to get the bottleneck view—a learning-centered view of their courses and teaching. The basic Step 1 Bottleneck team discussion of Exercise 1.3 can be preceded by elaborations that build community and extend cross-disciplinary practice.

Some teachers prefer to ponder their bottlenecks in advance before committing to them in the group setting. Others seem fine picking their bottlenecks on the fly as in Exercise 1.3. In addition, some academics prefer to approach a new topic such as Decoding the Disciplines by reading about it in advance, so we usually suggest a reading such as the introduction to this book or the chapter you are currently reading, or a favorite article about decoding, such as Shopkow and colleagues (2013b), which provides an overview of the decoding process. The facilitator chooses to assign "homework" based on where the Decoding the Disciplines workshop or seminar fits in the school year. (If it occurs near the end of a semester, faculty may be too overwhelmed with grading to do any up-front preparation.) Usually, not everyone will do it, but about half will. Thus, a week or two before the first team meeting, we may announce the bottleneck and reading assignments in something like the form depicted in Figure 1.10.

Having collected this "homework," we will show the bottlenecks to the group at some point to reward those who made the effort to complete

Figure 1.10. Bottleneck and decoding homework assignment.

Dear Colleagues,

To get the most out of the Decoding the Disciplines session on April 25, I would like to invite you to look at the following two questions and e-mail your answers to me:

1. Identify a specific moment in a course you teach in which your students face a learning bottleneck (i.e., something that is essential for their success but that large numbers of students fail to grasp).
2. Describe as precisely as you can what they are getting wrong. (What is the nature of the bottleneck?)

Also, you may wish to read the attached chapter/article to get an idea of the kind of work we will embark on in two weeks.

I look forward to working with you.

Joan

the assignment. We might compile a list of the bottlenecks and post them to a learning management system site where participants can read them. As an alternative, we might use them in an opening presentation as examples of bottlenecks.

Another way to create awareness of the patterns in bottlenecks is to create a concept map of the bottlenecks in a discipline. This helps faculty see both how their disciplines differ from other disciplines and what the connections are between the bottlenecks commonly found in their disciplines and the larger epistemology of the field. Comparing these concept maps across disciplines can help teachers step back from viewing the students as having the difficulty and begin to see the patterns in thinking that they may take for granted (see Exercise 1.4).

Doubts About Bottlenecks

On rare occasions, we have encountered teachers who report that they do not have any bottlenecks in their classes. This may result from teaching mostly facts and details, the most basic level in Bloom's taxonomy. If this is the case, the students are not required to do much critical thinking, just rote repetition. The teacher might report that students are not very good at retaining the factual material, but this is a problem related to memorization rather than incomprehension, and there are methods to help remembering (see Table 4.3).

Sometimes teachers feel uncomfortable with the implication of bottlenecks: that students might not be mastering the material in their courses. This challenges their sense of competence as teachers. Others may be resistant to the possibility that there are inherent bottlenecks in a discipline they themselves seemingly mastered effortlessly. Still other teachers may consider the bottleneck perspective a negative approach, in that we are focusing on student "problems," which they see as leading to "spoon-feeding" students instead of forcing students to struggle with the new ideas we present. However, instead of seeing the bottlenecks as something negative, we consider bottlenecks to be powerful diagnostics that point to blind spots in our teaching that can be uncovered (see chapter 2 on teaching blind spots). And faculty who have focused on student bottlenecks, that is, on the conceptual frameworks of the discipline, often report that students find this approach rigorous and challenging, not bland or easy, and rigor is associated with student success (Kuh, Kinzie, Buckley, Bridges, & Hayek, 2006).

Reassuringly, even accomplished teachers experience bottlenecks. David Pace, who won a national award for college teaching from the American Historical Association, finds the bottleneck framework useful to uncover mental moves in history after 40-plus years of teaching, referring to them as "gifts" from the students. Bottlenecks can be a challenge for disciplinary experts to see because they have, by definition, already mastered these blocks to learning. The very problems that pose such a difficulty to students may barely exist in a conscious way in the expert, but this is not an indictment of the expert's hard-won expertise; it is a prominent feature of expertise. True expertise often brings with it unconscious or tacit competence.

Summary

Most faculty can identify bottlenecks in classes we have taught. When we haven't taught a class, we can turn to other instructors or the literature as sources of bottlenecks. Either individually or in teams we will want to refine our bottlenecks by writing them as clearly as possible, comparing them to bottlenecks in other fields, and asking students about them. The more readily we can see bottlenecks, the easier it becomes to get the bottleneck perspective—seeing things from the student side—breaking down what is difficult about our disciplines.

We have provided some ways for both individuals working alone and teachers working in teams to move forward in refining bottlenecks to learning. Teams may jump right into bottleneck discussions or, if time allows, prepare for this work by reading about Decoding the Disciplines and writing their bottlenecks in advance. Decoding facilitators may introduce working across disciplines through concept mapping of bottlenecks and disciplinary icebreakers.

Identifying bottlenecks is the beginning of the process for increasing student learning, not the end. When you have decided on your bottleneck, you will be able to fill in the first space in the decoding template (Appendix B). In Appendix A, you can see how a biologist and a musicologist have addressed Step 1 in the decoding process.

CHAPTER 1 EXERCISES

Exercise 1.1: Bottleneck Brainstorm (for Individuals or as a Starting Point for a Team Exercise)

Think about a course you have taught—preferably one that you have taught several times. Where do students struggle to learn? Are there some places where you can predict they will go offtrack? These are the bottlenecks. List several here:

_____

_____

_____

_____

Exercise 1.2: Questions to Ask Experienced Teachers to Uncover the Bottlenecks

- What do students have the most trouble doing in this course?
- How does it manifest itself in student's work?
- Exactly what do the students get wrong?
- So you find that students are unable to _____? (repeat what they said back to them)

Exercise 1.3: Step 1 Bottleneck Discussion (Teams of Three From Different Disciplines)

What is a bottleneck in one of your courses—a place where many students get stuck?

- First member of group speaks (3 minutes)
- Second member of group speaks (3 minutes)
- Third member of group speaks (3 minutes)

If the speaker is finished in less than 3 minutes, teammates should restate the bottleneck. Do they have it right?

Debrief: What did you find out about each other's bottlenecks? Were there similarities or differences?

Exercise 1.4: Bottleneck Mapping Activity (Teams of Three From Different Disciplines)

1. Facilitator: Define the basic concepts that have to be understood to operate in your discipline. We are going to compile the paradigm-shifting bottlenecks (the places where students really need to acquire new sorts of thinking) along with the non-paradigm-shifting bottlenecks, such as taking effective class notes.

2. Facilitator: Provide directions for this concept map. Make a list of the main paradigm-shifting ideas and other bottlenecks that impede learning in your discipline. On a large sheet of paper, list the discipline in the middle, connecting the other concepts to it, using an organizational structure such as branches, arrows, or groups. More important bottlenecks can be closer to the center, less important ones farther. Use verbs for the connecting lines to identify the relationships between bottlenecks (causes, is an example of, etc.).

3. Individuals: Draw a concept map of the bottlenecks in your field, following the facilitator's instructions.

4. Teams (of three from similar disciplines): Compare and contrast individual concept maps. Create a larger concept map of a metadiscipline to share. For example, a biologist, a chemist, and a geologist create a concept map of the bottlenecks in the natural sciences.

5. Share (Gallery Walk): Post the combined maps from #4 using the gallery walk format in which faculty place sticky notes to make comments and clarifications on each other's concept maps.

Debrief: What did you learn from the bottlenecks/mapping activity?

2

STEP 2

Decoding Mental Actions

In Step 1 of the decoding process, we analyze the bottlenecks to learning that students experience. Experts don't encounter these bottlenecks because they have already mastered the type of thinking required to overcome the bottleneck. Within Step 2 lies the revolutionary kernel of decoding—uncovering the critical thinking of the discipline that we want students to learn. The task in Step 2 is to make explicit the expert's implicit way of thinking, so that in later steps these can be made available to students. Decoding the Disciplines uncovers mental moves that are so automatic to an expert that they are invisible and, therefore, may not be explicitly taught to students. This chapter describes methods to decode disciplinary expertise and reveal the "mental actions" of the expert. We will start with the decoding techniques individual faculty can use, such as analogies, rubrics, model building, reflective writing tours, and mind maps. Next, for teams we will explain the classic decoding interview and its variations. We provide a number of in-depth examples of interviews and discuss issues like what to do when the experts have difficulty explaining their thinking.

Uncovering Critical Thinking

There is no one, generic form of "critical thinking"; different kinds of reasoning are employed in different fields, are domain specific, and cannot be transferred to an area where our knowledge is limited (Christodou, 2014). When we decode we are trying to uncover the critical thinking of an expert within a discipline or field. Problematically, one's own disciplinary expertise is often tacit; it has become "natural" and is not available for conscious scrutiny. This unconsciousness is not intentional; it is a natural consequence of the functioning of the human brain. Experts process information more quickly and holistically, divide it into larger units than novices (Chi, Glaser, & Farr,

36

2014), and dispense results of their mental processes in larger chunks as well (Chase & Simon, 1973). Experts are also better than novices at monitoring their own performance. To deal with the many stimuli the expert brain encounters, many lower level mental processes must occur automatically.

For example, once we learn to drive a car, turning the steering wheel or judging the distance between vehicles occurs mostly without conscious thought, while attention is focused on other aspects such as evaluating the behavior of other drivers or calculating an efficient route. This economy of conscious attention (Rosch, 1978) is entirely functional for the experienced driver, but it can be a hindrance when we want to teach a teenager to drive. Even though we are experienced drivers, it is difficult to recognize all the practices a new driver needs to learn. Expertise means having our thoughts and actions highly automatized; it leaves mental capacity for higher order tasks such as monitoring progress and evaluating solutions.

In the classroom the "expert blind spot effect" (Nathan & Petrosino, 2003) may cause the expert to view student problem-solving from the expert viewpoint rather than from the student's perspective, making it difficult to recognize leaps that the instructor has made and steps that students have not been taught. This is why instructors have difficulty viewing problems anew as the students do; this is the point of Decoding the Disciplines.

The goal, whether decoding one's own expertise or that of another person, is not to understand the *content* of a lesson or a course—something experts can easily explain—or how to teach it—something experts are often eager to tell one—but instead to grasp the *mental process* faculty rely on to operate within their field. These mental processes are often more complex for experts to explain because, for them, mental processes are tacit knowledge and may never have been explicit.

Step 2 Decoding for Individual Faculty

Faculty are accustomed to thinking and speaking of their disciplines in terms of subject content (Carter, 2007). The transmission of inert content (the output from an expert's mental processes) is a prevalent practice (Hurtado, Eagan, Pryor, Whang, & Tran, 2012), which makes the underlying thinking students need to master particularly elusive. Decoding interviews are the classic approach to uncovering the implicit mental moves of the expert, but they are best conducted in teams of interviewers, and the interview is *not* the only way to decode mental actions. In the following sections we will decode methods that individuals can use. You will probably want to use more than one to ensure success at this very difficult task of unpacking a mental process.

There are two functions in decoding: to uncover a comprehensive list of expert mental actions and to describe these mental actions in detail. The first function of uncovering the list of mental actions that comprise a key disciplinary process such as interpretation in history, close reading in literature, or generation of hypotheses in biology is like opening up a set of nested Russian dolls to inventory the mental actions the expert engages in. The second function explores each nested doll to thoroughly understand and assess the mental operations it contains; we compare it to walking around a darkened house turning on the lights for those unfamiliar with the layout of the furniture. In decoding we move back and forth between these two functions throughout an interview, and this is something that someone working alone should also be thinking of doing. In the first chapter, we discussed some of this work when we talked about breaking down bottlenecks into their component parts. That was opening up the Russian dolls. The second part, turning on the lights in a darkened house, is at least as tricky—because it is difficult to find the light switches in the dark—but it is crucial.

One way to categorize Step 2 Decoding is to differentiate the methods according to whether they work best to inventory the subcomponents of a larger disciplinary process (e.g., close reading in literature) or to find the switches to turn on the lights in the dark house. For the first function, to do an inventory of the nested dolls, we have found that nonverbal modeling and creating mind maps work well. For the second function, to turn on the lights in the dark house, we use reflective writing, the creation of evaluative rubrics, and the use of analogies. The second function must include the first (in other words, to turn on the lights one has to have done an inventory of the rooms in the house), but the second process goes deeper and takes longer.

We begin with the methods that allow us to inventory the nested dolls.

Decoding Through Nonverbal Modeling

Susan Hines (Saint Mary's University of Minnesota) has invented a nonverbal approach to decoding. It makes the tacit thinking visible by modeling it using Play-Doh, although it can be done with aluminum foil or any other easily manipulated material. Instead of attempting to use words to describe what a teacher wants the students to be able to do or what an expert does, the teacher models the desired outcome and only then describes it in words (see Exercise 2.1).

Modeling the expert mental move and describing in words the model you just made reveals the mental action. For example, an instructor of a computer programming course used Play-Doh to model matching items from two different containers so that each item matched one, and only one, item

Figure 2.1. Matching materials from two containers.

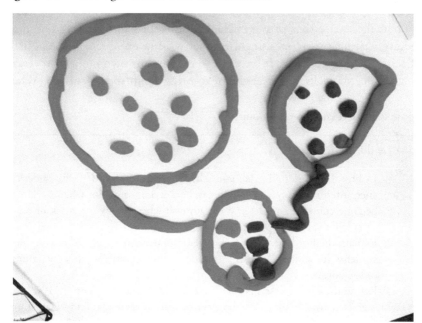

(see Figure 2.1). Deciding categories and matching items into them is an important mental action in the programming of databases.

Faculty have reacted positively to the Play-Doh decoding exercise, saying that they surprised themselves with what they produced—that "aha" moment that accompanies successful decoding. With this first attempt at uncovering our own tacit mental action, we might have laid out some of the "nested dolls," so we may want to try another method that probes the mental action to turn the lights on in the black boxes.

Decoding Through Reflective Writing

Another approach uses a series of prompts so faculty analyze their own mental actions in writing again and again. The reflective writing exercise in Figure 2.2 was developed by Swantje Lahm and Svenja Kaduk (2016) in the writing program at Bielefeld University, Germany. Faculty answer a series of questions about the bottleneck and then about the thinking they do to get through it. By responding to the prompts, they decode their own thinking. The exercise ends with one more chance to describe their own mental processes, this time to colleagues. Through the writing prompts and discussion, they further decode their own mental actions. This process begins with Step

1, so it offers an opportunity for faculty to revisit their bottlenecks before proceeding.

It makes sense that this exercise was developed in a writing program, because writing programs want to model writing exercises, and especially reflective writing exercises. It forces us to explain our own mental processes, to use different tacks to get at them, to bring them to the surface. When

Figure 2.2. Bottleneck writing tour.

Analyze the bottleneck:

1. Define the bottleneck. Ask yourself: What are the bottlenecks students encounter in my course(s)? This can be a certain moment when students become confused, a test, or a certain task where many get stuck or fail. Decide on something that really bothers you.
2. Explain the bottleneck. Describe the bottleneck in detail: What is it that students get wrong? What is it they don't understand? What is the nature of the bottleneck?
3. Refine the bottleneck: Look at the bottleneck and ask yourself: Is it too big? Is it too small? Is the bottleneck really essential for my course or discipline? Describe the bottleneck once again with as much detail as you can. If necessary, modify it.

Analyze your mental action:

4. What do you do yourself? Describe what you do as an expert in your discipline. Ask yourself: How do I deal with this bottleneck myself?
5. How does an expert deal with this? Describe one more time how an expert in your discipline would proceed when confronted with this bottleneck. What steps would an expert take to overcome the bottleneck? What would an expert do?
   Note: Many of these steps may seem so self-evident to you that they remain unconscious. Try to make these steps conscious and break down big steps into as many steps as possible. For example, a professor of literature asks his students to "observe" before they "interpret." The next question would be: What does a professor of literature do when he "observes?"
6. Get feedback. Explain your bottleneck to a colleague in another discipline. Then describe what you do yourself. The colleague asks for clarification of the things that were not understood.
   Note: The goal of the feedback is to understand exactly what the expert does! You want to get clear on the cognitive steps the expert takes. Don't divert into discussion of content—talk about the intellectual process.

Note. Adapted from Lahm & Kaduk, 2016.

faculty take the bottleneck writing tour, we see lots of writing and lots of pondering. Again, we find that discussion with a colleague from a different discipline and the cross-disciplinary comparison holds a mirror up to our own ways of operating in the discipline.

In Figure 2.3, Professor Laura Hurley of Indiana University uses the bottleneck writing tour to explore a bottleneck that is common in, but not limited to, biology. Note how she gets clearer about the bottleneck and about her own tacit thinking through the reflective questions.

Using the bottleneck writing tour format, Professor Hurley begins to understand that the bottleneck is more than the specific topic of hormones and behavior; it is ways of thinking about pieces of evidence and their relationship to concepts. The expert uses the concepts as models and tests the pieces to see which concepts they fit best. That way she is able to go back and forth between specific facts and the concepts to which they are connected. This insight will let her go up a level conceptually, to show students the mental action above the level of facts and details. The bottleneck writing tour as a Step 2 Decoding technique gets faculty describing their bottlenecks and explaining to themselves (and sometimes to another person as well) the reasoning they use to avoid getting stuck in the bottleneck.

Decoding Through Rubrics

Development of rubrics is another individual method for decoding the mental actions underpinning success in a course. For experts wishing to decode their discipline's crucial mental actions, a decoding rubric is another way to draw out their own unconscious competence. These are not generic rubrics aimed at some generic skill such as writing or critical thinking, but are instead custom designed to address the exact difficulties of a particular task. A rubric articulates the expectations for an assignment by listing the criteria, or what counts, and may describe levels of quality ranging from excellent to poor (Andrade, 2005). Decoding rubrics can make visible to teachers their tacit disciplinary mental moves that they might not have been demonstrating to students. Decoding rubrics are useful for probing the subcompetencies that make up the larger disciplinary mental move.

Because the decoding rubric is aimed straight at the bottleneck, development begins by making a list of the errors that students have made attempting to complete a particular assignment. To create this list, the instructor may examine student work on actual assignments. If the instructor has never taught the course before, a colleague who has assigned a similar task can explain what mistakes should be expected. Or the instructor can create the first rubric using errors the students are expected to make, adding to the rubric as the course goes along. The errors, in effect, are the

Figure 2.3. Example of a bottleneck writing tour in biology (Professor Laura Hurley of Indiana University).

1. Define the bottleneck
   General version: Students are having difficulty connecting a specific example to a larger point as demonstrated by being unable to retrieve specific information when given a conceptual prompt.
   Specific version: In the unit on hormones and behavior, on the exam students are unable to indicate hormones that fulfill specific roles. This has been a consistent problem, despite multiple reworkings of this lecture.
2. Explain the bottleneck
   This leads me to think that the problem is a general one, seen to a greater or lesser degree in other topics too, of being able to "hang" specific "facts" on to a larger conceptual framework. They are thus unable to retrieve information, even when I feel that what they are being asked to do is fairly easy, and even though I verbally emphasize the connection between concept and hormone in class.
3. Refine
   This bottleneck is absolutely essential to the course as a general example. Relating facts to a concept, and vice versa, is at the heart of being able to understand and do science. To restate the bottleneck, my hypothesis is that students are unable to relate specific information to larger concepts, even when this relationship is stated in class. This could be because they lack experience in the general process of doing this, and/or they are not given the opportunity to do this in this particular unit, due to the constraints I have felt in covering a large amount of content!
4. What do you do yourself?
   Act like a detective; start with a framework (hypothesis), gather facts based on this, and continually question whether/how the facts fit the framework. What is required is being given (a) the opportunity to arrange facts into different hypotheses and work with them directly and (b) the idea that concepts are not sacred and immutable, but are the result of creativity within a certain set of rules.
5. How does an expert deal with this?
   Experts have the advantage that they know how concepts are created, so they understand that they are not unchangeable. An expert will mentally view the facts in different configurations, to see which way they best go together, then create an overall statement/idea that fits the relationship among "facts."
6. Get feedback
   We focused mainly on describing the bottlenecks, not so much on feedback. Some of the issues we had were in common, in terms of relating smaller units of knowledge to overall concepts or interpretations. The idea of holding in mind potentially "contradictory" narratives of the same events was an interesting concept. We also discussed cultural obstacles to understanding different paradigms in both history and science.

bottlenecks or what students do not know to do. The example in Figure 2.4 lists possible errors from a summarizing exercise in history. Note that the summarizing task can vary in different disciplines (Graff, Birkenstein, & Durst, 2006).

Next to each type of error, the teacher can briefly explain what the expert does to avoid the error, creating a second list (not illustrated here), which can provide the basis for the operations that are essential in the assignment and, more broadly, to the disciplinary thinking that needs to be uncovered and decoded. It may be difficult for an instructor to clearly explain what steps should be taken to meet the challenge of the assignment. This is another place to hold a mirror up to our tacit thinking. Meet with a colleague from a different field who might notice assumptions and help us make sure no steps are missing. Writing what the expert would do to avoid the error is where the actual decoding takes place in writing decoding rubrics.

Once the teacher has created these two lists—errors students make and actions experts take to avoid them—they can a rubric create by (a) naming each category using a noun phrase and (b) calibrating the levels of student performance by spelling out the actions a student would take to exceed,

Figure 2.4. A decoding rubric for summarizing in history (identifying errors).

The Goal: For the student to provide a summary of an entire history article with appropriate detail in about 200 words, such that a reader would know what the article said without reading it.

Typical Student Errors:

The summary is not clear (the student may appear not to understand the article—a reading problem—or may write badly).

The summary does not hold together (the student may have simply listed material).

The summary leaves out one or more important points (the student may not see the significance of the omitted points and thus the thrust of the whole article).

The summary is too detailed (the student may not have known what to include or exclude, so included everything, an analysis problem).

The summary isn't detailed enough (the student may not recognize the specificity of the article or may think that specificity is unimportant).

The student writes "about" the article rather than summarizing it or says what the article "does" rather than what the author "says" (the student has not fully engaged with the material in the article and has perhaps only skimmed it for content).

meet, and not meet expectations. Without calibration between success and failure, it can be difficult to help students move toward mastery.

Completing the rubric guides experts in decoding their own thinking and the mental tasks that are crucial to the discipline that the students need to learn. The completed rubric can facilitate scoring student work and assigning a grade. In addition, because it succinctly delineates criteria, it can be distributed to students as the work is assigned to clarify the expectations for the assignment. The category titles one uses in a rubric are up to the teacher and can depend on the field and the item being graded and whether the course is graded on mastery or a curve. The second column in Table 2.1 shows a "way station" (Shopkow & Díaz, forthcoming), a predictable stopping place for students between the expert and novice ways of operating. Depending on the assignment, there might be more than three columns on the rubric, especially if the teacher recognizes more than three possible places students usually land. Table 2.1 provides some examples of the possible column titles, which have implications for student motivation.

As usual, if possible, get an outsider view to clarify your insider view to be sure the mental actions are clearly explained and the calibrations are differentiated. For example, "solves problem" might not explain clearly to someone outside of the field that an audio engineering instructor wants students to be able to "correlate the results of physical actions with electronic outputs and develop a system to bring a signal from one place to another." Nor is it clear that an anthropology instructor who says that "writing with lots of details" meets expectations means that the student is able to "select a critical incident from your observation notes to describe in detail."

TABLE 2.1
Titles for Decoding Rubric Columns

Stuck in the Bottleneck	At a Way Station	Mastered the Mental Move
Low	Medium	High
Does Not Meet	Meets	Exceeds Expectations
Beginner	Intermediate	Advanced
Novice	Developing	Exemplary
Needs Revision	Satisfactory	Exceptional
Unacceptable	Basic	Proficient
Incomplete	Passable	Excellent
Unsatisfactory	Competent	Proficient/Distinguished

A rubric of this kind has been developed by Jane Matranga for the daily journals kept by students in an overseas study course that compared U.S. and Paris design aesthetics (see Table 2.2). The list of student mistakes (the bottlenecks) in column 1 includes listing fashion items without explanation, repeating discussion points from class tours verbatim, and using photographic "selfies" as documentation rather than photos of design aesthetics. Each of these failures to demonstrate course competencies provides the occasion for an analysis of precisely what mental action is missing. The desired disciplinary mental actions are shown in the third column, while the second column shows a "way station" (Shopkow & Díaz, forthcoming), a predictable stopping place for students between the expert and novice ways of operating.

The rubric method for decoding has several advantages that make it particularly useful. First, it is not necessary to explain the decoding method, although it can easily be followed by an explanation of the approach. Second, it may provide the "aha" insights that will encourage further exploration of the bottlenecks and mental actions of a field. When they have experience using decoding rubrics with assignment expectations so clearly defined, teachers may understand the value of using rubrics (which many teachers still reject) and may no longer be satisfied with generic grading rubrics used in the past.

Decoding Through Analogies

Another highly effective way to clarify the instructor's mental action is to generate a commonplace analogy that exemplifies the action. As we shall see in chapter 3, analogies (and *metaphors*—some teachers/fields prefer this term, but for simplicity throughout the book we use *analogies*) play an important role in modeling mental actions of experts for students. But they also can help determine mental actions during the decoding process. Usually, the expert thinks of mental action in terms of disciplinary examples. Because of the content of a discipline (e.g., in biology, all the parts of a gene, embedded in a cell, embedded in a living organism), it is difficult to "see" the mental action of interest; it is "camouflaged" to the outsider. In a certain sense, instructors who have not decoded their disciplines use a language unknown to their students. In the "dictionary" of the discipline, all the terms are explained in terms of each other and are self-supporting. Since students do not know that language, the definitions themselves are circular or sometimes confusing, as when disciplinary experts use everyday terms as terms of art. When instructors are asked to provide analogies for the operations that confuse students, they must leave the echo chamber of their fields and describe these operations in broader language that is easier for students to understand. Conceptual analogies can be used to explain an unfamiliar

TABLE 2.2
Rubric for Fashion Design in Paris (Jane Matranga)

	Bottleneck	Way Station	Proficient/ Distinguished
Observing clothing design aesthetics in exhibitions or retail settings Description of collections or inspirations for designs	Provides lists of what was seen without explanations.	Describes design objects, collections, and store environment and presentation. Describes observations of themes, colors, and construction techniques. Gives descriptive examples.	Describes design objects, collections, store environment, and presentation. Describes observations of themes, colors, styling, and construction techniques. Gives descriptive examples. Provides annotated sketches and inspirations.
Analyzing fashion aesthetics Connecting observations to class themes and course objectives	Restates verbatim ideas or issues from the class discussion in relation to daily observation.	Analyzes daily observations in terms of course themes.	Applies course themes to daily observations to form new insights.
Documenting fashion aesthetics	Provides a quick snapshot or selfie on location as documentation.	Takes photos that show aesthetics observed in stores, windows, museums, or persons on the street.	Captions photos to explain aesthetic differences about what was observed in stores, windows, museums, or persons on the street.

domain in terms of a familiar one, importing the familiar domain's relational structure (Lakoff & Johnson, 2008). Decoding through an analogy is useful because it can isolate a particular mental action from all the possible mental actions people regularly use.

According to cognitive theory, analogies work because they are mental simulations (Shanton & Goldman, 2010). Of interest to us are cases in which one mental event, state, or process is the reexperience of another mental event, state, or process. The simulated mental action does not have to be an exact duplicate, but must bear a resemblance. One example of simulation is the construction of visual imagery. Visualization as mental action uses many areas of the brain that are also used by genuine vision. This suggests that visualization shows which "mental muscles" are used by genuine vision.

In biology, for example, students find it difficult to understand how the shape of a protein can change the function of the protein. Students familiar with the "Transformers" toy can visualize how the toy can change from a rocket to a car and recognize that rockets perform differently from cars on a racetrack. Similarly, the unfolding of a protein creates a linear arrangement with a new function. This example provides students the opportunity to see that form and function go hand in hand, importing the idea from a familiar area to one that is unfamiliar. An analogy can only help if the students are familiar with the analogy's domain; in this case, they need to be familiar with Transformers toys.

In a writing bottleneck in history, students struggle to balance the amount of evidence and explanation in an essay. To generate an analogy, we brainstorm situations in which two sets of items have to balance. To bake a good chocolate chip cookie, we want neither too much dough nor too many chocolate chips; we need a balance between the two. Such an analogy provides a link between a concrete experience the students have likely had before (baking chocolate chip cookies) and the new mental action (writing a historical essay). (Visit http://citl.indiana.edu/resources/teaching-resources1/teaching-handbook-items/Lecture_techniques.php to see the video of the cookie analogy.) The analogy helps students understand what the instructor means in asking students to balance theory, explanation, and evidence in writing assignments. (See Exercise 2.3 to develop an analogy.)

To give another example, a public policy instructor's students struggled to understand the basic work of policymakers and never seemed to understand how the three branches of U.S. government interact with each other. The instructor thought about what he does with a cause he believes in—he might start a grassroots campaign to build public pressure for his preferred policy, initiate a court case, or try to get a law passed by the legislature. Then he started listing possible analogies for what he would do, because this reminded him of chess moves as an analogy, or, if students are unfamiliar with chess, a quarterback's playbook, which, when internalized, allows the player to read a situation on the football field and immediately narrow down the possible plays to the best options. As he thought about the analogies, he realized this mental action is not just about choosing a strategy and disregarding others, but having a set of strategies to choose from.

We approach the process of generating analogies playfully because we might not hit on the right analogy right away. But when we do find one that represents the expert's thinking (according to the expert), the teacher will now be able (through the rest of the Decoding the Disciplines steps) to make the implicit explicit and available to students.

Decoding With Mind Maps

In a diagrammatic interview method, experts summarize the decoding interview by sketching mind maps that spatially and visually organize the mental actions and depict how these experts understand the parts of their thinking. Such mapping exercises assist experts in exploring their own cognitive structures (Austin, 1994) as they perform a mental action. The mind map can either lay out the "nested dolls" function or the "turn on the lights in the dark house" function, probing one or two mental actions in detail. This method is especially useful for the nested doll decoding—identifying the subcomponents that make up a larger mental operation, such as generating a hypothesis in science. A decoding mind map would look like Figure 6.1.

Step 2 Decoding in Teams

The remainder of this chapter describes Step 2 Decoding methods that are best accomplished in teams.

The Decoding Interview

The decoding interview is used to get at an expert's underlying critical thinking. Often we form teams from different disciplines to interview each other to decode tacit thinking. That way, when an expert lapses into "discipline-speak," something that frequently happens, the interviewers won't get caught up in it. However, there are also things to be learned when people in the same discipline (particularly when they already have some experience of decoding) interview each other. They may find that they can make their field's epistemology or ways of creating knowledge more explicit through this process.

When they are initially interviewed, experts usually offer relatively superficial responses or respond as if they are speaking to someone in their own discipline who knows what they do. The interviewer needs to ask probing questions to uncover the tacit knowledge and mental actions experts use. In short, we need to find out the "tools" they use. To decode an expert we cycle among the following steps:

1. Ask experts to start from a specific, recent example when they used the mental action. Then ask, "What do *you* do?"
2. Imagine yourself doing what they describe. Are crucial steps being left out?
3. Ask questions where you don't understand. Probe where the experts cannot explain.
4. Summarize what the experts say; restate their points.
5. Reassure the experts that it is okay to not be able to explain their tacit knowledge.
6. Gently redirect if the experts talk about how they teach their students, how they learned it, or if they launch into a lecture.

We have provided detailed instructions for a decoding interview at the end of this chapter (see Exercise 2.4). The interviewer moves back and forth between larger disciplinary moves and their subparts to inventory the subcomponents of a larger disciplinary process. As in the interview depicted in Figure 2.5 about writing for the disciplinary moves of history, the parts of the process are uncovered, like nested dolls, before the interviewer moves on to exploring any "dark rooms."

In the example in Figure 2.5, the instructor is sometimes able to answer each question, but only in a way that would make sense to another expert. For instance, the interviewee answers the question about how historians arrive at questions by saying that it is important to read for a while without expecting a result. Another expert would recognize the process of reading primary sources to see what questions these sources raise, but the interviewee has not explained how reading leads to questions (and indeed, for novices, just reading often doesn't). In the hundreds of decoding interviews others and we have conducted, only one time has an expert been able to fully explain his mental actions without a large number of probing questions.

The use of two interviewers, with one from outside the target discipline, will help ensure that no common blind spots will be left undiscovered. The outside interviewer will not know the disciplinary code and, therefore, will be more likely to recognize when a given response is coded in terms of the disciplinary field, since the answer may not make any sense to him or her. Since students are generally novices, beginning the interview with something students routinely miss is often a fruitful approach. Another reason for having at least two interviewers is because at the same time we are decoding the experts' mental actions we also need to keep aware of our own reactions and those of the interviewees. There are three things to be aware of throughout the interview:

Figure 2.5. Step 2 Decoding interview on writing in history—uncovering "nested dolls."

Bottleneck: Students Cannot Write Well in History

Interviewer: What do you do when you write?

Instructor: I read a lot first. [This is the first nested doll.]

Interviewer: How do you know what to read?

Instructor: I am usually in an archive or reading in my subfield, so the context is narrowed down. [This is the next nested doll.]

Interviewer: How do you know what to read?

Instructor: All the work I do is driven by questions. [This is the next nested doll.]

Interviewer: How do you know what question to ask?

Instructor: I am always working from a question. It is the heart of my research.

Interviewer: How do you know when you have found an answer?

Instructor: I think a willingness to read for a while without result— willingness to just get a sense of tone as opposed to looking for information that can be extracted. [Next nested doll.]

Interviewer: What do you get from that?

Instructor: To spend some time in another culture is hard and different moments in the past is hard and it's just a matter of getting people to sit like maybe if there's a puddle—be in that puddle of another culture or be in the puddle of another time period for a little while. Just get used to the feeling, not to learn everything about it but just to get used to the feeling for a moment. [Another nested doll.]

Interviewer: So, this is something historians do, imagining themselves in the culture, getting a sense of the context. What does this have to do with writing?

[As the interview continues, each one of these nested dolls might be probed.]

---

1. Confusion. As an interviewer you should not pretend to understand and skip over parts where you feel confused. Your lack of expertise is an advantage. As listeners we often fake understanding when experts delve deeply into their expertise—students are experts at this!—but in a decoding interview, the interviewer doesn't let the misunderstanding go unexplained. A sign that you are slipping is that you feel your eyes glazing over. When you feel this, or see that your fellow interviewer has tuned out, you need to ask more probing questions to reveal the assumptions the expert is skipping over. The interviewers drive this interview, which may be considered a directed conversation as much as an interview.

2. Digressions. You should try to avoid being sidetracked by digressions. Gently redirect interviews if the experts begin to talk about how they would teach their students (later steps will address this), how they learned a mental task (generally not applicable to others), or if they launch into lectures. These digressions often indicate that interviewees are approaching the tacit process but are finding it difficult to explain their mental processes.

3. Expert's comfort level. Notice if the expert gets uncomfortable from continued probing. The expert's discomfort is a signal that you have arrived at tacit knowledge. Experts (usually the "smarty-pants" in the room) are not used to being required to explain their tacit knowledge or having difficulty explaining anything. Reassure them that their responses are appropriate, but continue to probe at that point.

Finding the tacit knowledge is no small matter. Thus, we often start interviews by cautioning, "You are used to being able to answer questions put to you as an expert. But in this interview, as we explore your tacit knowledge, you may find it difficult to answer our questions. That is a good sign and means the interview is going well."

Experts are often surprised about what decoding interviews can uncover, the "aha" moment. As physicist Gregor Novak explained:

> Viewing my own interview [many of our interviews have been recorded], I was struck by the fact that it sounded so new and fresh to me. Obviously the ideas must have been in my head all along; I must be using this stuff with my students, but I was not conscious of it. It is clear to me now that a skillful probing interviewer can help the interviewee articulate thoughts and ideas from deep down in the subconscious. (Personal e-mail communication, April 12, 2016)

Once the interviewers have uncovered a number of possible areas to dig into, they need to turn to one mental action and to let no assumption remain unquestioned. To get a deeper understanding of the assumptions and tacit knowledge the expert uses to overcome bottlenecks, the interviewer must gently probe, digging deeper into the expert's thinking process until—like turning on the lights in an unfamiliar house—something hidden has now been revealed to him or her, or the expert becomes aware of something they do in a new way (see Figure 2.6).

Interviewers must pay close attention to the responses to ensure that all crucial steps are included, that disciplinary jargon is clarified, and that the task has been completely explained. As a mental action is probed, a more

Figure 2.6. Probing in a decoding interview.

Interview With Alberto Varon, Department of English, Indiana University

Interviewer: What is a bottleneck for students in Introduction to Ethnic American Literature course?

Instructor: Students cannot bring Latino Studies frameworks to reading a text.

Interviewer: Tell us about a time you have done this recently.

Instructor: I am not sure I can fully do this. But I am currently reading a memoir by Catarino Garza, an 1860s Texas bandit.

Interviewer: What do you do?

Instructor: Read the text. Translate the nineteenth-century Spanish handwriting. What do the sentences mean—this is basically understanding the plot.

Interviewer: What do you do next?

Instructor: Reread carefully looking word by word, phrases, and paragraphs. Stop and think about what some paragraphs mean. How does the author say what he says, why is he saying what he says? Read it at least three times or some novels six to seven times. Look for: What are recurring themes? What is it about? Family? Professional life? What is the context? He was a revolutionary. He wrote about his relation to U.S. and Mexican nation-state.

Generate some ideas about how the way he says things and the content are connected. What language does he use—similes and analogies? Is he bland or poetic? I found a nice turn of phrase in a different text recently, so I might notice the language used.

Interviewer: How do you pick themes to focus on?

Instructor: Why this focus? What is driving this? He says something more than once, twice. Can I find a space in my book for it? It relates to my research, which is about nineteenth-century print culture—texts that were printed, government docs, books, memoirs, letters, etc. (For example, weather and landscape might not be of interest to me, but if someone else were writing about environmental issues, these might interest them.)

If it related to banditry. I am writing a chapter about bandits and banditry. Latinos were bandits—wanted to fight colonialism and the U.S. Mexican Americans how did they understand their situation from their viewpoint? I am asking, "What matters to him? Why does he care more about his horse and caress his horse, but barely mentions his wife's name. What does he say about his gun?"

Interviewer: What would I see you doing when you read?

Instructor: I annotate the text; I draw and write in the text. I underline, circle (especially names), and write in the margins. If ideas that are raised connect to another portion of the text.

Interviewer: What does it look like?

Instructor: I mark the text with my own shorthand—I have a whole system:

Ha—if it seems funny

(*Continues*)

Figure 2.6. (*Continued*)

? if—I question the phrase

!? —means exciting raising issues

?! —means seems important but I don't know how

Interviewer: What do you do with the results of the annotations?

[I would probe further here—how does he use the annotation? How does he uncover the unexpressed, unconscious subculture of Latino banditry via close reading? I would bring it back to the previous bottleneck.]

Interviewer: How do you choose which text to read closely?

Instructor: In this case, serendipity. Someone at the archive, Nick, said, "Have you read this? No one has." So I photographed 470 pages (because they were too delicate to photocopy) and e-mailed them to myself.

---

complete inventory of the steps required to overcome the bottleneck slowly emerges. As interviewers, we ask for an explanation of steps that are vague or absent. We don't fake understanding. The instructor will provide the required explanation, but that in turn will contain more unexplained material. These new nested dolls will need to be opened, and the interview proceeds, with each item containing a hidden element embedded within it. In the process, the interviewers and the teacher will probe ever more deeply into the heart of the discipline. Interviewers need confidence that the mental actions can be revealed, even if this is a different discipline from their own. After all, the bottleneck comes from an undergraduate course, and a thoughtful layperson should be able to follow it too.

Sometimes the interview can seem stuck; the expert has left out some steps, and when we try to break them down, even seemingly simple procedures whose details are important parts of larger processes, the expert is unable to describe what she or he does. When such holes appear in trying to break down the mental actions of the expert, and the central decoding interview question ("How do you do that?") is not providing the breakthrough because the expert cannot readily answer the question, the interview can feel at a dead end. At this point the interviewer can often help the interviewee move forward by suggesting possible kinds of thinking that are invisible to the expert, but surprisingly often may be at work. The following are several effective metaquestions that can be asked:

1. Do you *visualize* something? What does it look like?
2. Are you making a *comparison*? With what?
3. Are you asking a set of predetermined *questions* (based on some unmentioned heuristic, such as race, gender, dollar amounts, or taxonomy)? What are the questions?

4. Do you choose an *option* (or strategy) from among several? If so, how did you know which to choose and which to leave out?

5. If all else fails, suggest an *analogy* for the mental action. Does this analogy properly represent the mental action?

From the hundreds of interviews we have conducted, we have found these questions often open up seemingly inexplicable mental actions. This is because experts often visualize a model or process, make implicit comparisons, apply heuristics, or select from a set of options or strategies, depending on the discipline. Being able to suggest these kinds of mental actions is key for getting an interview unstuck and helping the expert to decode a bottleneck successfully.

For example, in an interview where a math expert got stuck (see Figure 2.7), we resorted to one of the metaquestions. Because we were decoding in a field so very abstract and difficult for a nonmathematician, we needed examples and analogies to help us "walk around in the head of the expert" to uncover his mental actions. How did the interviewer know to suggest the Gulf oil spill as a function? (We admit that this question came from our previous experience working with a mathematician.) We (the interviewer and the interviewee) had to agree on the analogy (familiar context) and the target concept (the mental action to be clarified). The interviewer sometimes takes a stab in the dark to find a starting place, as in the example in Figure 2.7 where the interviewer offers up an educated guess, because it was all so "obvious" to the expert and he was not able to explain what he does.

One of us (Joan) was an interviewer in this case, and as a nonmathematician she was starting to feel lost about what these instructors meant. But the interview produced two foundational items: First, there is currently no agreed-on definition of a *function*. Students might think that calculus is like algebra—a mistake that Joan made—and think that the relationships between different numbers are static or predictable. Calculus is, instead, about change. Second, functions have base components, or input and output. These are conceptually different from variables and an answer to a problem, a concept that students may not readily identify as different from previous classes in math. To better understand these two areas, Joan interviewed another calculus professor (see Figure 2.8) who helped her come up with some analogies for these two foundational ideas.

From this instructor Joan learned that there was a core debate about functions. This is a point that could go unnoticed by students and is crucial to understanding how calculus is a different method of solving mathematical problems. The first and broadest definition, a relationship between input and output, is like the stock market. On any given day (input) stocks will all

Figure 2.7. Example of a probing interview in math.

The Bottleneck: Students Don't Grasp the Concept of Functions in a Calculus Class

Interviewer: Let me try coming up with an example of a function, even though I am not a mathematician. Is data from the 2010 Gulf of Mexico oil spill an example of a function? If I list for every day the *volume* and *spread* of the oil, two numbers appear side by side in a table. Then I can graph those numbers or make an equation from them. I could use them to predict what would happen in the future as the spill continued. Or compare them to other spills. Is this an example of a function?

Instructor: What you have described is algebra, not calculus, two different problem-solving methods in math. Your example is algebra because it has just two numbers for each day. Calculus is dynamic and continuous. So, there would be a lot of numbers in the table for each of the functions (volume and spread). But your example is a useful starting place.

Interviewer: Okay, so the oil spill example works if we think of it as two continuously changing numbers (volume and spread) related to each other. How do you relate the numbers to each other? Are you *visualizing* something, such as the oil spreading?

Instructor: I don't see the oil spill at all. As soon as I get the numbers, I immediately *visualize a GRAPH*. I can't help myself from doing so—the graph POPS into my head.

[The expert has just experienced what we call the "aha" moment, a frequent event in decoding interviews.]

Interviewer: So a graph is very important for thinking about a function in calculus—you transform the numbers into a graph. And from the graph you can make an equation?

Instructor: I can play with the graph in my mind and actually, there are two graphs, one for each of the functions (one for spread and one for volume). [He sketches a graph on the back of a napkin and then another]. Based on this graph, I can see that the spread will trail off after a while; after all, the Gulf is only so big, so the oil can only spread so far. With volume [points to the second graph] the line may go up as the volume increases and then down as attempts were made to shut the spill off. The graph is how I work with this.

Interviewer: So, the function is the relation that makes the graph?

[This is a terrible question—a stab in the dark.]

Instructor: No, the function is two sets of numbers graphed in relation to each other. With calculus, I can show the rate of change between the numbers. A steep curve shows a fast rate of change. A gentle curve shows a slow rate of change. The function describes this unique relationship.

Interviewer: But we are not showing the relationship between volume and spread—they are in two separate graphs?

(Continues)

Figure 2.7. (*Continued*)

> Instructor: The relationship is between a time stamp and spread for graph 1 and a time stamp and volume for graph 2. Given two sets of elements, each item in one set is uniquely paired with one in the second set. This creates a set of ordered pairs. The numbers from the first set are called the input and from the second are called the output. The first causes the second—the spill causes the spread. But actually, there are competing ideas about function—some say it has to have a formula or a rule. But that is not the official definition. Also, functions are all about curves.

Figure 2.8. Continuing to explore functions in calculus.

> ### Bottleneck: Understanding the Concept of Functions in Calculus
>
> Interviewer: I'm trying to understand what a function is in calculus.
> Instructor: Mathematically there's two concepts of function. One is any relationship with an input and output, so you put in a day and you get out a distance. Or you put in day two and you get out a distance. So one of them is input and output. It could be anything, any kind of relationship.
> Interviewer: Like for the mileage in your car? How far the tire has turned and the odometer reading?
> Instructor: Yes, but it could be anything. Think about the stock market, on a certain day the closing stock. So every day we plot how the stock market did. But there's no rule about it so the second concept is that it has to be a formula or a rule. Of course the stock market is a prime thing where there is no formula or rule. We don't know where it's going to end up at. So things that are done randomly, there's no formula and no rule. But I would still call that a function, in the sense that number one, that means there's definitely an answer at the end of the day there is a closing value. So to me that would be a function in the number 1 style. . . .
> Interviewer: So the function is just that there's an input and an output.
> Instructor: That's right. That's number one. And this formula rule, I mean people disagree about this, so it's not like there's a definite answer about this. Just like there's two different concepts people could be playing. So I wouldn't say that one is right and one is wrong. It's like disagreement.
> Interviewer: How do you think about that as a mathematician? You just use it one way one time and you use it another way another time? It's like this word that has two different meanings?
> Instructor: Well pretty much everything has two different meanings when you get right down to it. And you must know that.
> Interviewer: So you're not philosophically troubled by it?
> Instructor: This is the official story [points to #1 function = inputs + outputs]. So this is really the official story, "it doesn't need a formula." But I know that when scientists talk about it they really mean that [points to #2 functions = formula]. But I know that what's in the books is written as #1.

(*Continues*)

Figure 2.8. (*Continued*)

> Interviewer: In the math books?
>
> Instructor: In the math books, yes.
>
> Interviewer: And then scientists?
>
> Instructor: Scientists I think really only think about the formula—#2. That's my experience.
>
> Interviewer: I think #1 up here, input output, what's that like? I mean where do we see inputs or outputs?
>
> Instructor: In the real world?
>
> Interviewer: Yes, where's another place where we see it? I want a metaphor outside of math, something where you have inputs and you have outputs. I mean the stock market is kind of a good example of that.
>
> Instructor: I'm sure there's lots of others to use.
>
> Interviewer: But we're trying to describe function. Actually, we're trying to define function through a metaphor.
>
> Instructor: I recently was reading about the effect of various foods on your mood. So food and mood is input and output. So, let's say you're inputting alcohol, you're going to change your mood a certain way. So, your feelings are a function of your eating according to some people.
>
> Interviewer: Yes.
>
> Instructor: You're not controlling your thoughts. Your food is controlling them in some sense. So in that sense that's a function.

close at a certain number. There is no reliable rule that can predict or determine at what rate a certain stock will close, hence the need for analysts to examine stock trends. Other functions or relationships are more predictable (more like a formula), given certain conditions. This definition of a *function* is like the influence eating certain foods has on your mood and general well-being. If you eat bad food consistently, your mood and body will respond over time in a predictable manner. If you eat good food, your body and mood will respond accordingly, generally with a positive mood. If you eat good food most of the time, but have a few too many drinks one night out with colleagues, your mood the next day will more than likely be depressed or tired. While the exact degree isn't predictable, the overall effect is.

As you can see, getting to these differences within the field of calculus took some deep probing with questions from a nonexpert. Along the way, the probing also revealed a critical difference that divides calculus from algebra, dynamic change and curves. Because most students entering the classroom will have worked with algebra, they may mistakenly think that calculus works in a similar manner, that they can just input numbers to get a corresponding correct answer. What they will miss is the way in which calculus starts from a fundamentally different perspective that seeks to know the changing dynamics of relations between data rather than merely solving for an answer. Asking these questions of experts in the field reveals where students might encounter problems and can help instructors shape their courses to address these bottlenecks before they become problems.

We have outlined the basic interviewing process, but there are some other possibilities. Our methods of conducting interviews and our efforts to train interviewers to operate in different contexts have led to the development of new formats, including the use of "fishbowl" interviews and communal interviews.

The fishbowl interview is a public demonstration of how a decoding interview works. We select a "volunteer" to be interviewed—someone who is confident enough to think aloud in front of the group and be self-disclosing, while trusting enough to be brought to a place where the person might not be able to answer the questions. We ask for two volunteers from the audience to conduct the interview. We stop every few minutes to process the conduct of the interview, make suggestions, and confirm any findings.

For example, a biology professor whose bottleneck was that his students did not know how to read a research article revealed in his Step 2 interview that he usually goes straight to the results section of a research article, because he often knows the authors and thus knows the questions they are studying. Under questioning, we found that the results were usually data that appeared in the form of a statistical graph. Pressed further, he began to realize that as he read a recent graph of cell length, he pictured cell lengths. That is, he went directly from the graph to visualizing the actual objects in his mind.

During the interview, the "fishbowl" interviewers and interviewee sit in the middle of the room. Everyone else sits in a circle outside the fishbowl looking in at the interview; they are observers and notetakers about the discussion. At several points throughout the interview, the observers share their observations and ask questions.

If the group is not too large—less than 10—everyone can take part in a collective interview, such as when a group of 7 computer scientists laid out the bottlenecks in their fields and inquired of themselves and each other about how they think about recursion. This process may reveal that they approach issues in similar ways or differently, but getting explicit about it will help them teach it.

Janice Miller-Young and Jenifer Boman, working at Mt. Royal University, have added some innovations to the basic decoding interview at Mt. Royal University. In an ethnographic self-study of the decoding interview, faculty transcribed the interviews, followed by individual and then group reflection on the transcriptions. One cross-disciplinary faculty group decoded a bottleneck that was found in all of their service-learning classes—reciprocity

(Miller-Young et al., 2015; Pettit et al., 2017). Another intradisciplinary group of faculty (athletic therapy) interviewed each other on different bottlenecks in order to reorganize the curriculum. They, too, transcribed the interviews, read the transcripts, and wrote reflections about them. They discovered that they learned more from reading and reflecting on each other's interviews than if they had simply participated in the interview (Yeo et al., 2017).

Analogies in Teams or With Students

Sometimes when we have not quite decoded the mental action, we can deploy the analogy development we described for individuals as a team or as a whole-group practice, brainstorming possible analogies together (see Figure 2.9). Someone will suggest a possible analogy and the expert will be able to point out exactly what is wrong with it, which can lead to a better analogy. Usually we have to discard several analogies before we find just the right analogy that highlights the mental actions needed for success in the course. Generating analogies is a task faculty might not have experience with, but it can be learned with practice. We will return to analogies in chapter 3, as they can play an important role in modeling (see Exercise 2.3). And if we don't end up with a great analogy (which happens), later, at a class session, the teacher can ask the students to generate analogies, using Angelo and Cross's (1993) Simile CAT. From these responses, the instructor is likely to get an appropriate analogy that allows the students to understand the unfamiliar mental action through comparing it to something familiar.

Figure 2.9.   Generating a calculus analogy.

We asked a room full of faculty to help us come up with an analogy for functions, starting with the mental action of turning functions into a graph.

One teacher suggested visualizing a graph is like taking the parts of a jigsaw puzzle (with *many* pieces) and being able to see the solution immediately. The expert would use the edges and colors to see the patterns in the function; for someone who is not an expert, solving the puzzle would take a long time. This simplified analogy emphasizes seeing the patterns in a function.

After that we asked, "Where have we seen something continuous that we would sample and graph?" This question emphasized the continuous aspect of a function and soon an analogy was suggested: a strobe light shining on a disco dance. The data are like the flash of the strobe light—catching only certain moments. The actual event (the movement of the dancers) is continuous, so the graph and equation can represent the continuous dancing, not the jerky motions we see in the strobe flashes.

After trying out several analogies we hit on two that the expert agreed represented expert thinking well (see Figure 2.9). These two analogies would be useful in decoding the mental action of the expert, who, it turns out, can immediately visualize a graph when presented with data and who can also see that the data are continuous, while the graph is only capturing parts of it—some mental actions of which the novice is probably unaware.

Summary

Decoding the expert's "critical thinking" is the most challenging step in the Decoding the Disciplines approach because we are not used to thinking about teaching in terms of mental actions nor are disciplinary experts necessarily aware of their own mental actions. Methods for decoding consist of interviews, mind maps, Play-Doh, writing prompts, analogies, rubrics, and group decoding among others. Once the expert learns to make at least some mental actions explicit, teachers can present discipline-specific thinking in clear and effective ways. After this paradigm shift, teachers might wonder how they could have ever taught without knowing the underlying mental actions they wanted students to learn. The mental actions of experts have then become the foundation for instruction.

But the question remains: How precisely can we restructure students' conceptions of our fields? If the first two stages of decoding have been conducted successfully, we have identified a place where the learning of many students is blocked, and we have broken the barrier imposed by that large task into a series of well-defined mental actions. The next step is to identify the most effective strategies for modeling these ways of operating for our students, and that will be the topic of chapter 3. Then teachers can determine classroom methods that will get students through the bottlenecks.

In Appendix A, you can see how a biologist and a musicologist have addressed Step 2 in the decoding process.

CHAPTER 2 EXERCISES

Exercise 2.1: Decoding With Play-Doh

Action	Rationale
1. What do you want students to do at the end of your course? Make it out of Play-Doh or other material.	This is a bit of a warm-up so you can get used to handling the modeling material and make the leap to modeling the desired thinking in the course.
2. Pick a bottleneck where students struggle to learn. What does the expert do? Make it out of Play-Doh.	We are using a different means from what we usually do to get at hidden mental operations. By first creating a model without words, we can overcome any hidden assumptions or blocks to seeing and reveal the mental action.
3. Write in words the action that was modeled in the second Play-Doh figure. This is the mental action.	The verbal description of the mental action puts it in a form we can use (words) for later steps of decoding.

Variations of Decoding With Play-Doh

1. Other modeling materials may be used such as aluminum foil, LEGO, or a random assortment of natural objects.
2. For planning online or hybrid courses, pick a one-week course section or module in which students struggle. What would you do to get through the bottleneck?

Exercise 2.2: Decoding With Rubrics

1. List typical student errors on this assignment.
2. For each error, explain very briefly what the expert would do to avoid the error. This results in two side-by-side lists, which will form two columns in the rubric.
3. To create the actual rubric, draw a grid with four columns with these headings: Competencies, Stuck in a Bottleneck, At a Way Station, Mastered the Mental Move.
4. List the bottlenecks in in the "Stuck in a Bottleneck" column; the expert practice goes in the "Mastered the Mental Move" column.
5. Fill out the "Competencies" column by naming each one using a nominative phrase. For example, with a history bottleneck of difficulty

developing historical arguments, one category would be "Generating Possible Arguments."

6. To finish calibrating the levels of quality of effort, describe an in-between performance. What does the student who is between the expert and novice way do? Place this in the "Way Stations" column. Without calibration between success and failure, it can be difficult to help students move toward mastery.

7. If necessary, add a final column for comments or a numeric score.

8. Seek feedback on the rubric from a colleague outside your field. For example, "solves problem" might not explain clearly that an audio engineering instructor means "correlate the results of physical actions with electronic outputs and develop a system to bring a signal from one place to another." Nor would it be clear when an anthropology instructor specifies that writing with lots of "details" "meets expectations," that the instructor means that students should "select a critical incident from your observation notes to describe in detail."

Exercise 2.3: Decoding Through Analogies (The Analogy Game)

Inventing analogies to decode your implicit mental action is not as difficult as it may seem. To get started:

1. Begin with a specific mental action. What do *you* do?
2. Analyze it in terms of Bloom's typology—is it matching, visualizing, solving, and so on?
3. Ask the following: Where have I seen this function before in another context? What is this like?
4. Ask the following: Is this analogy relevant to the students? Can I think of a more relevant context for students?
5. A Boolean search of your topic along with the terms *analogies* or *metaphors* sometimes brings up an analogy that works.
6. Run your analogy by a colleague from outside the discipline—he or she might be able to suggest a more precise one.

Exercise 2.4: Conducting a Decoding Interview

1. Start with a recent, specific example of the expert successfully overcoming the bottleneck students struggle with—for example, the bottleneck is that students don't understand the concept of bias in scientific data. Then ask, "What do *you* do when you are doing this task so that you don't get

stuck at this spot? When was a recent time you came up against bias in data? What did you see? How do *you* do this? How did you handle it?"

2. When the interviewee responds, try to imagine doing the thinking described. Ask yourself, "What more do I need to know so I can (mentally) do it?" Performing the mental tasks as described allows the interviewer to see where expert thinking might be covered up. "How is this different from the way I think about bias? What sorts of things do I need to know to understand bias in data? How do I know what to look at to determine the bias in data?"

3. Probe any place where the interviewer cannot explain. (*Repeat this step* often in the interview.) For example, the interviewer might say, "So you say that the data are factual, but they are also biased. I don't understand how they can be both at once. Can you explain that to me?"

4. Summarize—reflect back to the interviewer what was said without the fine details. (*Repeat this step* several times in the interview, particularly when the expert has gotten stuck.) "So bias is not conscious selection of some data over other data, but is caused by methods of collecting data?" for example.

5. Toward the end of the interview, abstract and list the main three to five mental actions. Categorize the mental action in terms of one of Bloom's typology levels: analyzing (taking things apart), synthesizing (generation or combination of elements into a new idea), applying (using procedures to solve a problem), or evaluating (making judgments based on criteria). "So all data have bias because our methods always involve sampling. So I would need to identify the *sort* of bias that might be in the data (analysis). I would do this by thinking about the possible ways data might be gathered in this situation and how the method might influence the data (application). I would have to know what the authors did to compensate for the errors produced by their method of sampling (evaluation). And then I would determine whether given the inaccuracy inherent in data gathering there is still reason to see the author's conclusions as reasonable. I would have to know how much inaccuracy is likely to be in the data as well (evaluation)."

6. Continue to ask for more details until (a) the bottleneck has been fully explicated, (b) there's a reasonable expectation that the student will be able to perform the mental actions, or (c) the expert cannot explain further.

3

STEP 3

Modeling

Principles of Modeling

In our previous chapters, we did not address the issue of teaching. Step 1 focused on identifying bottlenecks to student learning and Step 2—the "decoding" step of Decoding the Disciplines—focus on making explicit the tacit mental actions that an expert uses to navigate through the bottleneck. Only after the expert's tacit critical thinking is uncovered does the Decoding the Disciplines model turn to teaching students how to perform it. In this chapter we focus on getting students through the bottleneck by demonstrating the mental action for the students in a way the students can readily grasp. In chapter 4 we discuss how to provide students with practice and feedback on their attempts to negotiate the bottleneck (Step 4). In chapter 5 we treat two issues: motivating students to persevere in their efforts to pass through the bottleneck and holding them accountable for doing the sometimes challenging work to do so (Step 5). In chapter 6 we turn to assessing the degree to which students are able to negotiate the bottleneck (Step 6).

Step 3 is the "lecturing" step; it shows the expert critical thinking in action. In this step, we want to take extra care to convey to students the information that we gathered in the first two steps of the decoding process. While some may think that they already practice this in their teaching, it is often the case that the first two steps indicated tasks that have not been fully explicated to students. Following a couple of principles will help increase the effectiveness of the modeling step for teachers.

- Modeling Principle 1: Use an analogy from outside of the discipline.
- Modeling Principle 2: Demonstrate the mental action on a disciplinary example using metaexplanation to show exactly where the expert's attention should focus.

Metaexplanation is particularly important, since many teachers will argue that they already provide examples of disciplinary thinking through their lectures. In fact, as of 2012, 70% of male teachers in STEM fields use lecture as their primary teaching method (Hurtado, Eagen, Pryor, Whang, & Tran, 2012). Lecturing is still extremely common in other fields as well. However, for students to recognize what is happening, the instructor needs to point out where the mental action applies in the example; the meta-explanation is crucial to that effort.

Through the power of analogies and meta-explanations, these modified lectures can clearly show students that a particular kind of thinking is needed in this class, a mental move that may differ from what they ordinarily do. Otherwise, students do not necessarily pick up on the thinking going on. In a similar fashion, teachers may observe good teachers, but their own teaching is more likely to be transformed by an understanding of the research behind good teaching.

We have stressed the creation of analogies in this section because they work very well for many teachers and students. The best analogies have the power to bring students into the new ways of thinking. This section describes the usefulness of analogies for flipped classes, taking the "lecture" from content delivery toward the modeling of how to perform disciplinary thinking. Because the modeling step is so effective in getting to students successfully overcoming the bottleneck, this chapter includes three exercises for developing analogies—out of your own expertise, from an expert, or from students.

Modeling Principle 1: Use an Analogy From Outside of the Discipline

Selecting Analogies

It can be difficult for students to know exactly which "mental muscles" to activate to reproduce the expert's thinking—if they are even aware that the expert is thinking differently from them—so modeling starts with the illustration of the mental action via an analogy or a metaphor. Almost every mental action we want students to do is something they have previously engaged in (with a few exceptions: quantum physics has few analogues in the everyday world). Analogies are modeling mechanisms on which we can draw to make unfamiliar domains familiar. Analogies and metaphors work as inferential frameworks by tapping into existing, related ideas and transferring their relational structures to other domains (Jones, Ross, Lynam, Perez, & Leitch, 2011). By making a comparison, analogies show students which mental actions to turn on for critical thinking in a particular situation or problem. Because analogies can make the strange more familiar, they are useful for making clear an unknown mental action.

For the purposes of decoding, a good analogy is based in content from outside the discipline and uses something familiar to students. Because new forms of disciplinary thinking are difficult to "see" (e.g., all the parts of a gene, which are embedded in a cell, which are in turn embedded in a living organism), the mental action of interest is "camouflaged" to the outsider. Those in a discipline share assumptions and jargon so that the insiders know every word used and the actions the words entail. If we remove the mental action from the disciplinary example, take off the disciplinary camouflage, and "dress" it in another outfit, we can isolate the mental action. For example, we can model RNA replication through the analogy of photocopying. For students who know how a photocopier works, replication is like a molecular photocopier that "scans" the gene and spits out a perfect copy.

The more familiar an analogy is, the more likely students will be able to relate to it. Familiarity depends on the age and context of the students. For college students, such topics as roommates, dating, friendships, and family can be good sources for analogies. However, culture constrains understanding; analogies that may be useful for some students might be less familiar to others. Analogies that keep cultural context in mind will avoid topics that students are less likely to understand.

- *Foods*—One might think that foods seem familiar to all people, but certain foods might not. Joan's family loves the German breakfast food *goetta*, but unless you are from Cincinnati (or even if you are), you may not be familiar with *goetta*.
- *Sports*—Doesn't everyone love football? Not really; that is a specialized kind of knowledge that may include a gender bias.
- *Holidays*—These vary widely by family context, religion, and other background.
- *Movies*—These date extraordinarily fast.

These limitations do not mean that analogies should be avoided, only that we have to keep the audience in mind (and not least, that we are not part of that audience anymore). When we create analogies, we map them to the target concept, taking the similarities and misunderstandings into account. It is important to anticipate the analogy-caused misconceptions and eliminate them by contrasting them with epistemologically appropriate analogies (Ubuz, Eryilmaz, Aydin, Bayazit, Universitesi, & Kayseri, 2009). (See chapter 5 for more about how to contrast inapplicable conceptions with conceptually useful ones.)

The analogies in Figure 3.1 work because they are from outside the target discipline and are likely to be familiar to students. More importantly, by

Figure 3.1. Examples of analogies.

Education—Students often get stuck choosing a research question. Finding a research question is like selecting a college to attend. Each person has a different combination of interests and criteria. Some may want to attend college in a certain locale, urban or rural. Others may concentrate on the campus culture, such as prevalence of fraternities and sororities; or a historically Black university culture. Cost and availability of financial aid may be the deciding factor for other students. They make a list of specific requirements, just as one would for finding a research question—problems to be solved, methodology to be used, research subjects, and theory. Tying the act of choosing a college to the process of selecting a research question enables students to transfer the same type of mental action from a familiar action to a less familiar task.

Social Work—Students have difficulty understanding a social theory of Max Weber's that posits that people with power constantly act on those without it and that power-wielding groups act to maintain their power over other groups. An analogy that helps students understand the way powerless groups constantly have their power undercut by those in power is beach erosion. Overpowering and relentless waves wash the sand away from the beach, but there are methods for halting beach erosion, just as in social work, there are frameworks that can be brought to bear to deal with the control of the powerful over the powerless. (*Courtesy of Tanya Putnam, Western Carolina University*)

Physical Therapy—In the field of physical therapy, students often do not realize that they need to pay attention to some signals more than others, depending on the patient and their muscular-skeletal issue. They can't just follow a recipe. An analogy can be made to the amplitude adjustments a sound engineer makes on a soundboard. Some bars are pushed up and others lowered, depending on the piece of music and the instrumentation. Comparing a signal from the muscular-skeletal system of a particular individual with the signal a sound engineer modulates for a certain piece of music helps students understand the importance of watching for the signals in a particular situation. (*Courtesy of John Carzoli, Western Carolina University*)

Library Science—An analogy for scholarly searches versus popular searches is online dating. When someone decides to date online, they have many choices of sites to use. A person is likely to choose their dating site based on the desired relationship outcome (a potential friend, date, hookup, companion, or spouse). Some sites use forms that ask for specific information about users and their potential matches, while others do not require as much information. Those that require more information are likely to provide fewer matches, but those matches will likely be better suited to the user's desires. However, the sites that ask for little information are likely to produce a far greater number of potential matches whose relevance will need to be assessed by the user. This is much like a search for scholarly information. When performing a scholarly search, one has to decide

(Continues)

Figure 3.1. (*Continued*)

> the kind of search engine to use—a general one or a discipline-specific database. Queries developed for a scholarly search are typically far more specific than those of a general search. Returns from a general search engine are numerous and sometimes are not very good or relevant to the searcher's needs. In contrast, a search that has a strong query and is conducted using a database that was developed about a specific source will typically produce returns that are specific and relevant but will produce fewer of them. (*Courtesy of Eiyana Favers, Indiana University*)

highlighting particular attributes of the target analogue, they show which mechanisms make up the mental action.

Analogies can make available the mental moves of the expert so students can get through difficult bottlenecks, such as choosing a research question (we match substantive and personal choices as we consider many features); viewing groups as structured with power or not, and frameworks for action; paying more attention to some signals than others; and evaluating different search engines to get our best search result. Not all concepts need an analogy; usually only the more difficult, critical bottlenecks do.

One of the bottlenecks that is found across disciplines and reliably trips students up is systems thinking. Analogies (and metaphors) influence thinking most where direct experience or perceptual understanding is limited, which is often the case with systems thinking; it's hard to get the full scope of the model all at once and on our own. Complex systems are at the heart of many of the world's most difficult problems: climate change or epidemics, for example. When many complex parts are connected, students do not know how to reason using the mental model of the expert to chunk parts together, analyze causes, and strategize solutions. For example, law students struggle to predict which precedent in which court will affect a current case; in sustainability studies, students struggle to keep the ecological and social factors interconnected; in feminist studies students struggle with methodological pluralism (which framework should they use?). The problem raised by the teacher in the calculus example in chapter 2 might also be thought of as a systems-thinking problem; students have difficulty moving beyond the direct relationships of algebra. Unbeknownst to students (and sometimes to the expert!), the expert has a model of the system in his or her mind. Systems are often represented by models, because models can represent abstractions, either physically or tacitly, in the minds of experts.

Thibodeau, Winneg, Frantz, and Flusberg (2015) experimented with metaphors to promote systems thinking. Their experiments demonstrated that metaphors that emphasize the complexity of a system, rather than simplify the parts, enhance holistic and relational reasoning. Students wrote more about systems when income inequality was compared to a failing organ of the body than when the metaphor compared it to a blemish, a surface detail.

Because analogies and metaphors help students apply existing knowledge to unfamiliar areas and do so powerfully, quickly, and precisely, they are very useful, but they are not always easy to come up with. In the next section, we provide some ways to develop analogies.

Inventing Analogies
In chapter 2 we used analogies to decode the mental action. Those analogies might be usable with students, although perhaps others would need to be developed. Creating analogies is not only a skill that can be learned but also useful in that it encourages both the teacher and the students to integrate what they know (Perkins, 2010). When we began to use analogies to demonstrate mental actions in various disciplines, we would ask colleagues who were good at generating analogies to help us come up with them. But over time we have learned to generate them by imagining doing the mental action; observing what that mental action feels like; and remembering where we did that, or something similar, before.

To come up with an analogy, we often compare the mental action to the basic categories of Bloom's typology. This quick mental review can help narrow down the kind of analogy we are looking for:

- *Analysis*—Am I taking things apart? Examining the parts?
- *Synthesis*—Am I putting things together in a new way? Creating something new?
- *Evaluation*—Am I judging or rating something?
- *Application*—Am I trying out a procedure or model in a new context or case study? With a new audience?

As we have worked with experts, we have often offered them analogies. Sometimes our ideas seem a little outrageous; planning an autobiographical art project is like . . . planning what to take on a camping trip? However, when we offer a less-than-perfect analogy, the expert is usually able to see what is wrong with our initial analogy and determine where it misses the mental action. At this point the expert can usually propose a better one. In chapter 2, for example, the biology professor whose bottleneck was that his students did not know how to read a research article had revealed in his Step 2 interview that he usually goes straight to the results section of a research article to visualize the actual objects represented in the data represented by a graph. So, the translation from a graph to the real objects being quantified in the graph is the mental action for which we wanted to create an analogy. In a room full of instructors, we asked everyone to suggest an analogy for reading a graph. The faculty suggested many analogies, including making a picture by connecting the dots or reading a map. The biology professor did not quite like these because they did not emphasize what he emphasized; however, the analogies got closer, such as imagining an actual landscape from the symbols on a map. We began to understand that this mental action involved translation. Finally, an audience member suggested it is like reading musical notes on a staff and hearing the sounds of the notes in your head. The biology professor agreed that this was a good analogy to demonstrate reading a research article. For nonmusical students (since music education has been cut in schools) we might suggest reading a graph is like reading written words on a page and sounding them out. Even though we had broken down reading a research article into several component parts during the Step 2 Decoding interview, creating the analogy for modeling at Step 3 helped us get even clearer about what the critical step consisted of. Now just as a reading teacher teaches children the sound each letter makes, the biologist becomes aware of the need to highlight translating the numbers in the graph into the actual objects the graph data represent, so his students will know on which aspect of the mental action to focus their attention when reading a research article.

Our goal at this point is not to offer the perfect analogy, but to help experts find one that demonstrates their mental action. At the end of the chapter, we provide an exercise (Exercise 3.1) based on the bottleneck writing tour (see Figure 2.2), in which you will reflect on the mental action and brainstorm possible analogies for the kind of thinking you want your students to do. This, or one of the exercises that follow, should give you a strong analogy.

We have assumed thus far that you are trying to teach a sort of thinking that is central to what you do. However, many teachers are asked to teach topics on which they are not subject matter specialists; this is nothing new for most teachers. Analogies can be useful in this situation as well, although without personal expertise, coming up with the analogies is more of a challenge. In this case, approach a colleague or an expert to help you develop analogies and metaphors to convey to students the types of thinking you want them to perform.

A third way to come up with analogies is to ask the students (in teams or individually) to offer analogies for the mental action. Angelo and Cross's (1993) Classroom Assessment Techniques (CATs) check on what, how, and how well students are learning. The Simile CAT, an adaptation, asks students to invent an analogy, which can both check their understanding and further it (see Exercise 3.3).

Students may need a little team practice when they are learning to generate analogies, but with repetition, they will be able to do it. The Simile CAT then asks students to reflect on their analogy and explain the comparison between the analogues. Such metacognitive work is instructive for students (because it reminds them that there are different ways to think about the material they are learning) and also provides feedback for instructors. As usual, taking a few minutes for formative assessment gives the students a chance to reflect on their learning and really think about what they learned, while giving instructors insight into what was learned and their teaching. For example, in Joan's graduate pedagogy course, students were prompted using the Simile CAT. Their prompt was "Matching teaching methods to mental moves is like . . ." They responded:

- Picking the right bait when fishing
- Putting a jigsaw puzzle together
- Identifying plants
- Selecting a recipe that mixes ingredients to get Grandma's golden biscuits

These analogies suggest a careful matching and attention to detail (the last one includes some affective issues). The teacher can use the new analogies built by the students to demonstrate the mental action in future iterations of the course. Students often come up with analogies that are particularly resonant for a teacher's audience.

By using analogies prior to a disciplinary example, students will have an easier time applying the same mental muscles within the discipline. Having considered three ways to develop analogies, the next section focuses on explicit modeling within the discipline.

Modeling Principle 2: Demonstrate the Mental Action on a Disciplinary Example Using Metaexplanation to Show Exactly Where the Expert's Attention Should Focus

Once you have shown students the mental action using the analogy, it is time to demonstrate it with an example from within the discipline, accompanied by metaexplanation. Providing disciplinary examples and case studies is a mainstay of teaching. However, in spite of all the time instructors spend on disciplinary examples, there are several problems with teaching through examples where there is no metaexplanation. Students often fail to recall pertinent examples (Gick & Holyoak, 1983). Also, students may not draw appropriate implications or conclusions from the examples or cases shown them, nor know how to deploy the expertise that was demonstrated because their knowledge is inert (Gentner, Loewenstein, & Thompson, 2003). For example, when historians provide evidence for an argument, some students may hear it, especially in lectures, as just a story, particularly if their attention has not been called to the fact that there *is* an argument. In other words, students fall back on the ways they are used to thinking about the material. Thus, the points that teachers hope will be understood from the presentation of disciplinary examples may not be evident to students because they do not necessarily know what the expert *did* or what *they* should do.

The solution to this problem is for teachers not only to work through the example but also to call explicit attention to their thinking as they do it, by thinking aloud. In other words they spell out each of their mental actions and make metacomments about why and how certain steps are taken. This is metaexplanation or metacognition, explaining one's own thinking. This shift from lecture-on-content alone to lecture-on-how-to-think-about-content is subtle but profound. It pinpoints exactly what the students should *do*. Of course, it is only possible for the teacher to lead students so explicitly through a disciplinary example once the mental actions have been decoded at Step 2.

Figure 3.2. A modeling lesson in art history (Stephanie Beck-Cohen).

An instructor described an analogy between the style signature of clothing designers and identifying an unknown work of art. Just as it is possible to identify fashion designers by their signature fashion style (Ralph Lauren = preppy and sporty, khakis and polo shirts), art historians can similarly recognize the elements that indicate different artists. To show where her attention is focused, she examines an unknown fresco, applying the concepts introduced in class: form and composition, line, color, texture, perspective and foreshortening, and proportion and scale. Disregarding the content—the cross, angels, crowd, halos—and not yet revealing the identity of the artist, she puts a "mental sticky note" on the elements important to the underlying structure. To mark the focus of her attention she places actual sticky notes on the slide image:

At the central focus point: everyone is looking at Jesus.
On the empty background: where there is only a single color.
On the front of the picture plane: where the scene takes place.
On a face: the faces are filled with emotion.

After looking at several other works by the same artist, she reveals the artist (Giotto) and the dates and titles of his works. Having repeated this demonstration with several other pieces, the students will be ready to practice what to look for in works by Giotto, even ones they have not been shown before.

Figure 3.2 shows modeling for an art history bottleneck in which students struggle to identify unknown works of art.

Once the teacher has presented the outside-the-discipline analogy (clothing fashion styles), and demonstrated the within-the-discipline example with explanatory metacomments (using sticky notes), students gain an idea of the mental action used to navigate the bottleneck.

Pointing out exactly what the expert does in the midst of a disciplinary example may seem like a minor detail, and without having decoded the expert's mental action at Step 2, the teacher may not know what should be pointed out. But if we want students to learn how to perform the complex mental actions of our fields, it is important to show them in detail what we want them to do. For example, the biology professor in the earlier example may want to create a cartoon showing him looking at a graph of numbers with a mind bubble that shows him visualizing cell lengths, so students can see him making the leap from the data to the objects that are represented in the graph. We provide an exercise at the back of the chapter to help you develop a way to highlight the mental action, whether you are working alone or in a team (see Exercise 3.4).

Ben Nelson, an educational reformer, argues that lecturing should go the way of the dinosaur. His Minerva Project (G. Wood, 2014) is trying to reinvent college by eliminating lectures—formal, prepared talks. Nelson's target is the lecture used largely as a form of content delivery, which we know to be inefficient for many students, even if some students—the students most like their teachers—learn well from them. We would agree that this form of the lecture is overused and inefficient. However, we would argue that lectures can be helpful to show what is expected of students, the form critical thinking takes in the field or class—in other words, as demonstrations of process rather than delivery of content or conclusions. Some forms of lecturing already accomplish these kinds of purposes: demonstrations in science; worked problems in math; and, yes, providing just-in-time content for students to put to use on the spot. Modeling most closely resembles the use of lecture for demonstration, but with the addition of a metacognitive element, an explicit reference to the thinking involved in moving through the demonstration. Of course, there are ways to model the mental action other than the professor giving an in-class lecture, including YouTube videos or the plethora of instructional videos (or clips from them) found on the Internet, or selected readings from books or articles. Lectures may not be necessary, but when designed to model thinking well (including analogies and highlighting), they can be very useful. When we think of modeling, we think of a demonstration of the mental process, not knowledge delivery.

Are We Spoon-Feeding Students?

Some people ask us whether making the thinking of the expert explicit is making things too easy for the students. They seem to feel that struggling with not understanding is a necessary part of student learning, and that if students cannot understand, they should choose a different subject to study. We have several answers to this objection. First, we would argue that the purpose of education is not to limit teaching to those learners who are able to intuit the ways of knowing of the discipline, but to open up—demystify or, to use the terminology we have chosen, to *decode*—those ways of knowing to make them accessible for as many students as possible. Most students will never become experts in our disciplines, nor do they want to, but in their lives as citizens they will need to know something about how various kinds of experts produce knowledge and thus how they think. For instance, they will need to know something about how scientists theorize, because they will be asked to vote on policy matters that are dependent on scientific arguments. Second, in many cases we are asking students to do cognitive work that they are able to do only with help; that is, we're asking them to reason in their area of proximal development, which is where the richest learning occurs (Vygotsky, 1978). Finally, it's not that when we decode the thinking of our disciplines students find it easy to do, just as we don't find it "easy" to work in our disciplines even though we know how to think in them. We (and the students) still have to do the work. But the *kind* of work we can get students to do is of higher quality, more authentic, and more valuable for them to do and more interesting for us to evaluate.

Summary

The modeling step is the time and place for lectures or other forms of exposition of the mental action, but with some additions: an analogy from outside the discipline, an example from within the discipline (the disciplinary content), and commentary that points out the key actions as the example is performed. Developing analogies is one of the best ways to check that the mental action is clear. It is difficult for students to know which mental muscles to activate without the analogy removed from disciplinary content. As the mental action is performed in the disciplinary context, metaexplanations of exactly what the expert focuses on point out where the critical thinking takes place. The modeling in Step 3 is just the beginning of teaching students to perform the mental action, but it is an important starting place.

In Appendix A, you can see how a biologist and a musicologist have addressed Step 3 in the decoding process.

CHAPTER 3 EXERCISES

Exercise 3.1: Reflective Writing for Analogy Development

1. Begin with a specific mental action—be very clear about it. State the mental action here: _____.
2. Imagine doing this mental action. What does performing the mental action feel like?
3. Analyze it in terms of Bloom's typology. Is it matching, visualizing, solving, and so on?
4. Where have you seen this mental action used in another context? For example, if analyzing, where have you seen this kind of analysis before? What is doing this like?
5. Brainstorm one more analogy. Is there another realm where you have seen this mental action in use?
6. Describe one of your analogies to a colleague to see if she or he can suggest a better analogy.
7. Once you have invented or collected three analogies, try them out with your students. Which one do they like best? Be sure to ask them why.

Exercise 3.2: Prompts to Get an Expert to Provide an Analogy

For individuals

Write to someone you know who is an expert on the topic and ask for an analogy. Be sure to do the following:

1. Describe the bottleneck—a specific place in the course where over and over again students get stuck. What is it that students get wrong?
2. Ask the expert to think about what the expert does when facing this bottleneck to avoid getting stuck. Can the expert think of an analogy for what is done to avoid the bottleneck? What is doing this like?

OR

Interview an expert who is familiar with the bottleneck.

1. Ask the expert to describe the bottleneck where students get stuck.
2. Ask the expert what is done to avoid getting stuck in the bottleneck—be sure to ask for a description of a recent time when that kind of thinking was used. What did the expert do? Be sure to probe to fully understand the answer.
3. Ask the expert to suggest an analogy for a key mental action—and be prepared to suggest one to get the ideas rolling.

Decoding in community (teams)
Break into teams of three. Help each person develop an analogy to show the mental process that will be familiar to students. (8 minutes each)

- Ask yourself: Where have I seen this mental action before?
- What is it like? Don't be afraid to suggest a "bad" analogy—team members often reject the first analogy, but their explanation of what is wrong will get the team closer to a better one.
- Keep taking analogies until the team is relatively satisfied.

Debrief afterward in the larger group: Can someone share a useful analogy? How do analogies help show the mental action?

Exercise 3.3: Simile CAT

Begin with the specific mental action—whether generating hypotheses, reading a research article or primary source, and so forth—and insert it in the blank space provided.

1. Compare _____ to something similar of your choice. What is it like?
2. Explain what makes this an effective analogy.

Exercise 3.4: Highlighting the Mental Action Through Modeling

Individual writing reflection
How can you highlight the mental action in a specific disciplinary example? That is, how will you indicate to students . . . what indicates where the argument lies? The style elements that mark a particular artist? What the data represent? How will you provide metacommentary so students know where to focus?

In teams of three
Help each person create a way to highlight mental actions during a disciplinary example. (15 minutes each)
   Debrief questions:

- Will someone share a useful highlighting technique?
- How is highlighting useful?

4

STEP 4

Practicing Critical Thinking in a Discipline

Imagine this all-too-common scenario: When an economics teacher worked a problem in front of the class, it seemed to make sense to his students. At the end of the class, both the instructor and the students felt like they had a firm grasp of how to work similar problems. But later, when students tried to do their homework, suddenly they were unsure what to do. After discovering the students' problem, the teacher made this analogy: It's like they can sing along with the radio, but once the radio is turned off, they can't remember how the song goes. The teacher learned a valuable lesson that day: Watching someone perform a task and performing the same task alone are two very different things. The lesson here: Most students can't learn just by watching the teacher; they have to practice, which is Step 4 of Decoding the Disciplines. Through practice and feedback, students will actually apply the mental action to acquire or maintain proficiency in what was modeled for them in Step 3. Effective feedback along the way shows students where to direct further efforts and indicates to the teacher when repeated practice may be needed.

While all teachers recognize the need for practice and regularly assign it to their students, there is more to practice and feedback than just choosing a method. Prior to the past few decades, college teachers did not have a lot of classroom teaching methods to choose from. With the advent of teaching centers 50 years ago (Cook & Kaplan, 2012) there are now seemingly thousands of teaching techniques available and the crucial question has become "When do we apply particular methods?" Still, teachers may not know very many methods, because most of us probably experienced only very traditional methods ourselves, so teachers' selection of methods may be haphazard. They may choose to use technology because it is cool (and much hyped). For instance, a teacher may have students make documentaries because videos are a popular medium, even though technology is only a means to an end and enhances learning only when the unique capability of technology supports the mental action (Oblinger & Hawkins, 2006). Furthermore, the introduction of a technology requires that students be taught to use it. If learning to use the technology is important to the class, this is justified. If it isn't, the time might be better spent elsewhere.

Or a teacher might choose a method that he or she has seen someone else use. For instance, a teacher might choose to stage a debate in a political science class on this topic: "Resolved: The role of the state is to ensure that justice is to be done." If creating a persuasive argument is the desired mental action, then a debate exercise is an appropriate method, as the intention of debate is to persuade others through argument that their position is the proper one. However, if the teacher wants students to analyze the philosophy of government in Locke's essay *Second Treatise of Government* and compare it to the philosophy of government expressed in the Declaration of Independence, then creating a reader's guide for both texts would be a better method.

Finally, a teacher may simply select an "active" method of instruction because he or she has heard that active learning encourages better learning, and there is considerable support for this belief. Numerous studies, especially in the sciences, have shown that when compared to the passive reception of lectures, active *doing* by students increases learning (Hake, 1998; Hoellwarth & Moelter, 2011). Meta-analysis of students in lecture-only classes found that they were 1.5 times more likely to fail a course than students in sections where they were required to apply what they were learning (Freeman et al., 2014).

However, not *all* forms of activity increase learning. One study of a random sample of biology classes found no relationship between active learning and student performance. The authors attribute the lack of gains from active learning to instructor proficiency (or lack thereof) with active learning methods (Andrews, Leonard, Colgrove, & Kalinowski, 2011). Simply having students "do" something doesn't work when the teacher is not clear on what kind of thinking the students ought to be practicing.

Here Decoding the Disciplines offers guidance on how to select activities that enhance learning, namely activities that are directly focused on the necessary mental action students should learn and perform. For example, a biology lesson's goal might be for students to generate scientific hypotheses. If the teacher simply asked the students to "discuss" the morphology of butterflies (their shapes and structures), given such a vague prompt, students might discuss the different butterflies in their locale, the range or colors of butterflies, or the unique features of some species. That is, this learning exercise would not necessarily prompt students to generate hypotheses. For effective active learning, the practice must aim at the specific mental action.

While working with teachers and instructors through decoding workshops and research, we have observed many unfocused practice activities. For example, some teachers show a movie in class without showing students their analytical frame, so the students react based on whether they liked the movie. Similarly, students in an interior design class were assigned to critique each other's designs; they were willing to say only what they liked about other students' work, even though the teacher wanted them to make formative critiques. However, she had not provided them practice in making comments about what could be improved. For active learning methods to be effective, they should foster practice of the mental action. In other words, practice is not just a matter of grabbing an active structure that seems fun or different. The mental task has to be matched to the type of thinking the students are to practice. The more active methods emphasize the desired kinds of thinking, the more these methods improve learning.

We also strongly suggest that the practice be focused on one particular mental action or sequence of actions rather than a holistic kind of exercise. We might compare this, as David Perkins (2010) does, to a skills drill in Little League baseball. It is difficult to develop competence at a particular task while also simultaneously performing others. This is why novice drivers are often taken to large, empty parking lots, where they can get the feel of steering the car without having to worry about changing traffic signals or other drivers. This doesn't mean he or she will not ever drive on the road, but a good driving teacher will pull the novice off the road to practice a skill the novice is struggling with.

It is very useful to have students practice a particular move or set of moves a number of times so that the moves are naturalized and available to be used in the other more complex tasks the students will also have to perform. So students in physics may practice interpreting graphs before they are asked to deploy this competence in a more complex problem. Art history students may practice looking for aspects of the styles of artists before they write an essay on stylistic development in Renaissance art. *This is why we usually recommend focusing on one bottleneck and teaching it thoroughly.*

Because designing the right sort of practice for students is so important, chapter 4 is organized around six principles of practice:

- Practice Principle 1: Create practice for the component skills.
- Practice Principle 2: Provide repeated practice for difficult mental actions.

- Practice Principle 3: Bring the component skills back together.
- Practice Principle 4: Match practice methods to mental actions through Bloom's typology.
- Practice Principle 5: Create awareness in students of their own thought processes and the ways of thinking in your field.
- Practice Principle 6: Design effective feedback after practice.

Practice Principle 1: Create Practice for the Component Skills

Difficult skills cannot be learned all at once or only by watching others perform them. Most students, for example, would not be expected to watch someone waltz and then, after only watching, stand up and be able to waltz. Problems with the practice step may arise because of a failure to model the component moves fully at Step 3. In a math class a teacher may solve several calculus problems on the board, or the instructor in a creative writing class may read several beautiful poems to his or her students. For homework afterward, they may assign the students to solve a calculus problem or to write a poem on their own. But the teacher has not broken the calculus problem-solving or poetry writing into its parts nor designed practice of those component skills, aiming especially at the most difficult parts—the bottlenecks. As a result, only a few students, often those who are educationally advantaged, are successful.

To give an example from calculus, when students are attempting to solve a calculus problem, they may not know the pertinent mental actions they need to deploy. They may not know

- where to start;
- how to translate words to symbols and then back again;
- what variables should represent;
- how to represent the relationship between the variables;
- procedures and concepts from earlier math classes, such as factoring from algebra, or knowing facts of trigonometry that may be necessary for this problem;
- what to do if they get stuck; or
- how to check their work.

To give an example from creative writing, students may not know the components of writing a poem, so depending on the course goals, the instructor may need to develop a series of practices that helps students who struggle with the components of writing a poem. They may not know

- that different genres of writing exist and what makes poetry its own genre;
- where creative writers get inspiration (or that they even need inspiration);
- how to come up with their first draft or that writing a poem will involve many drafts;
- how to write inductively, letting the reader experience concrete, specific images and feelings;
- how to find just the right words to describe that experience;
- how to generate effective metaphors;
- which literary devices they might employ; or
- how to judge when a poem is finished.

In designing practice for students, the teacher needs to build a series of assignments that focus on the bottlenecks and the underlying mental actions. What looked like one bottleneck may turn out to be several bottlenecks, the components of a more complex mental action. Once the components have been revealed, only then can exercises for these components be devised, giving more time and effort to where students struggle the most (see Exercise 4.1).

Teaching to the bottlenecks and sub-bottlenecks sets the priorities in the classroom and helps the teacher better design deliberate practice. When the components of critical thinking have been identified in Step 2 and modeled in Step 3, then the teacher knows the parts that should be designed for students to practice in Step 4. If the sorts of thinking the teacher desires to teach are truly central to the discipline, showing students how to do it is not "teaching to the test."

Teachers working in the context of the flipped classroom can take advantage of the portfolio of methods for practice to use class time wisely. Practice is the centerpiece of the flipped classroom: All of the difficult things a teacher wants students to be able *to do* get practiced in teams with the teacher available to help as needed. Once teachers learn how to bring active problem-solving into the class, they will be able to say what an experienced team-based learning practitioner claimed: "That is where the fun is."

Practice Principle 2: Provide Repeated Practice for Difficult Mental Actions

Just as students cannot learn a demanding new mental action through observation alone, even with explicit metacommentary, most students cannot master a new mental action in only one practice session. Repetition helps students firmly establish mental patterns so they become automatic. This is particularly true if the skill goes against the ways they have worked in previous years of schooling; in that case, they will need repeated practice to break old habits and overcome misconceptions about the discipline (see chapter 5 on motivation).

However, repetition of the same skill (drill) can become boring and ineffective. To show students that the mental actions may be used in somewhat different forms, variation in practice methods is called for. In an example from an advertising class (see Figure 4.1), we devised eight different methods for students to practice the mental action of choosing and inventing creative advertising strategies; teachers do not have to use all of these, but teachers can choose the appropriate ones to build students' skills.

Figure 4.1. Practice in an advertising class categorized by competency.

Creating an Advertising Strategy
Principles of Creative Advertising (300-Level Journalism Class)

Step 1 Bottleneck: Students want to execute the technical advertisement (e.g., produce a video or a magazine ad) before devising the strategy for the ad.

Step 2 Decode Expert Thinking: Experts generate a strategy that includes a creative construct (often visual) before they decide the format of the advertisement.

Step 3 Modeling Metaphor: Novices to any sport may watch the game without being aware of the strategy employed. However, when a soccer team is trying to kick the ball into the net, the team has a playbook with many plays to choose from and the players know when to implement a certain strategy. Next, the teacher shows numerous examples of creative strategy for advertising. The analogy helps them know what kind of thinking this is—it is like choosing from a sports playbook. This doesn't mean that they will never invent a new play, but it is more likely that they will use an already existing strategy than invent a new one. With all of the plays in mind, now it is time to learn how to select one for a certain advertising objective (which was taught as a previous lesson).

Step 4 Practice: How will you have students *practice* devising a creative strategy rather than execution of the advertisement?

1. List five creative strategies. (REMEMBERING)
2. Dissect the creative components of existing ads (Who is the audience? What characteristics of the product are emphasized? etc.). (ANALYZING)
3. Analyze the strategic metaphors of existing ads (What does the metaphor emphasize?). (ANALYZING)

(*Continues*)

Figure 4.1. (*Continued*)

---

4. Devise an advertising strategy. (CREATING) They pass their strategy to another team, who tells them whom they think it's for and what it says about the product (or whatever other aspects of the ad are important beyond the technical execution). (ANALYZING)
5. Practice generating multiple advertising strategies using Balderdash (the party game)–style creative pitches. The teacher provides prompts and teams or individuals have a few minutes to come up with a creative pitch. Everyone stands up and pitches one at a time. If a pitch is similar to another pitch, both sit down. Those standing at the end invented the most original pitches. (CREATING/EVALUATING)
6. Draw a cartoon of their creative strategy (either one frame or several frames). (CREATING)
7. Last one standing competition—Develop a creative strategy (CREATING). The team uses a free online voting tool (e.g., Socrative) to choose the strategy that will go forward from their team. The class continues to vote on the strategies, with token (even joke) prizes for the first, second, and third. (If the class is large, each section can put forward their winning strategy to the whole class.) (EVALUATING)
8. Summarize a creative strategy in one adjective. Describe why they chose that word in two sentences (Word Journal CAT). (EVALUATING)

The mechanics of practice can increase competency on the mental action two- and threefold (Rohrer & Pashler, 2010). "Retrieval," the simple recall of information, is a form of practice that increases learning and slows forgetting. From the example in Figure 4.1, students can practice retrieving creative strategies through self-quizzes, flash cards, or mnemonics.

Practice that is spaced over time also improves long-term learning. For students to remember advertising strategies over the long term, previously studied concepts need to be revisited at intervals. Mixed practice also improves learning; rather than studying creative strategy all in a block and then moving on to the next topic (execution and process), intermingle strategy and execution exercises. Requiring continued retrieval of the mental action through cumulative tests or assignments promotes learning better than teaching a subject once and not returning to it. So does giving assignments where previous mental actions are used across a semester along with new ones. For example, one might build and then continue to use a creative strategy as students work on execution and process and produce ads for different media.

In an example from a game design class (see Figure 4.2), the students practice developing and testing the unique features of their game first. In increasingly more complex assignments, the students continue to practice testing their unique game concept first.

Figure 4.2. Design for practice in a course on game design.

Will Emigh's Game Design Class (The Media School, Indiana University)

Bottleneck: When developing a game, students forget to keep an overview of the parts in mind and fail to prioritize the unique game concept, which should be developed and tested first.

Analogy: My metaphor for the key game concept is creating a recipe for a veggie burger. We know the parts of a burger (bread, toppings, cheese, patty) but we have to focus on only the core element at first—the burger. Then, later, we might adjust the toppings or cheese to support the new veggie burger.

Practice: Students will practice this process by identifying the major parts of an existing (known) game and describing which game concepts they would test first had they been the creators. Then, I will give them an unknown game concept and they will do the same thing. Finally, they will have to submit the pieces and testing plan for their own game concept—before they get too involved in its creation.

Students practice the mental action—prioritizing the game concept—several times before they develop any actual materials (whether cards and boards or digital programs). Practice gives students the chance to build or maintain new ways of operating. The mechanics of practice matter, but there is no getting around the need for repetition and spaced practice.

The challenge for many teachers is making the time for spaced, repetitive student practice. Teachers feeling the pressure of content coverage may march inexorably on to the next topic, hoping students will intuit critical skills along with content (Calder, 2006). The result, however, can be little retention of anything. Therefore, the more practice methods prioritize the critical mental moves of the discipline, the better students get at disciplinary critical thinking.

> Our students are not clear about the kind of knowledge history is or what they should do with that knowledge, and so they find no reason to retain the content knowledge. If content knowledge is the vocabulary of history, analysis and argument are its speech. Students have been asked to memorize vocabulary of history (its facts), and have sometimes been asked to read passages written by others (secondary works), but they have seldom been asked to speak the language of history. (Shopkow, Díaz, Middendort, & Pace, 2013a, p. 16)

Shifting to the bottleneck perspective can move teachers away from a content-coverage approach to teaching. It may sound counterintuitive, but as Sundberg and Dini (1993) found in a biology course, fewer topics that are taught more deeply actually increase student learning. Course goals can prioritize bottlenecks and misconceptions of a discipline for deep learning of disciplinary processes, not just rote memorization of content.

Practice Principle 3: Bring the Component Skills Back Together

Sometimes students practice individual mental moves, but they may not get to put them together and use them in an authentic way in the classroom. As a result, they may not understand why they should practice these skills or maintain them. David Perkins (2010), using the analogy of Little League baseball, emphasizes the importance of allowing students to play "the whole game." When children are learning to play baseball, the coaches don't simply have them run one skills drill after another. They do some skills drills, and then they learn to deploy those skills in a game. The game is not the same as the big-league version of the game; it cannot be, because the children are not ready to play big-league baseball. But it is what Perkins calls a "junior version" of the game, similar to the adult game in that it deploys skills that will eventually be of use in the adult game.

For students to master a complex task, we break the task into smaller component tasks and then let them practice those parts individually. With competence at these initial steps, we can then assign the culminating task (writing an original research paper or developing an experiment) that asks students to synthesize all of the smaller skills that make up the larger task. Building up skills to a larger task is known as scaffolding (D. Wood, Bruner, & Ross, 1976), implying a temporary structure that supports the building of a house. The beginning stages of building a house require support systems— scaffolds—to maintain the integrity of the structure and to ensure that previous work doesn't collapse. Over time, the scaffolding is incorporated into the structure of the house and the house itself becomes stronger and can bear more weight. Similarly, we scaffold student learning so that students build up a solid foundation of subcompetencies. As these are mastered and become stronger, the students can take on increasingly difficult tasks.

Some kinds of scaffolding over time become "unconscious"; the scaffolding is not taken away, but the competencies become implicit—as in a research paper or course project. In the example from journalism, all the separate components of an advertising campaign were modeled and practiced. For the final, authentic project, students had to bring all of the components together. They had to (a) clarify the primary objective of the advertising campaign, (b) define a target audience, (c) generate the creative strategy, and (d) execute the deliverable products. Students were asked to perform all of these tasks individually with practice, and feedback was provided for these exercises. By the time the students reached the culminating task, they already had a firm grasp of the component parts and were able to perform well on the advertising campaign.

Other kinds of scaffolding do go away. In learning some languages, students are often taught to explicitly identify the subjects, verbs, and objects in a sentence. This can help with learning the syntax of the language. But when it comes to actually speaking the language, thinking about the parts of a sentence might impede fluency. In translating from English to Chinese, for example, it might be easier to take a concept in the English, visualize it, and then construct it in Chinese, without first trying to think of what part of speech it is in English. In this case, the scaffolding is removed so that the mental action (speaking Chinese) can be performed more fluently.

These kinds of approaches generally come together within the practice of backward design, where the teacher has decided on the big learning goals he or she is teaching toward and what kind of student work will show how well the students have mastered those competencies (Wiggins & McTighe, 2005). Indeed, decoding is a natural partner of backward design, because it identifies the important disciplinary mental moves students need to learn and offers students opportunities to practice them so that students will be successful on the final, overarching learning goal.

For example, students in Leah's upper level High and Late Middle Ages history course work across a semester to write a microhistory in which they place an object (text or image) from the Middle Ages in its historical context (Shopkow, 2017). By doing so, she is addressing an overarching bottleneck: Students tend to think that history is about facts and events, rather than seeing history as an interpretive discipline. As a result, they do not understand the written discourse historians use to interpret the past. Practicing with the components, students work through a series of scaffolded assignments in class and in homework that they will need for the final product.

For the final project, the subcompetencies are applied in the creation of a synthetic document—the microhistory (see Table 4.1). Students explain the historical incident in context, having practiced the component tasks they may have otherwise neglected—describing the object with an emphasis on key themes, using the secondary readings to illuminate the ways the themes appear in the object, and offering an interpretation of the object.

The work is spaced across the semester because real conceptual change takes time to teach, practice, and master. The task is authentic, a form of cognitive apprenticeship (Brown, Collins, & Duguid, 1989; Lave & Wenger 1991). The students are not just looking up answers, but are also carrying out a junior version of a true historian's work. The final, synthetic task is

TABLE 4.1
Competencies for Writing a Microhistory

Subcompetencies	Task for Students
Match student interest to the available anecdotes.	Choose a microhistorical anecdote from a limited set made available by the teacher.
Analyze the elements closely; understand and identify the frameworks (themes and questions) that historians bring to a source.	Generate possible topics and critical lenses to explore in the anecdote.
Connect the frameworks and the anecdotes.	Choose several frameworks through which to interpret the anecdote.
Bring other historical arguments to bear on their chosen anecdote.	Conduct keyword searches to find relevant secondary source articles.
Make explicit connections between the anecdote and the secondary literature, practicing the components of analytical reading in history—this may involve several other bottlenecks.	Choose an article or book chapter to read (six assignments over a six-week period). Identify the author's arguments, counterarguments, and evidence used to support the argument for each article; ask a question raised by each article. Write this up as a review.

highly generative. It can lead them in many different directions; they ask questions that are original to them, and thus it generates an authentic form of assessment. They will need close teacher guidance, a form of cognitive apprenticeship. That portions of the assignment are unfamiliar is a good thing, because it makes it difficult for students to return to familiar habits and practices, ritual activities (Bain, 2006).

Practice Principle 4: Match Practice Methods to Mental Actions Through Bloom's Typology

To help students understand the ways of operating in your discipline, it is important to know the difference in types of thinking and what types are prevalent in your field. For this purpose we apply Bloom's taxonomy (Bloom & Krathwohl, 1984) in Decoding the Disciplines, not to bring students up from lower levels of thinking, but to classify different types of mental actions particularly at the decoding, practice, and assessment steps (2, 4, and 6). Bloom's categories help us differentiate the very different functions of mental actions, from analyzing (taking things apart), creating (bringing things together in a new way), or evaluating (making judgments or ratings). Consequently, we are calling it "Bloom's typology" (rather than taxonomy) to signal this different usage: Bloom's "types" are very large categories of mental action. Once you categorize your mental action into its Bloom's type, then you can select teaching methods that correspond to the desired type of thinking.

The first three categories of Bloom's typology are hierarchical (see Figure 4.3); thus, to answer a question that requires analyzing satisfactorily (the fourth level), students must also have mastered skills at the levels of remembering, understanding, and applying. The three remaining categories (analyzing, evaluating, and synthesizing) require higher order thinking skills but are not necessarily hierarchical, meaning that a question categorized as evaluating does not always require the skills of analysis and synthesis but will require mastery of the lower three levels (remembering, understanding, and applying). Once we have identified the Bloom's type at which the mental action occurs, we select a teaching method that fosters that type of thinking. Eventually this process will become automatic for the instructor. But until it does, it helps to keep Bloom's categories, and the verbs that give rise to these types, front and center. To encourage the appropriate type of thinking and not have students work on the wrong type of thinking or on lower orders of thinking—in "Bloom's basement"—be sure to choose the verbs that control that type of thinking in wording student exercises.

A series of analogies related to the topic of "the hospital" can help illuminate the different functions in Bloom's typology (see Figure 4.4).

In applying Bloom's typology for Step 4 Practice you need to determine the type of thinking you want your students to do and which methods are appropriate to teach them to do it; then have them practice the skill (see Exercise 4.4). In biology, if a teacher simply wants students to memorize genetic pairs—Bloom's "remembering" type—they can play an online DNA base pairs matching game (www.nobelprize.org/educational/medicine/dna_double_helix/dnahelix.html). Or the teacher may want students to practice visualizing protein synthesis at the molecular level, imagining all the parts of the inner cell and how they operate, which involves the analyzing type of Bloom's classification. For practice, the teacher might have students draw the different parts of the cell. However, drawings are two-dimensional and difficult to capture dynamic molecular processes. To get a better sense of these processes, students can role-play Protein Synthesis, which is based on Weiss (1971; see also www.youtube.com/watch?v=eOqFlynf8JA). In other words, the activity depends on the kind of mental action to be practiced. The example in Figure 4.5 shows a mental action across all six types.

Figure 4.3. Bloom's typology.

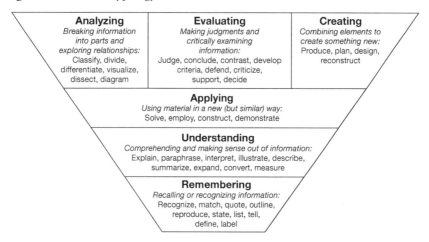

Figure 4.4. An elaboration of Bloom's typology.

6. *Creating:* Combining elements to form a new, original entity. This might be compared to designing a new hospital in my hometown. While plans for other hospitals may be considered, our hospital will have to fit the needs of our specific location, population, and medical educators. In research, creating might mean looking at ideas from other fields that can be brought to bear on a specific field or that field's ideas and concepts. For example, applying "big data" methods to the field of scholarship of teaching and learning provides a new way to consider classroom research.

5. *Evaluating:* Making judgments based on criteria and/or standards is like judging the quality of hospital care, from qualitative measures such as the responses of patients to their care to quantitative measures such as the time patients wait in the emergency room or patient readmittance rates (revealing inadequately treated illness). Evaluating with criteria is very different from relying on gut reactions, thumbs up or down, with no criteria specified.

4. *Analyzing:* Breaking material into constituent parts and determining how the parts relate to one another and to an overall structure is like taking hospital bills apart to see what people were charged for different parts of the bill, the proportion of each part in the total bill, and the responsible parties for parts of the bill. An itemized bill would show, for example, the interrelated, yet separate, departments of a hospital that rely on the radiology department to diagnose and treat patients.

3. *Applying:* Using procedures to perform tasks or solve problems in similar situations is like the way the hospital uses many procedures. There are procedures for check-in of patients—which may differ depending on the patient's form

(Continues)

Figure 4.4. (*Continued*)

> of insurance—and for blood draws—a procedure I personally would not want someone to get creative with! In these tasks, personnel use a learned set of protocols to direct incoming patients to the right place or department.
>
> 2. *Understanding:* Integrating new materials into existing schema and being able to explain in our own words. So we might explain the role of our local hospital in the community to someone—there are probably several ways to describe this, but the meaning is similar.
>
> 1. *Remembering:* Recalling or recognizing information from memory is like recalling the address of my local hospital—there are no steps involved; it is simply a fact. Methods for remembering emphasize the rehearsal of information in order to repeat it back. For example, when I was a child, my mother taught me my home address as a song, a form of rehearsal so I could memorize and recall the address easily. During the Medieval period, people sometimes used grotesque images for the same purpose—visualizing the image brought the memorized material to mind.

Note. Adapted from Pilgreen, 2012.

Figure 4.5. Different tasks in physical therapy using Bloom's typology.

> **Bloom's Typology in Physical Therapy (Capi Scheider, Riley Hospital for Children, Indiana University Health)**
>
> In the field of physical therapy, range of motion exercises help preserve flexibility and mobility of the joints on which they are performed. Design a physical therapy range of motion program for a patient:
>
> 1. Remembering—Define the range of motion procedure.
> 2. Understanding—Explain the range of motion procedure as it relates to the patient's diagnosis.
> 3. Applying—Measure a patient's range of motion according to APTA guidelines.
> 4. Analyzing—Differentiate the meaning of the measurements by comparing this patient's measurements to a normal or "standard" range of motion.
> 5. Evaluating—Assess the need for physical therapy intervention.
> 6. Creating—Develop a long-range physical therapy plan.

Although the example shows how students might demonstrate competence at all the different types of thinking in Bloom's typology, the students are probably not having difficulty with all of these levels, meaning practice exercises should not be addressed to all of them. The teacher needs to decide what the most significant impediment is and direct practice to that point. To give an example, many disciplines, especially in the humanities, still rely on written communication as their main method of analysis and practice.

Doing lots of writing, however, does not improve writing as much as doing writing assignments that focus on the bottlenecks where students are known to have difficulty. For instance, there are predictable weaknesses in parts of biology research proposals, such as

- poor statement of a hypothesis and ways to test it,
- faulty reviews of literature to identify gaps in knowledge,
- failure to state adequately the broader scientific and societal significance of a study,
- weak interpretation of the data, and
- failure to show the relevance of a pilot study (Crowe, Dirks, & Wenderoth, 2008).

Identifying the weaknesses that appear in the different components of writing in biology makes it easier for teachers to help students write better proposals. Writing assignments that emphasize the construction of meaning in the discipline with clear explanations of the mental components of the writing process improve learning (P. Anderson, 2013).

It is helpful for teachers to have a tool kit of teaching methods that correspond to the disciplinary skills they want their students to practice. Table 4.2 matches Bloom's types of thinking and the verbs that govern the types of thinking with several methods and techniques for practice. Certain methods are chosen because they structure student practice of the desired mental action and intentionally promote a level of thinking. When unsure, the teacher can analyze the mental action in terms of Bloom's typology and then select a method for that type. We have included CATs (Angelo & Cross, 1993) at every level, because CATs are useful structures for student practice, as well as for assessment.

Specific practice methods can be developed for mental actions in every field (and should be). In fact, Crowe and colleagues (2008) created some for biology, which we have adapted in Table 4.3. Note the verbs used throughout: They control the category of thinking being invoked.

It would be useful to create a chart like Table 4.3 for your field, but of course, to do so you would need to decode the major ways of creating knowledge in your field to ensure a focus on the key mental actions. Exercise 4.6 will help you learn to put the mental action front and center in selecting your teaching methods. As always run your ideas by a colleague or develop them with a team; a reader from outside your field will help you make your discipline clearer and help you develop more effective practice for your students.

TABLE 4.2
Matching Mental Action to Practice Methods

Bloom's Type/ Mental Action	Verbs to Elicit	Practice Methods
Creating	Produce, plan, design, reconstruct	Writing a poem, a book, a puzzle; creating a work of art; inventing a metaphor; writing a research proposal; constructing a model; creating a question, hypothesis, experiment; developing a plan; synthesizing multiple case studies Invented Dialogue CAT
Evaluating	Judge, conclude, contrast, develop criteria, defend, criticize, support, decide	Peers evaluating one another's products, case studies, mock trials, editorials, and evaluation reports using explicit criteria Student-Generated Test Questions CAT; Paper or Project Prospectus CAT
Analyzing	Classify, divide, differentiate, visualize, dissect, diagram	Carrying out case studies, simulations, role plays, discussion, labs, interview with experts Save the Last Word; Analogy CAT
Applying	Solve, employ, construct, demonstrate	Demonstrating problem-solving or application of rules, laws, theories with case studies; worked problems; scenarios; practice in multiple contexts Applications Cards CAT
Understanding	Explain, paraphrase, interpret, illustrate, describe, summarize, expand, convert, measure	Summarizing readings; creating graphic organizers; doing a demonstration; participating in discussion Directed Paraphrasing CAT; Human Tableau or Class Modeling CAT
Remembering	Recognize, match, quote, outline, reproduce, state, list, tell, define, label	Reporting on lectures, readings, podcast, video Creating mnemonics, flash cards

TABLE 4.3

Biology Mental Actions Matched With Methods

Bloom's Type	Mental Action	Method
Creating	Generate a hypothesis or design an experiment.	Generate five hypotheses for the following: Design three ways these hypotheses can be tested.
Evaluating	Assess understanding of a given biological concept.	Develop criteria for understanding a given biological concept; provide a written assessment of the strengths and weaknesses of your peers' understanding; critique the hypotheses, models, and experiments generated by other teams.
Analyzing	Analyze and interpret data in a research article or textbook.	Without reading the author's interpretation, analyze and interpret data in a research article; then compare the author's interpretation with your own. Turn the data section of a research article into an infographic.
Applying	Visualize a biological process and the changes that would result from altering the activity of a component in the system.	In teams, graph a biological process and create scenarios that change the shape or slope of the graph. Invent an analogy for the biological process.
Understanding	Describe a biological process.	Take turns teaching your peers a biological process; quiz peers on biological processes.
Remembering	Identify biological concepts or components.	Practice labeling diagrams; quiz yourself with flash cards.

Practice Principle 5: Create Awareness in Students of Their Own Thought Processes and the Ways of Thinking in Your Field

In every class, students work with content and complete assignments. Many students use the same study methods even in very different fields—and find success in doing so—without becoming aware that different fields use different approaches. Knowing the different types of thinking required for different disciplines is a key skill in critical thinking. Thinking about one's own thinking is called "metacognition," and Decoding the Disciplines can help teachers foster metacognition so students become aware of disciplinary differences and plan different strategies for their different courses. In the example in Figure 4.6 Dan Buckland (2012) points out the different approaches to the same problem taken in three different fields.

Similarly, the meaning of "reading" varies widely across fields, as does the way evidence is collected and used. Students are often not aware of these differences, and this goes back to the implicit knowledge of disciplinary experts (see Step 2). To the teacher, it is obvious that the enterprise in an economics class is very different from that of a math class, but this difference may not be apparent to students, particularly if the same language is used in each class to describe different activities. Students can take a giant leap in performance if they develop the language for talking about what they are doing conceptually.

For example, in an expository writing class, Cynthia Scheinberg (2003) realized that discussions did not connect to the skills needed for the writing. She hypothesized that some composition teachers were such good facilitators—synthesizing the readings, asking probing questions, bringing up larger themes, and summarizing the end—they were rendering these writerly tasks invisible to the students. And yet teachers do not hold class discussions because students need practice in talking.

In response to this problem, Scheinberg created the "Conversacolor" game so students could connect class discussion to the skills they needed for writing in her field. Students had to classify statements made during class

Figure 4.6. Disciplinary differences in problem-solving.

Dr. H. removed a patient's gallbladder laparoscopically. She is unhappy with the tools she uses; they don't work the way she wants them to. She feels that she spends too much time struggling with the equipment rather than doing the procedure. Other surgeons say they have had the same problem too. What should be done?

- *Physicians* would ask what other surgeons have done to compensate for the unwieldy tools. Do any of those methods fix the problem of taking too much time struggling with equipment?
- *Scientists* would design a brand new laparoscopic (or alternative) system to view the gallbladder.
- *Engineers* would study what the surgeons like and dislike about the system. Then they would modify the current system to keep the benefits and lose the difficulties.

discussion using categories related to writing. In order to speak, students would hold up colored cards to signal the kind of discussion comment they were about to make: a new idea, the further development of an idea, a challenge to someone's card choice, a transition between ideas, or a request for clarification. Through the cards, students practiced articulating aspects of the writing process with each comment, not just discussing the content of the reading. The Conversacolor structure helped students become aware at the metacognitive level of writing for the field of rhetoric and composition. A teacher in a different field would employ different categories for the cards based on critical reasoning necessary for the class, but the teacher could certainly use a similar technique.

One way to help students develop metacognition is to have them practice in teams in class, followed by individual practice outside of class. For example, students in a history class, who think the task is to memorize dates and events, may not have the language to describe analyzing a source, explaining evidence to make an argument, or taking the perspective of a historical person. By having to explain to fellow students when and how to marshal these historical thinking skills and contrasting that to what they do in other classes, students hone their understanding of historical thinking. As a student in the History Learning Project said,

> I never actually encountered the term *dualism* before. So I had to have someone explain that to me. . . . And then I started seeing that everywhere. So it was like, "Oh, they're teaching something as if there's a good and a bad! We're not getting all the perspectives here."

The in-class teams provide social support as students develop the language that goes along with developing a new skill—students collaboratively practice new mental actions through a socially mediated sense-making process.

A frequent bottleneck in math courses is that students do not know what to do if they get stuck. Awareness of their thought processes can help students realize that getting stuck is a common problem and that there are a variety of approaches to getting unstuck. Discussions in teams in a math class provide a community where students can become fluent in problem attack strategies.

Math and the STEM fields can use worked examples to counteract the "plug and chug" approaches many students use to solve problems, in which they substitute trial-and-error searches or focus on surface-level understanding rather than analyzing the structural features of a problem (see Figure 4.7). When they use low-level "plug and chug" approaches in traditional homework problems, their skills might not improve as much as instructors might expect. The worked example approach developed in algebra and geometry asks students to analyze the logic of a particular problem type by asking questions about an expert's solution to the problem. With modeling from the instructor and practice on the reasoning used in a problem-solving calculation, students can be asked to explain their reasoning and apply it to the next case, instead of being left to plug numbers into formulae with little conceptual understanding.

Worked examples function particularly well when the prompts are aimed at the bottlenecks, the places where students get stuck. Showing students incorrect solutions and having them explain the mistake is one way to do this. Using the "worked problems" approach can enhance students' understanding of the mental action and their confidence. At the U.S. Air Force Academy, 85% of surveyed students approved of the worked examples approach (along with just-in-time teaching warm-ups) because of the structure and confidence it provides (G. Novak, personal communication, October 21, 2013). In a computer science course, instructors found that students were getting hung up on the syntax of commands rather than learning the logic of programming, such as recursion or algorithm creation. When worked example analyses became part of the homework, the student failure rate decreased significantly (Moura, 2012).

Figure 4.7. Worked examples.

The Worked Examples Method for Analysis and Explanation of Problem-Solving

Before class, students are presented with a few "worked-out examples" (i.e., problems with the solution already provided in a step-by-step fashion). They are asked specific questions on the key operations in solving that kind of problem. For example, in a physics course, they are given a scenario about the liftoff and acceleration of the space shuttle. Then they are given three to six questions prompting them to explain the reasoning of the answer (and sometimes pointing them back to the textbook for explanations). Thus, first exposure to the concept occurs in the context of explaining the example. That way, students immediately see relevance of the new concept to the real world and how it is applied.

With the concepts further clarified through lecture, students are assigned to solve problems similar to the worked examples in class and after class. The worked problems method works well in "flipped" classes and in STEM fields, because it prompts students to explain their reasoning, thus making them more aware of their reasoning and preventing them from plugging numbers into formulae without following the logic.

To practice critical thinking about complex systems in environmental or life sciences, teachers often assign students to memorize models. This is another place where metacognitive practice can improve student performance on the mental action. To think critically about systems, students need to do more than memorize them; they need to create their own models and to identify the claims and evidence that are embedded in their models (Sorenson et al., 2015). Reflective discussions and writing about how to develop a sense of the parts, their relationship to the other parts, and their dynamic interactions in systems can help students become aware of something that they cannot be expected to intuit, because it is difficult to get the full scope of a system all at once and on one's own.

Crowe and colleagues (2008) helped biology students develop their metacognitive skills by showing them Bloom's taxonomy as applied to biology. In practice exercises, students ranked test questions according to the taxonomy prior to the test. They also calculated the Bloom's levels for an old exam (i.e., what percentage of points were given for questions at the level of knowledge, comprehension, analysis, and so forth). This helped students prepare for the cognitive challenge level of an upcoming exam. Also, student groups wrote four questions at each of the first five levels of Bloom's taxonomy and submitted them to the teacher at the beginning of the week. Students reported that fluency with Bloom's levels helped organize their studying and was useful in approaching subsequent courses. At the end of a course, students were asked to write one or two paragraphs about how using Bloom's taxonomy to analyze exam performance changed their learning strategies.

In short, with cognitive strategies students construct their knowledge; with metacognitive strategies they direct, regulate, and evaluate their learning. Metacognitive skills—"thinking about thinking"—can be taught to students to improve their learning (Thiede, Anderson, & Therriault, 2003). By encouraging "metacognitive conversations" in teams, students articulate their own reasoning processes and the ways this differs in diverse fields.

Practice Principle 6: Design Effective Feedback After Practice

Gregor Novak argues that giving feedback only after major exams or papers is too late to clear up confusion or for students to even care about the feedback because they do not have time to try again before the class moves on (De La Harpe, Terry, Novotny, & Novak, 2014). In general, early and frequent feedback can prevent students from repeating mistakes (Hattie & Timperley, 2007). Important though it is, practice without corrective feedback is less effective and could even could lead students down the wrong path. Feedback is formative, given to help the student move forward rather than to justify a grade. For that reason, Maryellen Weimer (2012) calls it "feedforward" rather than "feedback." Good feedback is focused on just a few (no more than three or four) things students might do to improve their next assignments or revise the current ones. When one is teaching to a bottleneck, it follows that the feedback should be addressed to clarifying for students the mental moves that will help them negotiate the bottleneck successfully.

Some teachers feel that giving explicit feedback is somehow cheating, as though when students are told exactly where to change what they are doing, they are somehow getting off easily. If the teacher's goal is for students to learn disciplinary moves, the students need to be shown this kind of thinking and not have it hidden and guessed at. To use a golfing analogy, explaining to a student exactly what he or she needs to do (not just what they have done wrong) is like gently taking her or his arms to correct the student's swing. When a golf coach does this, the student experiences what a good swing feels like, but it will still take practice to master the swing. Alternatively, some teachers snow their students under with feedback. In an effort to be helpful, they give so much feedback that they leave students unsure of what to focus on.

Problematically, even if the teacher provides clear feedback on the mental action, students tend not to read the feedback (Crisp, 2007). A reflective step encourages students to consider the feedback. In Leah's class, if a student wants to redo an assignment, the student e-mails a summary of the grader comments and how they intend to respond to them. This vastly improves the rewrites because students cannot just tweak the next draft, but must seriously consider how to implement the feedback. This is a technique garnered from the Duke University Thesis Assessment Protocol in Biology (Reynolds, Smith, Moskovitz, & Sayle, 2009). Another reflective feedback exercise, the "exam wrappers" in *How Learning Works* (Ambrose, Bridges, DiPietro, Lovett, & Norman, 2010), provides a review form that students complete when an exam is returned to them so they consider why they received their scores. Adding the following question to an exam wrapper helps students consider what kind of *reasoning* they are being asked to do: "What were you being asked to do in question 3?"

Feedback is ineffective if students don't have a chance to repractice the skill, whether they write another draft or continue solving more practice problems. For teachers who feel rushed to cover content, allowing students to practice correcting their mistakes pinpointed in feedback may present a problem. Students, however, may feel stuck and incapable without such practice.

Summary

For active learning methods to be effective, they need to focus clearly on the mental task. The task at Step 4 of Decoding the Disciplines is to match methods to the mental action. To do so, teachers need to create practice for component skills, scaffold complex tasks, and pay attention to the mechanics of practice, the technical considerations that, when accounted for, produce best results and aid students in fostering stronger skills. They need to know different methods to choose from and which methods promote which kinds of thinking and foster student practice at reflection on their own thinking. Finally, they need to provide feedback that does more than justify a grade or point out errors. Students need directive feedback and a chance for more practice with that feedback in mind.

To return to the anecdote at the beginning of the chapter in which economics students were unable to solve homework problems, you now probably have some ideas about how the professor might deal with this situation. Keeping Step 4 Practice and Feedback in mind, the professor might design practice assignments that would focus student efforts on bottlenecks in economics. Since economics relies so much on interpreting graphs, economics students would need practice at reading and interpreting graphs to apply course concepts to authentic problems. In a field in which models are used to understand important relationships in the economy about equilibrium and marginal utility, students would need practice at creating models and justifying the components they include. Reflective exercises would help them do so. They would need practice at evaluating the relative effectiveness of different models. They would need to begin with the less complex mental moves, such as interpreting the graphs, and to work toward the more complex problems that would have to be supported by a thorough understanding of the earlier mental actions. Without practice to build competence on bottlenecks, many students will struggle to learn.

In Appendix A, you can see how a biologist and a musicologist have addressed Step 4 in the decoding process.

CHAPTER 4 EXERCISES

Exercise 4.1: Practicing the Component Mental Actions

1. What is the critical mental action you want students to practice?
2. Make a list of the component skills that comprise this mental action. (If you are unsure of the components of a mental action, or the smaller steps necessary to think in a discipline-specific way, go back to Step 2 to decode the expert's critical thinking process.)
3. Place a star next to the ones that students find most difficult. (Collecting frequent small assessments of student efforts can provide crucial information about what students find most difficult to ensure these components of the mental process can be modeled and practiced.)
4. Next to each starred critical subcomponent, list one technique to be used for student practice.

Exercise 4.2: Repetitive Practice of Component Skills

1. What mental actions will require repeated practice in your course?

_____

_____

_____

_____

2. In what form and where will students encounter the repeated practice?

_____

_____

_____

_____

3. Which principles of practice will affect your design of practice the most?

_____

_____

_____

_____

Exercise 4.3: Bring the Component Skills Back Together

1. What synthetic task in your course will allow students to bring the component skills back together?

_____

_____

_____

_____

2. What are the components or subskills students must be successful at for the large, synthetic task?

_____

_____

_____

_____

Exercise 4.4: Matching the Cognitive Task to Teaching and Practice Methods

1. According to Bloom's typology, what *type* of thinking is your target mental action?

_____

_____

_____

_____

2. What are several available teaching methods or techniques for this *type*? (See Appendix D.)

_____

_____

_____

_____

Exercise 4.5: Getting Control of Bloom's Typology (for Individuals and Teams)

Silent writing (for an individual)

a. Jot down a test/essay/project question you have assigned your students previously. Don't spend long on this.
b. Rewrite this prompt so that students would practice the mental action in three categories in Bloom's typology to see how the question would change depending on the type of thinking desired. Be sure to select appropriate *verbs* to match the desired type of thinking.

In a team

   a. Ask a colleague to do the same exercise and exchange lists.

   b. Discuss:

     1. How will student practice change for the different types of thinking?

     2. What are the similarities and differences between your two sets of exercises?

Exercise 4.6: Matching Teaching Methods to Bloom's Typology (Developed by Susan Hines, 2015)

In this three-part activity, instructors evaluate their usual teaching methods, suggest teaching methods for peers, and select one for themselves. If you attempt this exercise individually rather than in a group setting, you will not be able to do all the steps; certain steps in the exercise require interaction with at least one colleague.

   I. Decode the mental action individually. (This is a reprise of Exercise 2.1, but it is a useful reminder of the key mental action for choosing teaching methods.)

     a. What do you want students to do at the end of your course? Make it out of Play-Doh (other modeling materials, e.g., aluminum foil, LEGO, or random natural objects may be used). (Play-Doh object 1)

     b. Pick one bottleneck where students struggle to learn. For an online course what is a bottleneck in one module? What would the expert do? Make it out of Play-Doh. (Play-Doh object 2)

     c. Write on a Post-it note the action being modeled in Play-Doh object 2.

     d. This is the *mental action.*

  II. Evaluate teaching methods.

     a. On a Post-it note, jot down the mental action.

     b. On the other side of the Post-it note, write down your go-to teaching method for this mental action.

     c. Exchange notes with a colleague. Tablemate reads Post-it note: What level is the teaching method on Bloom's taxonomy? (Refer to Appendix D.)

     d. Write it on the Post-it.

     e. Pass it back to the "owner."

    f. Three-minute writing exercise: Does your teaching method match the type of thinking you're trying to teach?

    g. Discuss: Do our teaching methods match the type of thinking we are trying to teach?

III. Shop for teaching methods.

    a. Jot down your mental action, again, on a 3 × 5 card.

    b. Rephrase it for three *different* Bloom's taxonomy types.

    c. Exchange cards with a colleague.

    d. Select a teaching method for each type. (See Appendix D.)

    e. Write your suggested methods on the back of the card.

    f. Pass it back.

    g. Discuss: Did you receive a teaching method you liked?

5

STEP 5

Motivation and Accountability

When a teacher has modeled the mental action the students need to do (Step 3) and provided students with practice and feedback in carrying out the action (Step 4), the students should be well on their way to success in learning the desired critical thinking. Sometimes, however, even after we have carefully planned lessons and provided opportunities for students to practice, they still struggle. When students struggle because they don't understand, it is hardly surprising if they lose any motivation to continue with the work, but our previous chapters have discussed ways to enhance student understanding. To the degree that we explicitly acknowledge to the students that the work we are asking them to do is difficult and express our confidence that they will be able to master it and that we will help them, they may be encouraged to continue plugging away at the problem. However, sometimes even this sort of encouragement doesn't work. When this happens, it is time to consider whether or not there are additional obstacles to learning that are sapping student motivation.

We have found two such obstacles, which we will address separately in this chapter. The first obstacle is the emotional bottleneck, where students' prior ideas and ways of operating get in the way of their learning. These ideas may lead students to reject disciplinary thinking, perhaps by arguing, but more commonly by going through the motions by rote, lapsing into sullenness or fatalism, or dropping the class. The second obstacle is that students may simply not be doing the work we are asking them to do because it is difficult and perhaps time-consuming and because there are not sufficient accountability structures and incentives in place. To learn, one has to physically change, break old habits, and foster new connections in the brain. No wonder humans sometimes resist learning (Timmermans, 2010)! Students tend to use the same mental patterns they have always used. They've had lots of practice at them in their previous schooling and it's more comfortable than trying something new. In the past their usual ways of thinking have frequently worked well enough, and in many contexts they are quite effective (Zhou, 2012). We will spend most of our time in this chapter on the first obstacle, as it is a particularly challenging and critical issue in a pluralistic society, although the second is no less important and transformative.

In this chapter, we will be discussing four principles to reinforce disciplinary critical thinking and motivate students. The first two address the issue of emotional bottlenecks, while the second two address how to encourage students to try new ways of thinking by disrupting their learning rituals and how to hold them accountable for doing so.

Our four principles:

- Principle 1: Identify the emotional bottlenecks.
- Principle 2: Address the emotional bottlenecks.
- Principle 3: Disrupt learning "scripts" through course design.
- Principle 4: Structure in student accountability.

The Emotional Bottleneck

Emotions and learning are inseparable. Students learn most when they are highly engaged (at those "aha" moments) but less when they are bored, conflicted, or just plain tired (Dragon et al., 2008). Attraction and attention are important factors in learning; even the most logical argument cannot be processed through pure cognition (Immordino-Yang, 2011). But emotions may also interfere with learning. This may happen because students have prior beliefs about their abilities ("I'm not good at math"), about their prior training ("I *already* know how to do this"), about what they ought to be doing ("I didn't come here to think; I came here to learn"), or because they feel that their beliefs are being dismissed or derided ("My faith group says that the earth is 6,000 years old, and you're telling me we're wrong"). As teachers we tend to assume that we can simply "tell" students they are mistaken or present them with "the facts" and that they will change their thinking. There is considerable evidence, however, that these approaches don't work well in the short run (Redlawsk, Civettini, & Emmerson, 2010), and the short run is all we have with most students. Teachers are sometimes blindsided when emotional bottlenecks emerge in their classrooms, so the first step is to find out what ideas are out there in the classroom and how many students hold them.

Principle 1: Identify the Emotional Bottlenecks

Just as the navigator of a large ship wants to anticipate the location of icebergs to avoid a catastrophe, we want to avoid or at least be aware of emotional bottlenecks, predictable upsets that can disrupt classroom learning. We can suspect emotional bottlenecks are in play when we encounter active resistance to course methods or ideas. However, faculty tend not to notice the role of emotions because, among their other competencies, they have learned to manage the interaction of their emotions and cognition effectively, remaining emotionally engaged but keeping a critical distance as well. That distance permits faculty to continue to update their understanding even when their findings challenge their beliefs. Like so many other aspects of knowledge, this ability to achieve an appropriate critical distance was largely learned tacitly, and those who did not learn it either avoided fields where this ability was necessary or left the discipline entirely.

As we came to realize that cognitive aspects of learning alone were not enough to get students through certain bottlenecks, we began to pay specific attention to the emotional aspects of bottlenecks that interfere with learning. By revisiting our 24 interviews with history faculty we noticed that emotions did not primarily affect the process because of feelings, such as being happy or sad, nor was the issue that students possessed or lacked passion for the academic subject. Instead, we found that students often had powerful and emotional preexisting *narratives* about the class, the material, or the discipline. If, for example, a student narrative is that what is important in the field of religious studies is personal or church-based spiritual experience, the students can be upset when asked to set the experiential and spiritual aside to analyze religious texts as works of literature. When course tasks do not match students' prior narratives, their emotions are aroused, interfering with their ability to update, that is, to change their ideas based on new information (Redlawsk et al., 2010; Smith, 2017).

Analysis of our interviews with history faculty revealed that there are two kinds of emotional bottlenecks students encounter: procedural bottlenecks and worldview conflicts (Middendorf et al., 2015). Examples of both kinds of emotional bottlenecks appear in Figure 5.1.

Procedural bottlenecks concern the nature and function of a discipline, and failure to master the procedure hampers a student's ability to operate in the discipline. In history, for example, students often naïvely believe that history is about finding out exactly what happened, like detectives, including events and dates, ending with "stories" about lessons to be learned (Barton & Levstik, 2004). The historian, in contrast, analyzes and interprets historical evidence in order to narrate what happened in the past (which

Figure 5.1. Some examples of procedural and worldview bottlenecks.

Procedural Bottlenecks

Biology (or many sciences)

Students do not use different reading strategies for different parts of a research article, such as for the data and results sections. Instead of applying a variety of rhetorical approaches, they may only skim or look for the plot, "what happened."

Computing

Students get stuck trying to debug and fix their programs, because the errors can be subtle and one can be blind to one's own errors.

Geoscience

Students do not know how to understand very long periods of time—millions and billions of years. They think of time in human terms.

Polar Science

Students do not know that there is sea-based ice and land-based ice. All ice is the same to them.

Composition

Students resist writing multiple drafts, because they do not realize that professional writers write multiple drafts.

Worldview Bottlenecks

Service-Learning

Students view service as the fortunate helping the less fortunate and earning moral merit, rather than as a reciprocal process in which they too must learn.

Climate Change

Some students believe that climate change or the current increase of carbon in the atmosphere is a natural phenomenon, a belief often coupled with particular political positions.

Diversity and Inclusion

Students may resist the idea that some groups are treated to systemic and structural exclusion and unequal treatment.

---

students expect that they have to do) and to explain why these things happened (this explanatory step is the one the students do not expect to have
to perform themselves), while withholding moral judgment (judging being
something many students think is the whole point of history). When students harbor procedural preconceptions, they may resist unfamiliar disciplinary practices and criticize teachers who use them. So, a history teacher
who asks students to explain may meet with complaints that he or she is not
telling the students "what they need to know." Students confronted with
procedures they do not understand may simply drop the course, as in the
example from introductory computer science courses we give later in the
chapter (see Figure 5.6).

Preexisting worldview bottlenecks, however, have to do with the way the
subject matter of disciplines conflicts with students' prior conceptions. In
religious studies, for example, the students' sense of self may cause discomfort in relation to class content, for instance, if they have been raised in their
faith to see certain religious teachings as right. Students have powerful emotional attachments to their worldviews, the basis for their beliefs about their
self-identity, religion, politics, and ethnicity, just to name a few. Worldview
bottlenecks arise in many disciplines, not just religious studies. In a geology
class, students were asked to respond to a reading about the history of earth
going back 4.6 billion years. One student wrote, "It is difficult for me to complete this homework because I believe the earth was formed 6,000 years ago."
Contradictions between worldview bottlenecks and the demands of the field
can generate resentment and confusion, among other emotions. Without a
challenge to the students' narratives, they are more likely to retain their original worldview rather than adopt a more critical and disciplinarily appropriate
concept, particularly since these worldviews derive from communities very
important to the student and of which they wish to remain a part, as shown
in Figure 5.2.

We don't necessarily have to make a distinction between procedural or
worldview emotional bottlenecks. Some bottlenecks combine features of
both. When students don't follow disciplinary procedures as, for example,
when they plug in numbers to calculate formulae without conceptual understanding or resist writing multiple drafts of papers, they may be also telling
themselves that they are not good at math or at writing, so these bottlenecks
comprise both procedures and worldviews. However, there is an important
distinction to be made between the two kinds of bottlenecks. Procedural bottlenecks and meta-misconceptions about the nature of the disciplines; frus-
trations when students don't understand; and panic at subjects they feel they
"aren't good at" are easier to deal with than worldview bottlenecks, because
worldviews are not just the creation of a particular individual. They are

Figure 5.2. Evolution as a worldview bottleneck.

Susan Fisher (2013) found that 55% of students in a 700-student Biology 101 course for nonmajors at a large Midwestern university did not believe in evolution. Specifically, they believed they were direct descendants of Adam and Eve from the garden of Eden about 6,000 years ago. Rather than denigrate this position as unscientific, Fisher wanted to give students permission to hold both religious and scientific viewpoints, as George Zhou (2012) recommends.

One of the strategies she used was to show them a continuum of 14 different positions on evolution that ranged from flat earth to atheistic evolution (E. Scott, 2004). There are several important motivational strategies at work here. She surveyed the students to become aware of the extent of their religiously based conceptions, so she was able to put a number on it (55%); this helped her realize the extent of this bottleneck. She could then focus on what needed to be shown more explicitly and could help students become aware of the choices they are making (Shopkow, 2017).

Rather than take a "my way or the highway" approach when students are subtly or overtly resisting a discipline's modes of critical thinking, we can teach them how to switch from one epistemic viewpoint to another (Gottlieb & Wineburg, 2011) and get them to think about when it might be useful for them to do so.

socially constructed through education and negotiated between individuals and the communities to which they belong. To hold certain worldviews is a requirement for membership in some communities, and to abandon them may be to leave those communities, to feel that one is holding part of oneself apart from those communities, or to become marginalized within those communities. In other words, although individuals hold worldviews, those worldviews are often socially constructed and reinforced. As George Zhou (2012) argues, in supporting a culturally sensitive approach to science education that sees the classroom as a place where different sorts of knowledge creation can be discussed without jeopardizing disciplinary knowledge,

> The replacement of the life-world cognitive products with the intellectual products of the scientific community is not realistic and justifiable for all students and for all concepts; rather the classroom discourse between the life-world culture and the school science culture should aim at the students' enriched understanding of both sides. (p. 124)

It is counterproductive to present our disciplinary ways of thinking as true, even though we are committed to them, and other ways of thinking as wrong. We can acknowledge the communities that hold these worldviews and situate the thinking we want in our particular environment. It is probably necessary to take on a discipline's ways of making meaning, if only in the disciplinary context, to become really accomplished in that discipline, because that is the entry ticket to the discipline. This means that some students will never enter our disciplines, because they will be unwilling to buy the ticket, but by laying out the options clearly for them, we can allow them to make an informed choice (Shopkow, 2017). Some students will choose to adopt disciplinary ways of thought when they work in the discipline, but not when they work outside of it. For instance, if they are working as economists, they may treat all transactions as monetized with a goal of maximizing gain, while in their personal lives, they may prioritize ethical choices over economic ones. This sort of epistemic switching (Gottlieb & Wineburg, 2011) is a perfectly good goal for us to aim for (see Figure 5.3).

Michelene Chi's (2008) work on student misconceptions in science provides us with key insights into emotional bottlenecks, even though her work does not deal with emotions. She points out that student misconceptions often arise because students are using different conceptual categories than experts do. A very similar phenomenon of category confusion occurs in relation to emotional bottlenecks, with the addition that students are emotionally committed to the narratives they bring with them, whereas when students confuse direct and indirect processes, they are not particularly committed to either. In other words, emotional bottlenecks are symptoms that students are using a nondisciplinary conceptual category, to which they are committed for whatever reason, for accomplishing course tasks, and that they either do not understand or are rejecting the disciplinary way of accomplishing the mental task. The history student who thinks doing history is like collecting shells on a beach (probably

Figure 5.3. The Pocahontas costume as a worldview bottleneck.

When a student in an ethnic studies class asked if it was appropriate to wear a Pocahontas outfit for Halloween, the instructor explained that it could seem to boil down a Native American group's social institutions, habits, lifestyle, and spiritual beliefs into a superficial costume. Another student in class, a self-identified political conservative, resisted the teacher's explanation by passing notes to his classmate, writing, "It's okay with *me* for you to wear a Pocahontas costume."

Besides the gender and class disruption issue, analyzing this reaction as a worldview bottleneck helped the teacher prepare a response. The teacher developed a class exercise in which student teams first analyze the Pocahontas costume from the two contrasting epistemic frames—ethnic studies and conservative politics (or any other episteme the students chose to use). Second, they list the strengths and weaknesses of each frame, and finally they decide when it would be appropriate to use each frame. Epistemic switching helps students become aware of the intellectual choices they make and empowers them to make them more consciously.

because of years of schooling to think this) will not try to make an interpretation as historians do. The geology student who thinks about the age of the earth in theological terms (because his or her faith teaches this) will resist the geoscientific understanding of earth processes. To the degree that we can avoid triggering a sharp emotional response, we will be more successful at conveying how our disciplines create meaning (Smith, 2017). So, we begin by identifying the emotional bottlenecks likely to crop up in our classes so that we don't inadvertently trigger them but can address them in a more deliberate way (see Exercise 5.1).

In doing this, we are actually starting at a different point than we start from in working on cognitive bottlenecks. With cognitive bottlenecks, we may simply let the students' work tell us about where they are experiencing difficulty. Because emotional bottlenecks are so problematic, however, we can't wait for them to emerge from student work. We need to collect systematic information about them, either at the beginning of a class when we have reason to expect that students will experience such bottlenecks, or as soon as they appear in student work; in other words, we start with an assessment. (For more about assessment, see chapter 6.)

Collecting detailed assessments of the emotional bottlenecks at the start of class can be delicate. We do not want to ask students outright, "Describe your beliefs that may interfere with learning science or [insert your field here]." Instead, we have to ask indirectly and subtly in ways that address course topics and get students to engage in metacognition—thinking about their own thinking—and we have to ask the students to fully articulate their answers. The following are some of the questions we have found useful:

1. Besides hard work, what does it take to do well in this [math, programming, insert your topic here] course?
2. What happened during [the Middle Ages, Cultural Revolution]?
3. What have you heard about [global warming, calculus]?
4. What is present in a sophisticated [historical/textual/data] analysis that is missing in a simple one?

And we always follow these questions with "Why do you say that?" Students tend to write what they expect we want to hear first, which is usually what they've heard in school, but if they write enough they reveal their preexisting narratives. The second part of the question pushes them to explain how they have arrived at their answers and so reveals the basis for their thinking going into the course, which is often not the disciplinary thinking we want them to do. We tailor such questions to our own courses and students. Figure 5.2 showed how one teacher approached assessment of the emotional bottlenecks of her students. However, to come up with good assessment questions initially, we are often making a guess about where we think nondisciplinary modes of thought may catch students in emotional bottlenecks. We give several examples of possible approaches in Figure 5.4.

Figure 5.4. Assessment questions to get at emotional bottlenecks (School of Health, Western Carolina University).

Social Work

Students think the basis of social work is compassion and intuition. In reality social workers use theory and research as the backbone of their work.

1. Pretest: "In addition to hard work, what does it take to be an effective social worker? Why do you say that?"
   Post: "What would you advise your best friend do to be successful in social work?"
2. Pre- and posttest: "Social work requires . . . compassion/intuition 1 2 3 4 5 theory/research." Students are asked to locate their views along the numeric scale from 1 (strong preference for compassion/intuition) to 5 (strong preference for theory/research).

Nursing

Students are repelled by pus or unpleasant odors; expert nurses, however, continue to work in the presence of (what may seem to a nonprofessional to be) disturbing symptoms.

"What features of wounds might distract a nurse from using sterile techniques? Why do you say that?"

Emergency Medical Technician (EMT)

Students may think an EMT is an adrenaline-driven hero. Expert EMTs, however, follow a set of safety and medical procedures.

Pre- and posttest using the Visual CAT. Ask students to draw an EMT and annotate details showing what it takes to be a good EMT.

Physical Therapy

Students may think physical therapy is a hard science with no room for qualitative work. But there are physical differences among clients and you have to make a hypothesis about the cause and best treatment for a physical problem.

1. Pretest: "In addition to hard work, what does it take to be an effective physical therapist? Why do you say that?"
   Post: "What would you advise your best friend do to be successful in physical therapy?"
2. Pre- and posttest: "Physical therapy requires . . . art 1 2 3 4 5 science." Students are asked to locate their views along the numeric scale from 1 (a strong preference for art) to 5 (a strong preference for science).

Principle 2: Address the Emotional Bottlenecks

Once we have identified the emotional bottlenecks and collected specific details about them through assessments, we are ready to address them just as we addressed cognitive bottlenecks, although emotional bottlenecks tend to take extra emphasis and planning. Similar to dealing with cognitive bottlenecks, we identify the emotional bottleneck and then find out what exactly experts do to avoid it. Using the usual Step 2 tools (interviews, rubrics, and analogies) clarifies the mental task. In the case of procedural bottlenecks, this is a cognitive task. In the case of worldview bottlenecks, this is both an affective and a cognitive task. Once we understand how the expert avoids the emotional bottleneck, the rest of the decoding process we have discussed so far can be used to address it: modeling the mental action and providing practice and feedback (see Figure 5.5).

However, we don't just want to model the expert mental moves for the students as we might with a less emotionally charged bottleneck. If you've gotten to this point in the book, you may already have tried that without success. We begin instead by getting students to see that there is more than one way to think about the material and to be aware of how they are thinking about it, where that thinking comes from, and how it differs from disciplinary forms of knowledge. For students to become aware of which category to use within a discipline, it helps to place evidence of the assessment of their emotional bottlenecks side by side with the disciplinary mental action. Only now can they begin to recognize the new way of thinking they are to use in class. For example, in one class 43% of students relied on media reports rather than historical evidence to think about Mexican migration patterns (Middendorf et al., 2015). Following a lesson, they might still listen to media reports outside the class, but we want them to understand that historians use different sorts of evidence. Figure 5.6 gives an example of addressing procedural bottlenecks in computing.

Figure 5.5. The conceptual shift from emotional bottlenecks to mental tasks.

1. Assess the emotional bottlenecks—what do they think about the topic before you teach it? (Step 6)
2. Analyze the results of preassessment to determine student conceptual preconceptions—the emotional bottlenecks (Step 1).
3. Make a side-by-side comparison of their preconceptions and how those are distinct from the new disciplinary way of thinking (Step 2).
4. Use Decoding the Disciplines Steps 3 and 4 to model and practice.

Figure 5.6. Addressing a procedural bottleneck in computing.

For example, testing the code is a regular part of programming. Students in the beginning courses are told to test small parts of the program along the way, so that debugging larger, multifaceted programs later on, and in more advanced courses, is less onerous. But students don't like to test first. They want to write code first. Tests illuminate the code and they have to understand the interface to be able to develop the tests, and they frequently don't want to put in this effort. So, no matter how much a teacher can tell them to TEST THE CODE, they don't see the point. Don't you have to write the code first, and then test it later? This is a classic procedural bottleneck that leads to frustration when their code won't run. Without having tested incrementally, they can't pinpoint where they went wrong, causing some students to just give up.

How does thinking about this as an emotional bottleneck help? Once we notice the reasons that students drop the course, Step 5 Motivation gives us three motivational suggestions. First, collect assessments from students about why they resist testing, and give them feedback on the results. Second, don't make testing the code optional. Hold them accountable to test their code from the get-go. Give students a grade for the code and a grade for the test, and let them count the same amount (see principles 3 and 4). Curricula such as "Program by Design" enforce a framework where students write checks (i.e., tests) before writing code. Third, elevate testing to a course topic and provide scaffolding to help students learn test-driven development as part of your course design. At first, require them to write detailed purpose statements instead of code, and the teacher can then suggest appropriate tests. Later, the teacher can provide partial tests for a function and ask students to add enough tests to cover all possible code paths. Soon, you can require students to write their own component tests, and eventually a whole unit test. These test suites can be shared with the entire class so students can test their code against tests written by others. By building up facility with testing, side-by-side with coding and across the course, students become acclimated to testing as a natural part of the development cycle. (Adrian German and Suzanne Menzel, Indiana University)

The contrast between the students' vernacular way of thinking and the expert's cognitive process involves "discrimination"—making a distinction. By placing the two things side by side, students can better see the category differences and start using the disciplinary appropriate category when thinking in the discipline. Table 5.1 shows several examples of the contrast between vernacular thinking that may trap students in an emotional bottleneck and the expert's mode of thinking. (Exercise 5.3 provides individual and team exercises to contrast emotional bottlenecks with the desired mental actions.)

TABLE 5.1

Examples of Emotional Bottlenecks and Their Contrasting Mental Actions

Field	Step 1: Emotional Bottleneck	Step 2: Mental Action
Mental Contrast	Students use a conceptual category inappropriate for discipline	Experts use disciplinary mental moves
Evolutionary Sciences	Recent earth creationism as a belief based on received wisdom (as religion)	The age of Earth as known through fossil record, isotopic analyses of the elements, and an understanding of radioactive decay (as science)
Graph Reading (sciences and social sciences)	A graph as a "picture" of the data, rather than a representation of the data (the graph goes up, the object must have gone up). Some students don't know where to start in looking at a graph	Translation from graph to what is represented (data sets, functions, or actual objects)
Biology/Any Science	Learning biology or any science as the memorization of facts and the results of science	Visualization of biological processes and making predictions based on the mental visualization
History	Determining winners and losers in the historical past; making judgments based on current frameworks	History as explaining why persons in the past acted as they did, backed by evidence showing why their position was shaped and constrained by the societal norms of the time

We can further help students recognize the difference between the conceptions they entered the class with and disciplinary critical thinking by creating contrasting analogies for the two; analogies emphasize the differences between the different sorts of mental actions (see Table 5.2).

Teachers can use these analogies to remind students, and students can use them to check their own mental processes ("Am I just grabbing the top apple from the stack or have I really examined it?" "Am I basing my claim on evidence or am I just going with what the textbook says?"). By showing images of the analogies side by side, we can help make the contrast between the two sources of mental actions even more vivid. In Figure 5.7 the colorful swimming board is floating on the surface, representing the way students

TABLE 5.2
Analogies to Capture the Contrast Between Mental Actions

Misconception/ Field	Analogy for the Preconception/ Emotional Bottleneck	Analogy for Expert Mental Process
Authority for claims in evolutionary science	Having the principal make all the rules about the school dance	Having students draw up rules based on what had happened at the previous 10 school dances
Culture (in social sciences or humanities)	Implying national identity or otherness with festive or exotic costumes	Iceberg metaphor that implies customs, habits, and beliefs that may not be explicitly stated
Humanities/social science—close reading as	Understanding a story: Being able to narrate the "plot"	Forensic investigation: The reader is looking for clues in the words
Scholarly library search as	Using the heel of your shoe to hammer in a nail (because your shoe is right there)	Going upstairs to get the hammer (because it is the right tool)
Creative writing—choosing the right words as	Picking up the top five pieces of fruit in the stack in a supermarket	Turning each piece of fruit over to check for blemishes and bad spots before selecting five pieces to serve to your friends
Biology/any science as facts versus the generation of explanations and tools by which to further studies	Following a recipe	Inventing a new recipe based on the ingredients one has on hand
Geologic time scale	Like watching water drip on rocks and not seeing a change Or Like taking a picture of a mountain every year to see if it is getting shorter or taller	Time lapse photography stopping at 10 million years or 100 million years Or Like time lapse of evening primrose bloom over one summer's evening versus the plant's life over a whole summer Or Like taking a picture of the same mountain every thousand years for a million years

Figure 5.7. Contrasting analogies for culture in visual form.

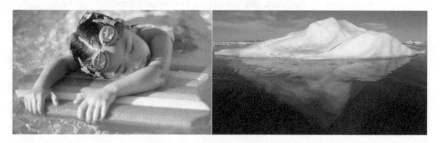

Note. Girl with Styrofoam Swimming Board, photograph by Tommy Wong, Wikimedia Creative Commons; Iceberg in the Arctic, photograph by A. Weith, Wikimedia Creative Commons.

assume that culture is both colorful and surface, while the iceberg, with most of its mass below the surface, symbolically represents the way much of culture lurks unseen below the surface.

Again, we want to respect the conceptions students bring into the classroom, which may be quite functional outside of that classroom. Well-chosen analogies can help create critical distance for the students and situate epistemic positions as choices and not as absolutes. They can allow students to get involved by considering the pros and cons, so they can feel respected and when they challenge the teacher's stand they can do so from a disciplinary perspective.

After we have used Step 6 of decoding to assess student thinking and thus have shed light on Step 1—where the students are getting stuck—when we have done Step 2 to uncover expert thought, we can go on to use Steps 3 through 7 of Decoding the Disciplines to build a lesson that helps students make the cognitive shift to the appropriate category. Depending on the emotional bottleneck, this may entail coming up with an anchoring metaphor; that is, a metaphor creating an especially strong association with the new category (Savion & Middendorf, 1994). For example, in service-learning classes, students sometimes find it difficult to understand reciprocity, and thus they may lack empathy for the community partner. For Step 3, Joan Linton developed a metaphor for reciprocity, the "yes, and" strategy of improvisational comedy, by which students and community partners listen very carefully and build on each other's ideas. Students practiced "yes, and" exercises in class to learn improv before applying it to service-learning. "Yes, and" served as the anchoring metaphor for reciprocity: It showed students what to pay attention to and how to value and build on what the other person brought to the service situation, not just what the students were "giving" (Asai et al., 2013). Linton's complete bottleneck lesson appears in Figure 5.8.

Figure 5.8. Service-learning "reciprocity" emotional bottleneck.

Joan Linton's 300-level public writing course at Indiana University integrates service-learning with a health and wellness focus. When students perform a minimum of 20 hours of public service, the experience serves as the basis for producing a written document for the organization and a final research paper for the course. However, students' unstated beliefs and values come up again and again to block development toward relationship-based coproduction with community members.

1. *What is the emotional bottleneck?*
   Students view service as helping those less fortunate than themselves, judge them as "other," do not value their ideas, and feel good about themselves for engaging in this work.
2. *Expert thinking*
   Experts view service as reciprocity—all participants, including community members, are colearners, coeducators, and cogenerators of knowledge and solutions (Pettit et al., 2017).
3. *Model/metaphor*
   The "yes, and" strategy of improvisational comedy, by which each person builds on the previous person's ideas. Students watched YouTube videos on this variety of improv (www.youtube.com/watch?v=nXl_51uED7Q). There are also course readings from authors such as Nobel Prize winners Elinor Ostrom and Mohammed Yunnus about coproduction of knowledge.
4. *Practice and feedback*
   Student teams play improv games. In weekly reflective assignments they write about ways they could apply the "Yes, and" improv formula to their interactions with clients at a domestic abuse shelter or a food pantry.
5. *Motivation*
   The improv comedy metaphor and team exercises added fun to the class as well as conceptual understanding of reciprocity.
6. *Assessment*
   Pre- and posttesting using student reflections about reciprocity showed an increase in conceptual grasp from 15% (pre-) to 60% (posttest). The reflections revealed a change in the student viewpoint about the community partners: "Even though it may seem like a person is abusing the system or lacking initiative, they ultimately know and understand their lives and experiences much better than we do. That's why our role is to help, not to judge."

Because the anchoring metaphor is added to practice and critical feedback on their efforts, students are less likely to respond angrily to the need to think differently and are more apt to change their learning patterns. Linton concluded about the effect of the bottleneck lesson on her students,

I learned that the cognitive intervention can indeed be quite simple, like the "yes, and" formula of improv, but that its force as metaphor is tremendous because it reconfigures relationships and the way one positions oneself in social interactions. Without this figurative force, no amount of received virtue or rehearsed empathy could dislodge one from deeply held values and beliefs about the other—in this case, those who live in poverty. (Asai et al., 2013)

In Linton's course, students had to switch their perspectives from seeing poor people as abusers of the system and "takers" to seeing them as people with challenges, just as in their own lives. The ability to switch perspectives is relevant to almost every field. However, because different disciplines require different mental actions, the ways in which the students' perspectives affect their understanding will differ from discipline to discipline. For example, in problem-solving fields, generating creative solutions almost always involves a change of perspective (Osborn, 1963).

Worldview bottlenecks lurk in many disciplines, but procedural difficulties can also produce emotional responses that impede student learning. For instance, teachers of polar science struggle to get student and lay audiences to understand the process and extent of the melting polar ice caps. One small part of the problem is a procedural emotional bottleneck; some of the line graphs of the underwater polar ocean data take some getting used to. Students are frustrated when they encounter graphs that must be read differently from the ones they are used to (see Figure 5.9).

Figure 5.9. Emotional procedural bottleneck in polar science.

Step 1 Bottleneck
> Even if students have learned to read other graphs (a big assumption), some graphs of ocean data are different, and thus difficult to read, not least because they contain multiple layers of information.

Step 2 Decoding the Expert's Mental Task
> For some of these graphs (e.g., temperature and salinity graphs), zero is not at the origin of the x-y axis; it is at the top left of the graph. The top of the graph represents the top of the ocean and we go down the y-axis, not up, as the numbers represent the depths of the ocean (expressed as decibars, where pressure is a measure of depth). The bottom of the graph, the data that lies along the x-axis, is a jagged line representing the various depths of the bottom of the ocean. There is a time sequence running along the x-axis, because the data in the graph were gathered by "gliders," probes that swim across the bottom on a path over a period of time. (Unlike in physics, this kind of graph DOES represent the physical environment, whereas in physics, graphs DON'T.) The shadings in the graph represent the temperatures.

(*Continues*)

Figure 5.9. (*Continued*)

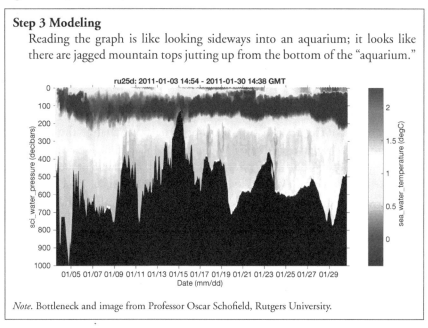

> **Step 3 Modeling**
> Reading the graph is like looking sideways into an aquarium; it looks like there are jagged mountain tops jutting up from the bottom of the "aquarium."
>
> *Note.* Bottleneck and image from Professor Oscar Schofield, Rutgers University.

Graph interpretation is just one aspect of the tacit mental action of polar science that makes it difficult for students to interpret data about the north and south poles. Analogies can help students better understand the role the melting of the polar icecaps has on water temperature/salinity/pressure, as might practice exercises where the students look at graphs from different disciplines and discuss what the graphs are intended to do. For faculty familiar with the decoding process, Exercise 5.4 provides advanced work designing practice and assessment to address student resistance.

Disrupting Rituals and Ensuring Accountability

Principle 3: Disrupt Learning "Scripts" Through Course Design

Just as existing mental actions interfere with student learning, so do routines students learned in their prior schooling. Students come to us after many years of "ritual interactions" about learning (Bain, 2006). In all disciplines, students may study and practice using the same internal "scripts" that have been successful for them over many years, not changing their brains to try new ways of reasoning for different fields. They often memorize answers just prior to exams, and as a result ideas are easily forgotten, because they are inert (Perkins, 2007). Instead of understanding why and when to use certain formulae, they plug in numbers and crunch answers. Arlene Díaz found that even after repeated efforts to get her history students to use evidence and make arguments, when it came to the final exam, they reverted to writing a five-paragraph essay, a script from previous courses, instead of what she taught them, to generate an argument arising from the evidence (Shopkow, Díaz, Middendorf, & Pace, 2013b).

To create courses that disrupt learning rituals, we change the nature of the assignments we give students using either frontward or backward course design. By dropping traditional exams and papers, we can signal to students that they have to think differently in this class. For example, if we want students to select advertising strategies in a journalism class, instead of having them take a test on advertising, they might repeatedly practice creating the advertising strategy with an advertising campaign as their final project (see Figure 4.1). This not only disrupts their ritual responses but also provides projects and activities that are more authentic and less like "school activities" (Brown, Collins, & Duguid, 1989; Perkins, 2010).

Having a repository of nontraditional assignments that bring together the components of the mental action can broaden our teaching horizons and prevent us from falling back on the traditional assignments used when we were in school. If our store of possible assignments is limited, our repertoire of thought-provoking assignments may likewise be limited. Table 5.3 lists possible disruptive major assignments matched to main mental actions.

The major assignments become central to the classes as students focus on working in new ways to create products that have real-world relevance, so that students aren't just doing assignments for the teacher. For example, Sarah Neal-Estes's journalism students created audio stories for American Student Radio and as a result earned internships with syndicated National Public Radio shows. The major project prepared them for real radio journalism, building across the semester as students created narrative arcs for the ear, taped interviews, edited, practiced their radio voices, and used sound design to produce their own stories for radio. To give another example, all first-year students in an Indiana University procedural law course participated in an access to justice service project (see Figure 5.10) that had been designed with this disruptive assignment as a major focus of the course. (See Exercise 5.5 for a process to design a disruptive course.)

Disruptive final assignments focus on the crucial mental tasks that we want students to do. Previously when students wrote essays, many tasks, such as close reading, critiquing arguments, and creating arguments, were

TABLE 5.3
Disruptive Major Assignments

Major Assignments	Mental Actions
Team Posters	Show evidence (data) and make inferences.
Web Pages	Construct a technical design; organize knowledge.
Video Podcasts	Analyze the elements of style of an artwork in a campus gallery.
NPR Radio Story	Identify and present a compelling narrative.
Museum Exhibit	Dig into something students are interested in, applying disciplinary practices (evidence and arguments).
Game Design	Define tasks, brainstorm alternative solutions, derive tasks, estimate time usage, form and lead teams, and test solutions.
Enter a Competition	Submit a game to a juried competition: Understand criteria, lead teams, apply competencies to specific tasks, design engaging game play.
Teach a Lesson to Local Schoolchildren	Demonstrate a complete grasp of the processes of cellular growth or photosynthesis by translating this knowledge into another simpler form.
Visual Essay	Narrate images or videos to show how popular movies do cultural work—reflecting or reinforcing shared values.
Service-Learning	Relate course topics to an authentic service project in which students reciprocate with community members.

jumbled together and difficult to assess. Students might perform poorly because they did not know how to do one of these operations. But which one? Leah asks her students to make posters in one of her lower level courses, highlighting the use of evidence to make an argument. So there it is in large print—the inference, the evidence, the conclusion, all in plain sight and easy to judge if parts are weak or missing. Assignments that focus on a few crucial processes allow the instructor and students to determine if a competency has been developed or not, motivating the students to focus on it. After taking Leah's upper-level Crusades course, a student told us that his outlook on the course changed after reading in the syllabus that there would be no tests, but the students would create an exhibit about the Crusades to be displayed in a public coffeehouse. To accomplish this, the students had to be self-starters. A lot of the history was told through images

Figure 5.10. Backward and frontward course design in procedural law.

Transforming a Law Course

In a previous iteration of a procedural law course, we had developed the cognitive bottlenecks: legal theory, legal analysis, and drafting pleadings. Using backward design (Wiggins & McTighe, 2005) we wanted to address three of the IU Maurer School of Law Program goals: commitment to the rule of law and public service, empathy, and the role law plays in society and advancement of justice for both sections of the 170-student course. Because these program goals covered a lot of ground, we used frontward design to identify three affective bottlenecks in the course: systems thinking, empathy, and dry book learning.

We used service-learning on the topic of access to justice for a series of disruptive course assignments. Twenty-nine teams of six students interviewed people who lack access to justice and community partners who were trying to enhance the justice delivery systems for them. Focusing on the three bottlenecks allowed students to experience the following:

- Authentic, complicated problems, where there are no simple right and wrong answers, modeling claims and assumptions, to develop systems thinking
- Service-learning NOT as those who have resources helping those who don't, but doing and being with one another to advance the collective understanding (Clayton et al., 2014) to develop empathy
- Injustice and doing something about it to develop passion

Using a human design model, teams proposed projects such as improved readability of legal documents along with wider availability and a streamlined process for expungement of criminal records. At the end of the course students made statements like, "The A2J project was incredibly challenging (especially the group work aspect), but it really pushed me and made me understand the reality of our legal system for a large number of individuals," and "As a first-year law student, you get bogged down in theory. This project was a breath of fresh air, because we got to do something real that mattered." On the end-of-course evaluation, students rated strongly agree or agree on these Maurer Law Schools Program Goals:

- #4: Understand the values that guide our profession: 70% (120 students)
- #5: Develop and put into practice empathy: 70% (120 students)
- #6: Understand the nature and the power of Law 75% (125 students)

(Quintanilla, Middendorf, & Kile, 2017)

---

in the display. Students had to read and investigate their own specific area and then engage in dialogue with fellow students. In effect, each student had to become a micro-professional in a specific aspect of the Crusades. One student, so engaged that he spent a great deal of time working on the exhibit at classmates' apartments, told us he wished he could do the semester again. That is motivation by course design!

We often use social pedagogies in disruptive course assignments, which feature innovative projects used to translate course knowledge into authentic tasks; the act of translating focuses students on the representation of the most difficult concepts, which deepens their understanding. Because social pedagogies are intended not only for presentation to the teacher but also to others—a more authentic audience (peers and frequently public audiences outside the class)—students are more motivated because their efforts will be public. This is what makes disruptive assignments more motivating than traditional ones (see Table 5.3). For such assignments, students may prepare and teach a basic biology concept to middle school students (Bass & Elmendorf, 2011); design a museum exhibit that answers the question, "What do Americans need to know about the Crusades?"; or help community members write memoirs of their life experiences. Instructors may ask students to use digital media tools such as online blogging, podcasts, websites, or tweets where pedagogically appropriate. Alternatively, student teams may create hands-on products such as team posters, museum exhibits, or pamphlets for community agencies. Social pedagogies make use of the power of social learning; students focus on creating class projects and products, reinforcing the new mental actions. Compared to learning new mental moves for tests and papers, students often enjoy the intellectual community they develop as they practice new mental actions, problem-solving and analyzing ideas together. The more we structured assignments to be social and public the more students internalized responsibility for the work and seemed to enjoy themselves while trying out new mental actions.

Principle 4: Structure in Student Accountability

With courses designed disruptively, how can instructors ensure that students come to class with course assignments prepared and readings completed? Students often ignore vague assignments, such as "read this article" or "write a question based on the readings," because these neither structure analytic processes nor give students a sufficiently specific task. Many college students will not perform required work without accountability structures in place, or will do so only if the teacher will see it. Courses need structures of accountability that hold students' "feet to the fire" by setting incentives so they are less likely to slip back into old, generic ways of operating that don't match with critical thinking in disciplinary fields (Díaz, Middendorf, Pace, & Shopkow, 2008).

Most students want to look good in front of their peers; by placing them in teams, using social pedagogies, and structuring assignments so students show their work to classmates, we can take advantage of the natural motivation of peer pressure. Teams can also improve learning because teams help students practice new ways of thinking, using new terminology and completing new tasks in a supportive group. However, many students have had negative experiences with "group work." This generally happens because there are no accountability structures in place, so that there is "free-riding." As Leah tells her students in her syllabus, "Accountability structures are especially important in team learning situations. True teams—where everyone is pulling his or her weight—aren't easier or faster to work in than working alone, but they produce superior results." When there are accountability structures, however, students may find teamwork more rewarding. A senior comparative literature major interviewed by us about her experience with teams in Leah's course reported that she enjoyed the team even though she was a "sit in my own corner in the library kind of gal." The team generated more ideas and did more research than she could have done alone, with less pressure than when she worked alone. She and her teammates communicated about the individual homework because, eventually, they would use the individual homework as a basis for their team posters. In short, they wanted to be on the "same page" from the beginning.

Michaelsen, Knight, and Fink (2004) developed team-based learning (TBL) structures to prepare students for class through in-class quizzes, participation in team problem-solving, and competion to create good products. TBL creates a motivational framework in which students increasingly hold each other accountable for coming to class prepared and contributing (see Figure 5.11).

The TBL method and variations of it have been used in every imaginable discipline, not just computing. TBL is a great system for experienced teachers, but it may fit poorly with the culture of some disciplines or some modes of teaching it. For example, if we want students to stop associating history with facts and events to be remembered, giving quizzes might not be the best way to achieve that goal. We found the individual and team quizzes cumbersome and time-consuming for history classes as a weekly practice (when more spaced out and alternating with other

Figure 5.11. Example of TBL in a database class.

Dan Richert uses TBL in his 300-level informatics database design and data retrieval class, where students encounter three bottlenecks to learning. The first bottleneck is the concept of entity-relationship diagrams—placing the everyday words of a customer into categories for a database. Designating the categories and matching items to the categories is a new kind of thinking for most students. The second bottleneck is reasoning in SQL, a relational database that differs from the programming languages they previously learned.

What makes these even harder to learn are two accompanying emotional bottlenecks: dualism (the students want to find a "right" answer [Perry, 1999], yet there are many ways to design a database and multiple acceptable designs) and the frequent mistakes common to writing a computer program. With these bottlenecks in mind, Richert designed the course so students would be sure to know what the expert does to get through them.

Richert selected the TBL method, which uses authentic problems, so students would create the database categories and try out various designs for the database, practicing the new concepts while explaining ideas in their teams. For effective practice students need repeated practice and they need the subskills to be built up over time. Richert is able to add one new skill onto another as the teams gain confidence with each one.

TBL also addresses motivation issues. Students hold each other accountable for coming to class prepared and contributing to the team projects; they can tell if a teammate is not keeping up. Richert has overheard his students tell teammates, "I'm sorry, I didn't get a chance to read it before class. I'll make sure not to do that again." TBL classes are "flipped" so that first exposure to content takes place outside of class (Walvoord & Anderson, 2011) and much of the in-class time is used for teamwork. On some days students must come to class prepared for an individual quiz, and then immediately retake it as a team.

How do students react to the TBL method? Overall they like it and say that it helps their learning. One student explained, "If you make a mistake and someone else makes a different mistake, you learn off of each other." Another student said, "It's intimidating to ask questions in a quiet room with just the teacher speaking. . . . I don't know how I could [learn databases] without asking my peers around me for help and going over things." Richert's students feel more comfortable asking questions and taking feedback in the team format.

assignments they can work), but, in general, the reason TBL works so well is the accountability factors that anyone can adapt. TBL's three accountability factors, along with Decoding the Disciplines, motivate students to persevere and comply with course requirements. They ensure that students do the following:

1. Prepare for class.
2. Contribute to the team.
3. Produce thoughtful materials.

Class Preparation

A bottleneck for many faculty is that students do not come to class prepared. If they follow a traditional format where homework entails applying mental tasks after exposure to course concepts during in-class lectures, students may be reluctant to do the homework because they feel they have mastered the concepts. In flipped classes, students may get their "first exposure" to course content outside of class (Walvoord & Anderson, 2011). In these classes, students need to come to class prepared, or they will not have the background to undertake the in-class problem-solving. Preparation methods for flipped classes should ensure that students have engaged with course materials and are ready to apply them.

Many systems can ensure preparation: quizzes, charting, drawing, discussion, interview analyses, or blogging answers to questions (just to name a few), and, whether digital or in hard copy, these could be brought to class like a "ticket" for entry. One approach we have found very useful is just-in-time teaching (JiTT) warm-ups. JiTT is a form of teaching to difficulties in which the teacher reviews student warm-up assignments a few hours before class (Novak, 2011). Warm-ups are short, web-based exercises that help the instructor identify potential student difficulties in time to address them in the upcoming class. Warm-ups present students with a problem or big questions that require digging into course readings to solve or answer. Warm-up questions can be quite elaborate or quite simple. In Figure 5.12 we give an example of a simple one from an introductory chemistry course. You will notice that it doesn't simply ask students what you get when you mix sodium and chlorine—ha! table salt!—but what the process of getting there looks like. The warm-up, in other words, reveals the students' level of understanding of basic chemistry.

Figure 5.12. JiTT warm-up in Introduction to Chemistry.

A JiTT Warm-up from Bob Blake, Indiana University–Purdue University at Indianapolis, Introduction to Chemistry

You allow sodium and chlorine to react. Describe what you see from beginning to end.

There are many possible methods besides JiTT warm-ups to ensure students have completed the preclass assignments. Grading schemes that assign a substantial part of the course grade to preclass work also incentivize preparation.

Team Contribution
A bottleneck to performance in teams is that most likely no one has ever taught students what collaborative team behavior entails (Weimer, 2015). A simple list, such as the following by Crutchfield and Klamon (2014), can set expectations for team contribution:

- contribute to the team's work
- communicate effectively with teammates
- care that the team produces high-quality work
- pull your own weight
- actively help solve problems that face the team (p. 290)

Many students' team performance improves dramatically after they receive feedback from their teammates, whether qualitative or quantitative. From our experiments on the History Learning Project, the two questions that have gotten best results are:

1. What has each team member (including yourself) contributed to the team?
2. What could each team member do to improve team efforts?

We summarize the comments before e-mailing them to students so that peers can comment freely. We administer this team evaluation three times during the semester (see Figure 5.13).

There are new systems that can automate the team scoring process, such as the Comprehensive Assessment of Team Member Effectiveness (CATME) (Ohland et al., 2012), which is useful for large classes. Whether teachers use their own homegrown method or an online product, teams work more effectively when students learn how to perform in them and receive feedback on their performance.

Product Quality
This is the grade a teacher gives for intellectual quality on the completed projects, such as posters; component projects on databases and queries; and final database projects, team presentations, and written reports. Sometimes we have an authentic review panel choose the best final projects, adding

Figure 5.13. Example of peer evaluation form for individual team members in a college pedagogy course.

> Comment on your own and the contributions of your teammates to the *bottle-neck lesson development* (discussions and blog comments).
>
> *Peer Contribution* (2% of course grade)
>
> 1. What was Mary Smith's most significant contribution to the bottleneck lesson development?
> 2. What could Mary do to improve contributions to team work?
> 3. What was Juan Martinez's most significant contribution to the bottleneck lesson development?
> 4. What could Juan do to improve contributions to team work?
> 5. And so on. (Place remaining team members' names on form.)
>
> Your feedback will be evaluated on the following criteria:
>
> - Readings—addresses the degree to which this person synthesizes the readings and applies them to his or her field; gives evidence or examples for judgment
> - Bottleneck Discussion—describes the degree to which the teammate gives thoughtful analyses and truly answers the questions
> - Feedback—specific, constructive; tells what teammate needs to do to improve comments

motivation to students to make their best efforts. Some element of making the students' work (but not their grades) public prods students to do their best work, because the quality of their performance is not just a secret matter between them and their teachers.

Instructors wishing to use any form of team learning effectively will want to change their grading schemes. In traditional courses much of the grade may be based on the intellectual product, whether exams, papers, or projects. With team learning (and even with individual learning where emphasis is on students learning a process), the grade needs to be distributed across all the accountability structures: for the intellectual products, preparation, and team effort. To incentivize preparation and discourage free-riding in teams, the grading schemes of three different instructors are contrasted in Table 5.4. We compared three courses that all used different accountability structures for preparation, team effort, and intellectual effort.

In designing accountability structures for these three grading schemes, instead of the whole grade coming from a few tests or papers, it is distributed

TABLE 5.4
Comparative Accountability Structures

Course Components	Course		
	Informatics	Medieval History	MBA Accounting Capstone
Main Mental Actions	Turning everyday language into databases	Interpreting historical narratives	Developing a strategy to address a client problem
Form of Teamwork	Team-based learning (Michaelsen)	Hybrid of individual homework, three team posters	Team project with real client—teacher as business partner/boss
Preparation	45% individual and team readiness quizzes from outside class videos and course readings	50% individual homework on subcompetencies	25% each team member documents weekly time allocation
Team Contribution	15% score teammates three times using a rubric	Score teammates on CATME. Team score can raise or lower poster grades by 10% or more in extreme cases (three assessments, second and third may lower score).	25% score teammates on 14 items (twice)
Team Products	40% for databases, queries, and final database project	40% for team posters	20% for team presentation and 30% for written report

across the accountability tools. In many lecture courses, however, most of the grade comes from a few exams or papers (with a small participation grade). These accountability structures improve student perseverance on mental tasks. We found you can't just teach to the bottlenecks or even to the emotional bottlenecks; rather, the whole course has to be designed to motivate students to persevere on new and difficult mental actions. Collaboration (through social pedagogies and accountability structures, through trying out new ideas with peers and showing that work to peers) reinforces students' understanding of the mental actions and thus is catalytic in helping students learn new disciplinary ways of operating.

Summary

The concept of emotional bottlenecks provides a powerful framework for understanding student resistance to learning. Work on emotional bottlenecks starts with identifying the emotional bottlenecks, the narratives students bring to the class. Because it is hard for experts to know where students get stuck, we want to assess the emotional bottlenecks and we do so through carefully worded questions. To show the difference between the categories students are using compared to disciplinary constructs, we place extra emphasis on the modeling and practice steps of decoding to ensure students incorporate new mental habits. When teachers encounter emotional bottlenecks, they may also want to restructure the course to prioritize student learning of the bottleneck. This might include new grading structures to hold students accountable for class preparation, contributions to the team, and the production of thoughtful materials so that students persist on new and difficult mental actions.

In Appendix A, you can see how a biologist and a musicologist have addressed Step 5 in the decoding process.

CHAPTER 5 EXERCISES

Exercise 5.1: Identifying Emotional Bottlenecks

For individuals

What is an emotional bottleneck for the students in one of your courses? What is the nature of the problem?

_____

_____

_____

_____

After writing an answer to these questions, you may want to discuss it with a colleague and hear the colleague describe an emotional bottleneck. As usual, try to pair up with someone from outside your department in a field different from your own.

For teams

For discussion in teams of 3, each person gets 3 minutes to discuss the question. If someone doesn't use the entire 3 minutes, the other group members should try to explain the emotional bottleneck back to that person.

1. First member of group speaks (3 minutes)
2. Second member of group speaks (3 minutes)
3. Third member of group speaks (3 minutes)

Exercise 5.2: Emotional Bottlenecks Pre-Assessment Questions (Individuals and Teams)

What question(s) would you ask to uncover the narratives or preconceptions students bring to your class?

_____

_____

_____

_____

After individuals have written, the question can be discussed in teams of 3, allowing 5 minutes per team member.

Exercise 5.3: Contrast Emotional Bottlenecks With Expert Mental Actions

For individuals

1. Brainstorm students' emotional worldview/procedural bottlenecks and the contrasting expert mental moves by adding your discipline to Table 5.1. Or contrast analogies for the student bottlenecks with those of the expert mental moves in Table 5.2.
2. You may want to collaborate with a colleague to fill in the blanks. As usual, try to pair up with someone from outside your department in a field different from your own.

For teams

1. Teams of three help each other contrast the expert thinking with the thinking students deploy when they are caught in emotional bottlenecks to fill in the bottom of the table.
2. The whole group practices generating analogies for one emotional bottleneck and the expert mental action to get the idea of generating analogies using Figure 5.8.
3. Teams discuss ways to apply this approach to their own contexts, reporting out to the whole group.

Exercise 5.4: Practice and Assessment of Critical Emotional Bottlenecks

Step 4 Practice: What practice and feedback would you give students to enact the cognitive shift of their emotional bottleneck?

_____

_____

_____

_____

Step 6 Assessment: What student assessment could check student competence in understanding the difference between their preconception/the disciplinary construct—such as the mental action of perspective switching?

_____

_____

_____

_____

The questions could be discussed in teams of three, allowing five minutes per person.

Exercise 5.5: Designing Disruptive Courses (Reflective Writing for Individuals)

1. What do we want students to be able to *do* by the end of the course. What is the overall mental task (e.g., textual analysis, computational thinking—creating directions for a computer to do a task, etc.)?

_____

_____

_____

2. What is a major assignment that would demonstrate students have achieved course competencies—tasks that would showcase textual analysis, computational thinking, and so on?

_____

_____

_____

_____

3. What are the earlier scaffolded assignments that will prepare students with the competencies needed for the final assignment? What mental tasks does each of these assignments require? (What are subcomponents of textual analysis, computational thinking, etc.?) You should have two side-by-side lists.

_____

_____

_____

_____

Exercise 5.6: Radical Course Redesign Note-Passing Activity (in Ongoing Teams of Three)

On a piece of paper jot down two ideas for possible final course projects for each of your teammates that will do the following:

1. Disrupt learning rituals
2. Hold students publicly accountable

(6 minutes writing, 2 minutes for each teammate)

Discussion:

1. Pass notes to teammates. Read the notes you received. (2 minutes)
2. Each person discusses the projects he or she received and how he or she might use them. (2 minutes each.)

6

STEP 6

Decoding Assessment

Twenty-four graduate students in a college pedagogy course were assigned to teach bottleneck lessons in real undergraduate classes. This included pre- and posttesting the mental actions and placing their findings on the class blog. However, three of them did not collect the pre- and post-CATs; all three concluded in similar fashion that they were confident their students had learned the concepts—though they had no data to back up this assertion. In contrast, the 21 who collected data arrived at a different conclusion: Those who collected data found that students had not gotten as far as expected though they were able to document specific improvements. They reported such things as, "The students learned five of the eight concepts; I will have to work on the other three." Or, "Before the lesson, 22% knew how to do the action, but after, 68% could."

Step 6 Assessment sets up a feedback loop so teachers can gauge students' performance on the mental action based on evidence, not based on assumptions. In Steps 1 and 2 we identified bottlenecks to learning and the underlying expert thinking to identify the mental action we want students to perform. The mental action then becomes the goal of a bottleneck lesson. Steps 3, 4, and 5 show how to teach to the mental action, model it, provide practice and feedback, and motivate students to persevere. Step 6 explains how to assess student performance on the mental action and assemble the evidence of student learning and where it fell short.

Chapter 6 is not the first mention of assessment in this book, because assessment is an essential part of acquiring the bottleneck perspective. In earlier chapters we use simple CATs in Step 1 to clarify the bottlenecks and in Step 4 we use CAT structures for some practice. In fact, practice exercises *are* assessments, whether graded or not. With Step 5 we immediately assess student preconceptions to uncover emotional bottlenecks students may bring to class. Chapter 6 is a more in-depth explanation of ways to check the extent to which students have mastered mental actions.

By exploring various methods to assess learning data *beyond* graded assignments, we can gather, visualize, and use learning data to improve teaching and learning. This chapter will explain the difference between assessments for learning versus assessments for grading, describe some categories for choosing assessments, present a variety of assessments, and discuss how to summarize the results.

Chapter 6 is organized according to the following six principles:

- Assessment Principle 1: Focus on evidence of mastery of one specific mental action.
- Assessment Principle 2: Become familiar with a variety of learning assessment techniques.
- Assessment Principle 3: Match assessment techniques to the mental action and Bloom's type of thinking.
- Assessment Principle 4: Use multiple assessment techniques, especially pre- and posttests, or "two is better than one."
- Assessment Principle 5: Summarize and interpret the evidence. (How do we make sense of the results?)
- Assessment Principle 6: Track the mental actions in assessments for grading—the final course products.

Assessment Principle 1: Focus on Evidence of Mastery of One Specific Mental Action

Assessment for grading can give an overall idea of the state of the student's learning, but not specific feedback highlighting areas for the teacher or the student to improve. For example, an instructor in a large 100-level gender studies course asked students "What is feminism?" for the final essay exam (Shopkow, 2010). We interviewed him to decode the mental actions for writing a successful essay. Figure 6.1 shows some of the many mental actions it would take to successfully complete the essay.

Assessments for grading can involve so many mental actions—critiquing arguments, creating arguments, recognizing different genres of texts, reading "closely," bringing other ideas to the text, and even tolerating ambiguity—that it can be difficult to separate out what a student has mastered or missed in the learning process. This kind of assessment has its uses, since it mimics the kinds of performances expected of experts, but it is less useful

Figure 6.1. Mental actions for writing a successful essay on "What is feminism?"

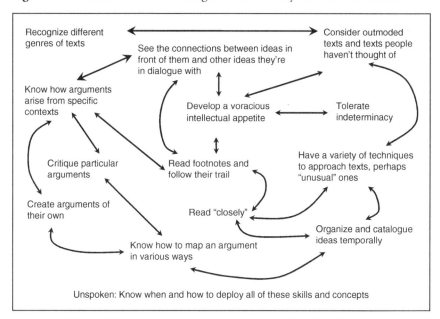

in determining how to get students to give more expert performances. It can be eye-opening for faculty, who primarily assess for grading, to learn how to assess student performance of a specific mental action.

Let's look at two types of assessments as delineated in Table 6.1: assessment for grading and assessment for learning. Grading assessments traditionally consist of the main course assessments, midterm and final exams or final papers. They are summative assessments, meaning they are obtained at the end of an instructional unit to measure the level of proficiency, compared against a standard or benchmark, and are usually high stakes and high pressure for students (and teachers). Because assessments for grading often take place at the end of a unit of study, students are not going to get a chance to redo their efforts. Thus, Gregor Novak compares them to autopsies, in that they come too late to help the patient (Novak, Pace, & Novotny, 2010). Grading assessments can also be compared to blood pressure or heart rate as measures of overall wellness; we get an overall sense of how well students performed in the course.

Sometimes a deeper, more targeted look may be useful. For example, doctors can diagnose diabetes with the hemoglobin A1c test or visualize muscles and organs with an MRI. These medical diagnostic tests are

TABLE 6.1
Assessment for Grading and for Learning

Category	Assessment for Grading	Assessment for Learning
Focus	Global, multicomponent competencies	Specific mental actions, the scaffolded components of larger competencies
Purpose	Measure student proficiency at end of a unit; classify students	Provide feedback and improvements to teachers and students
Methods	Exams, term papers	Learning assessment techniques (CATs), quizzes, homework assignments
Grading	Graded	Often ungraded
Stakes	High	Low
Terminology	Summative assessment	Formative assessment

comparable to learning assessments, small, frequent checks on what, how, and how well students are learning (Angelo & Cross, 1993). Whether graded or ungraded, these low-stakes assessments provide feedback for improvement to teachers and learners. Buchanan (2015) compares learning assessments to Fitbits, tiny monitors attached to wristbands by which people track specific, small measures of personal health: exercise and activity levels, food, weight, and sleep patterns, to name a few. Like Fitbits for teaching, CATs provide feedback to students and teachers on the "health" of specific competencies in a course. Low-stakes learning assessments help diagnose problems before students are asked to perform on high-stakes graded assessments. Having this kind of feedback from students can help teachers notice when students need more modeling and practice prior to summative assessments.

Learning assessments can help student performance because they diagnose a particular component, rather than award an overall grade or offer general praise or criticism (Black & Wiliam, 1998). Even so, many teachers still mainly rely on global student evaluations, such as midterm and final exams or large end-of-course papers. Learning assessments and grading assessments are quite different from each other, and it is a bottleneck for teachers when they do not know the difference between the two. At Step 6 Assessment in Decoding the Disciplines, we check student efforts on the mental action before they encounter the major, graded assessments. That is, we drill down to assess how well (or not) students are able to perform on a specific mental move.

Assessment Principle 2: Become Familiar With a Variety of Learning Assessment Techniques

We use CATs to get a clearer idea of what happens when students are trying out the mental action or to find out more about the bottleneck. Because teachers have often had bad experiences with assessments, which may have been used to evaluate their teaching and from which they may have received negative feedback from students or supervisors, some are leery of adding more assessment to their classrooms. Understandably, assessment can make teachers feel uncomfortable. We like to introduce CATs in friendly terms that imply felines: house cats! We want teachers to like CATs and to adopt some CATs in their classes. Only much later after teachers are used to collecting evidence of student learning through CATs do we introduce the great scarlet letter A-word (for Assessment) instead of CATs. (Throughout this book we use the term *CATs* more often than its synonym, learning assessments.) Thinking of these assessments as CATs can also help teachers avoid treating "assessment" and "grading" as synonymous.

Just as with the rest of Decoding the Disciplines, wherein faculty choose their own bottlenecks, analogies, modeling exercises, and forms of practice that all align with the mental action, there is freedom of choice in selecting the CATs (or other learning assessments) that will best reveal student competency on the mental move. In order to make their choice, it helps for them to become familiar with a range of different CATs. CATs can be considered in terms of four modes, or different ways students can experience them: kinesthetic, written, visual, or verbal.

Kinesthetic CATs

Kinesthetic CATs use tactile methods to check student learning through physical, whole-body techniques rather than traditional ways of measuring student learning on written tests or papers. Kinesthetic CATs can be used when class energy is low or during the doldrums of the semester when student (and instructor) energy is flagging (Duffy & Jones, 1995). They get students up and moving, using their bodies to show their position or response, before being asked to justify their position. Because kinesthetic CATs involve the whole body, they are especially memorable, so a teacher might assess kinesthetically for particularly important mental actions.

ConcepTests are short, targeted, informal quizzes interspersed throughout a class. The ConcepTests consist of one to five multiple-choice questions, and students have to indicate their choices by raising their hands, holding up a color card associated with a response option, or using an input device (clicker or phone) instead of writing a response. The primary purpose of

ConcepTests is to get a snapshot of the current understanding of the class for the teacher and all students to see. ConcepTests are particularly valuable in large classes, where it is difficult to assess student understanding in real time.

The Stand Up/Sit Down CAT, a simple variation of the ConcepTest, is a multiple-choice test with only two options. Students are all asked to stand up. Then the two choices are presented and students either stay standing or sit down in response (e.g., see Figure 6.2).

A variation on a Number Line CAT, the continuum dialogue asks participants to stand physically on an arc according to where each person places himself or herself between two statements that form the beginning and end of the continuum. The statements that establish the ends of the continuum must allow for difference without a right and wrong place to stand. When the statements at the two ends have been established, the facilitator asks people at different points in the continuum to explain why they chose to stand where they did (Wentworth, 2009) (e.g., see Figure 6.3).

Figure 6.2. The Stand Up/Sit Down CAT (education).

Mental action/prompt: Diagnose the biggest source of learning problems for second-language learners in your class.

- *Sit down* if it is one of communication/language *translation.*
- *Keep standing* if it is one of *conceptual* comprehension.

When everyone is standing or seated, ask a few students in each position to explain why they chose to stand/sit.

Figure 6.3. Continuum dialogue (sports management).

Mental action: Take a position and support it with evidence from course readings on the topic of paying college athletes.

Prompt: Student athletes should be paid to play on teams in addition to the free tuition they receive.

Place yourselves along this continuum: *0, no compensation* → *through 10, paid to play.*

Ask a few students to explain why they chose to stand where they did. Prompt them, if necessary, to provide evidence from course readings.

GOAL: Analysis of the pros and cons of the treatment of student athletes in college athletics/getting students to do the reading.

Written CATS

For written CATs students compose their thoughts or find words to explain what they have learned. Most of the CATs in Angelo and Cross's (1993) book are written ones, but we have included a few here that we find especially revealing. Written CATs have not only the advantage of providing a permanent record of student responses but also the disadvantage of requiring more work and time on the part of the teacher to analyze and respond to them.

Word Journal (CAT #14)

Summarize a text (or an assignment or a problem, etc.) in one word. Write a paragraph explaining why you chose *that* word.

This CAT seems very simple at first. Students choose just one word. But the added metacognitive reflection—students have to explain their thinking—means they stop and take a minute to explain it to themselves first. This can provide students insights into their own thinking, as well as provide clues to the teacher (e.g., see Figure 6.4). Thinking about their own thinking is an important addition CATs can make to the classroom. Of course, what students report they can do may differ from what they can actually do.

Simile CAT

Ask students to describe the relationship between two key concepts. Again, we are taking advantage of metaphors and analogies, because the brain can act as a simulator, applying a known mental action to a new and different context. Moreover, this transfer is something we wish to encourage in

Figure 6.4. One-word CAT example from Arlene Díaz (history).

Bottleneck: Students don't know how to read as historians do. They read the same way they do in other classes.

Mental action: Understand history as an interpretive field, not one of recording and remembering facts and events.

Prompt: Summarize in one word what reading in history entails. Then explain in a few sentences why you chose that word.

Pretest results: All (*N* = 11) students were looking for "facts," "details," "dates," or "stories," which is considered to be operating at a low level of expertise.

Posttest results: Five out of 11 students explained they were looking for explanations of why things happened (midlevel of expertise) while 6 out of 11 looked for evidence to support the claims and interpretations being made (high level). All of the students moved up to at least a midlevel on the posttest and just over half had moved to a high level of performance.

students, as it may help integrate their learning. A simile CAT is a good check to see the connections students are making.

Categorizing Grid CAT #8

Ask students to sort subordinate information into superordinate conceptual categories (e.g., see Figure 6.5). Categorizing grids are also good for getting students to understand and learn how taxonomies work in a given discipline. That is, students need to learn the rules for what pieces of information or concepts go together in the context of a discipline, one marker of expertise (Chi, Slotta, & De Leeuw, 1994). Categorizing grids can be a useful diagnostic aid in these situations. With the categorizing grid, the instructor and students can see at a glance if anything is missing from the grid.

Invented Dialogue CAT #17

To show their understanding of the viewpoints or theories of others, students invent a fictional conversation between characters by either inventing reasonable quotes or inserting actual quotes. The characters can be real ones (a conversation between Martin Luther King Jr. and Abraham Lincoln) or invented characters, and the exercise may entail students synthesizing theories, adapting stories, or extrapolating from data.

Visual CATs

Unbeknownst to students, experts in many fields visualize problems. Visual CATs can provide insights when the graded assessments require students to perform calculations or answer in text. For example, experts in many STEM

Figure 6.5. Categorizing grid in law (Victor Quintanilla, Maurer School of Law).

Bottleneck: Law students often stumble in analyzing cases because they have not identified all of the critical facts in a case as well as the civil procedural concepts and legal standards that apply.

Prompt: For the following cases, identify ideas in the correct categories: critical facts, civil procedures/procedural concepts, and legal standards.

Case	Facts	Civil Procedures/ Procedural Concepts	Legal Standards
1. Ashcroft vs. Iqbal			
2. Hickman vs. Taylor			
3. International Shoe Co. vs. Washington			

fields implicitly visualize processes and actual objects such as cell lengths or ocean depths and all the things in the ocean depths represented by the numbers in a graph. Yet the primary grading assessments may ask students to write words or perform calculations. Visual CATs can get students to sketch out the way ideas look to them in their minds. Visual CATs can take many forms, such as a visual representation of the details in a text (see Figure 6.6).

Like written CATs, visual CATs provide a permanent record to which the teacher can return at need, but they do take time to process.

Figure 6.6. Annotated Figure CAT.

Leah invented the Annotated Figure CAT for the mental action of understanding the audience of a historical source, the Beowulf poem. What evidence is there of Beowulf's role in society and character portrayed to the audience? Her instructions were to "Draw what Beowulf looks like to the audience for the poem. Point to the passages that support the elements in your picture." She provided students an example of a crude drawing she made of another character in the Beowulf poem, to drive home the point that drawing skills were not the point of this assignment. Each detail in the drawing was to be annotated with the line from the poem and the words from the poem to show where in the sources the students located that evidence.

Photo 6.1. Student conceptual drawing of Beowulf, showing connection to points in the text.

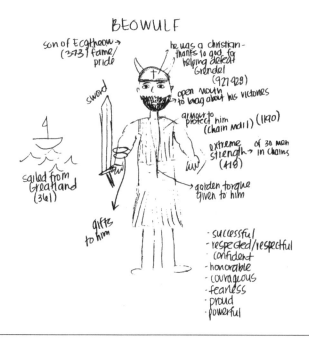

Concept Map CAT #16

A concept map is a graphical way for students to show the patterns of relationships around a given concept as they conceive of them. That is why they are also called "mind maps," since they literally show the connections students make between concepts. Teachers can use them to assess students' cognitive and metacognitive skills. Students can scrutinize their own conceptual networks and compare them to those of their peers and experts.

Meme CAT

Meme CATs require students to analyze and then represent the contagious information patterns of a concept, the various facets of an idea that spread differently depending on the viewpoints of different social group members. This works well for topics to which students feel some resistance (see Step 5). For a controversial construct, students identify various groups that might have differing viewpoints regarding the construct, possibly through the use of social media. Then they find images to represent the ways the different groups view the target construct. A follow-up question would ask students to explain in words what the different images portray (e.g., see Figure 6.7).

Figure 6.7. What an evolutionary biologist does.

Students make a digital slide of six comparative images (borrowed from the Internet) that show what an evolutionary biologist does:

- What my mom thinks I do (shows picture of a boy holding a model dinosaur)
- What my friends think I do (shows Sigourney Weaver hugging a gorilla in a jungle scene)
- What the media think I do (shows a photo of Richard Dawkins under a banner: "There's probably no god")
- What creationists think I do (shows a scary demon holding the world in its grip)
- What I think I do (shows Darwin in front of a chalkboard with diagrams on it)
- What I really do (shows computer program language with functions about tree tips, roots, and height)

Written reflection: Which source of knowledge does each group use to think about evolutionary biologists?

The Meme CAT combines a simile CAT with a visual CAT; it works especially well assessing emotional bottlenecks, because it helps students to compare various viewpoints related to a concept for which viewpoints may differ.

Cartoon CAT

Students use the frames of a blank cartoon (one to six frames) to explain in narrative form (with word bubbles and stick figures) a difficult concept. Some of the most effective cartoon CATs make use of metaphors. Susan Strome of UC Santa Cruz has her students draw a cartoon using symbols to represent the various proteins of a gene activation event. They also have to briefly explain each panel. The mental action involved is one of visualization, with the results similar to the Annotated Figure CAT, although this approach is particularly useful to assess how students visualize change or process.

The critical thinking of experts does not always involve words, such as when molecular scientists study the processes that happen at the molecular level. As they think about these processes, they "see" them in their minds. We can get at mental actions that don't involve words when we use visual CATs. Also, categories organize our thought, action, perception, and speech. We can get students to roughly "map" their categories so we can see the relationships they "see" in their minds. Roughly drawing what is in their mind's eye as in a cartoon CAT assesses skills that students might not be able to explain well in words alone.

Verbal CATs

By having students respond to prompts or teacher behaviors verbally, certain mental actions can be readily assessed. Students use their voices to respond. We are, again, trying to capture what is going on in their heads in a way that is different from the grading assessments. For some students, talking out their ideas helps them clarify their own thinking to themselves.

Callout CAT

One of the recognizable bottlenecks we have seen across many fields is that students do not know the difference between evidence (or data) and arguments (or interpretations or conclusions). When Eric Sandweiss (Indiana University Department of History) noticed that many students in his history class didn't take useful notes (the bottleneck), he decided to devote some class time to teaching them useful note-taking categories. He modeled three kinds of information they would be working on in class: main ideas (the big points he wanted students to get from the lectures), examples (facts illustrating the main ideas or points), and interpretations (analysis of the facts and ascription of meaning to them). During one lecture, he divided the class into three sections, assigned each section a sound to make (e.g., Homer Simpson's exclamation, "D'oh!"). For a 15-minute portion of the lecture, when they heard their designated category, the section was to make their sound. He followed up this CAT with several written assessments. While at the midterm less than half the students were able to recognize different categories of historical ideas from a previous lecture, by the end of the semester most of the students could. By becoming conscious of the ways in which their lecture had been deliberately constructed from themes, examples, and interpretations, he wanted them ultimately to become better able to reconstruct such elements into their own narratives (Eric Sandweiss, personal communication, April 2007).

Faculty may find it challenging to adopt new assessment strategies, so we have developed specific exercises for individuals or teams to consider the possibilities and commit in writing to their choices (see Exercise 6.1). In addition, we would add that teachers are not confined to Angelo and Cross's 50 CATs. There are innumerable methods for assessing student learning, with new ones being invented all the time by creative teachers for disciplinary purposes.

It will not escape alert readers that CATs also frequently provide students with practice of the relevant skills and feedback, even as they are assessing student mastery. We will not belabor the blending of assessment and practice in the following discussion, as this chapter will primarily focus on learning assessments: pinning down student mastery of a specific mental action. Most teachers will want to own a few CATs. CATs that can catch two sorts of mice, that both contribute to practice and give the teacher information about student learning, are particularly useful beasts.

Our major point with Step 6 is to check performance of a specific mental action or bottleneck before students are tested and graded and to make sure students have sufficient mastery of a component mental action before an instructor builds on that skill. We have just shown the range of techniques CATs use and the CATs that we have found most effective. Familiarity with at least a few CATs provides several different ways to measure student performance and is an important tool for classroom teachers.

Having selected a CAT to use, teachers still may find it difficult to make time in their busy schedules to actually collect the assessments. That is why when we are working in a team we often give them a hard deadline for collecting their assessment and completing an analysis, the topic for the next section of this chapter. The course planning template (Appendix C) was developed by Leah Shopkow and Arlene Díaz as part of the History Learning Project to structure planning for learning assessments.

Assessment Principle 3: Match Assessment Techniques to the Mental Action and Bloom's Type of Thinking

Just as in Step 4, when we matched practice methods to the desired Bloom's types of thinking for the mental action, Bloom's types can also be useful in selecting assessment techniques. Table 6.2 matches Bloom's types of thinking, along with the verbs or mental actions that establish that type of thinking, with several methods and techniques for learning assessments. Learning assessments are chosen for the way they intentionally structure assessments to check on a certain type of thinking.

With a specific mental action and the action's level in Bloom's typology in mind, we can select a learning assessment that will provide focused, specific feedback.

CATs can be applied to different types of thinking depending on the specific prompt. Angelo and Cross organized their CATs book's table of contents according to Bloom. CATs 2, 4, and 5 test declarative knowledge; CATs 19, 20, 23, 24, and 26 check skills in application; CATs 8 through 12 test analytical thinking; CATs 13 through 18 test creating and

TABLE 6.2
Bloom's Types Matched to Assessment Techniques

Bloom's Type	Mental Action/Verb	Learning Assessment Technique
Creating	Produce, plan, design, reconstruct	Simile CAT; Invented Dialogue CAT; Word Journal CAT; Cartoon CAT
Evaluating	Judge, conclude, contrast, develop criteria, defend, criticize, support, decide	Student-Generated Test Questions CAT; Paper or Project Prospectus CAT
Analyzing	Classify, divide, differentiate, visualize, dissect, diagram	Categorizing Grid CAT; Analytic Memos CAT; Annotated Figure CAT; Meme CAT
Applying	Solve, employ, construct, demonstrate	Applications Cards CAT; Human Tableau or Class Modeling CAT
Understanding	Explain, paraphrase, interpret, illustrate, describe, summarize, expand, convert, measure	Directed Paraphrasing CAT; Concept Map CAT
Remembering	Recognize, match, quote, outline, reproduce, state, list, tell, define, label	Focused-Listening CAT; Memory Matrix CAT

synthesizing; CATs 19 through 22 check problem-solving skills; and CATs 25 through 27 check evaluation skills. But the action of the specific learning assessment can determine the type for which the assessment functions. If students were asked to summarize a lecture into a concept map, that exercise would assess understanding. But if concept map CATs are used to compare the arguments and evidence found in different articles as synthesis in preparation to write a paper, then it might be of the analyzing or creating type. The point is that CATs are flexible and not married to one type of thinking: Changing the prompt of a CAT can make it assess a different mental action.

Some of our more useful insights come from assessments that use a different mode from the grading assessments in the course. These provide a different angle from which to consider student performance. When multiple-choice exams are the tests of choice, though well-designed ones can test higher-order thinking, they often largely test recall. Even when they test higher-order thinking, they test only recognition; they don't test the ability of students to articulate that thinking themselves, much less deploy that sort of thinking. An accompanying verbal or more metacognitive reflection may provide a different insight into student thinking, such as a Directed Paraphrasing or Word Journal CAT, which would show what information students are actually able to deploy. In math classes where students solve formulae and calculate solutions, CAT 21, Documented Problem Solution, which asks students to explain their process in words at each step of the calculation, can provide insights into students' mental processes, revealing where, if anywhere, they get off track and how good their conceptual grasp is. Using methods that are different from graded assignments keeps the students working with the information in different ways, and, more notably, could reveal problem areas in student thinking that might otherwise go unnoticed. Table 6.3 shows some learning assessments that can be used to check on student performance on a variety of mental actions. Placing the mental action in Bloom's categories allows us to more precisely assess what we want students to do.

Assessment Principle 4: Use Multiple Assessment Techniques, or "Two Is Better Than One"

Why use more than one CAT? The straight answer is that we are trying to capture some measure of student learning, or get into the "black box," as some scholars in this field put it. We can't weigh their brains to see if they learned. We can only measure what we put in (the assignments or CATs)

TABLE 6.3
CATs Matched to Mental Actions to Get a New View of Student Thinking

Mental action	Learning assessment (CAT) for new insights	Rationale	Examples
Solve word problems with appropriate equations or code.	Documented Problem Solution CAT	Students can't just copy and paste code or "plug and chug," they must explain what they are doing at each step in problem-solving.	Solve Problem 5 in two columns. Column 1: show your work. Column 2: explain and justify each step.
Explain a concept.	Cartoon CAT	Use pictures and words to explain a concept.	Draw a cartoon of a certain character's "persona" in English or the "longue durée" or "social class" in history or sociology.
Use evidence to support an argument, a thesis, or a conclusion.	Concept Map or Visual CAT	Students draw a concept map of their essay or use a visual CAT to show where they got their evidence.	Draw El Cid's worldview. Include the number of the line in the poem from where the evidence came.
Sort information into conceptual categories.	Categorizing Grid CAT	Students have to demonstrate which category they are using for different actions, which takes them a level above the actions to analysis of what different actions involve.	Given a list of different organisms, place them in the appropriate class (amphibia or reptilia) on the categorizing grid.
Classify statements made during class discussion using categories related to writing.	Applications Cords CAT or Categorizing Grid CAT	Assess whether students know the moves used in the writing process for one's discipline.	(Show five statements made in today's class.) At which part of the writing process might they occur?
Take the viewpoint of another person, historical or fictional.	Invented Dialogue CAT	Represent or invent the position of another person with a different opinion.	What would Marx and Smiles say to each other if they discussed capitalism?

and what students put out (their responses and work). Our best option, therefore, is to use different measuring tools, like different Fitbit measures, from the ones used for grading assessments in our classes. So rather than just using bath scales to measure our health on a weekly basis, we can check how many steps we walked and we can coordinate the information from both of these. Maybe we will find that the two measures correlate. In the analogy we are using they may do so or perhaps more steps will simply correlate with some other measure (e.g., a greater perception of vigor). What interpretive angle can we get on student learning? With several different learning assessments, we have a better chance of capturing how effectively students engage in disciplinary moves.

We often add "Why do you say that?" after a CAT question. This gets students to reflect on their own thinking, and metacognition can bring new insights to the students. We find the results very useful.

Another reason to use more learning assessments has to do with ever-increasing class sizes, which tend to be accompanied by increasing use of multiple-choice tests, especially in large STEM classes. Multiple-choice tests can be written so that they are not just testing recall, but it still can be difficult to discern the level of student conceptual understanding or reasons students selected a wrong answer. Learning assessments can provide insights into student thinking at higher levels of Bloom's typology (Crowe, Driks, & Wenderoth, 2008).

CATs and learning assessments can be used also as pre- and posttests. Pre- and posttesting is important because they demonstrate learning gains (Hake, 1998); they also show how much student error has been corrected through instruction (Bao, 2006). A measure of how much error has been corrected makes a good match with Decoding the Disciplines, which starts from the bottlenecks—the places where students get stuck—or initial error. Using pre- and posttests we can make refined checks on student performance on a specific mental action before building up the skills and then checking afterward for gains. Nilson (2013) asserts that while no measures of student learning "are perfect, direct pre and post measures are probably the least flawed" (p. 297). Figure 6.8 describes how several assessments were used to narrow down the bottleneck and pre- and posttest student performance on them in a game design course.

We urge teachers to save all of their students' work—learning assessments and other classroom assignments and graded assessments (in electronic form, of course!). It can be hard to predict which data may prove useful when we start to assemble the evidence.

Figure 6.8. Pre- and posttesting in a game design course (Indiana University).

Will Emigh identified the ability to create a short pitch appealing to a specific audience as a core skill with which students struggled. He assessed the students multiple times over several classes during the section on pitching. The results from these assessments made it easy to identify which aspects of that skill the students were learning and which held major bottlenecks. In particular, students had difficulty separating the parts of an idea that they were excited about from the parts that would be exciting to a layperson. In the fall, a new in-class pitching exercise was introduced that forced students to pitch another person's concept. In pre- and postassessments, students moved from one-fifth to two-thirds being able to make an appealing pitch to audiences who are new to a game idea.

Assessment Principle 5: Summarize and Interpret the Evidence (How Do We Make Sense of the Results?)

Once we have collected the learning assessments, what do we do with them? We will compile them in order to make sense of the individual responses so we can draw conclusions. This section explains how to do "quick and dirty" analyses to process the responses, and with that completed, it is time for interpretation and conclusions.

Teachers often have no idea what to do with the assessments they have collected. They ask questions such as "I have 200 pre- and posttests; what do I do with them?" Or they may request that others look at their assessments. A teacher whose students used social media for the mental action of critiquing race and analyzing media structures produced hundreds of learning assessments in the form of tweets. The teacher asked, "Would you like to see the tweets my students have written? I have attached them to this e-mail." Most people do not want to read raw data, nor would they know how to make sense of assessments without knowing more about the goals of the course. While it is important to collect assessments, they are not worth much unless they have been summarized. We need to analyze the results to see what we have and ultimately provide a synopsis of the responses. There are several basic approaches to analyzing the evidence.

We assemble the evidence, using either a qualitative or a quantitative approach (the approach may depend on the assessment we chose in the first place). In qualitative analysis we implicitly compare the evidence to something. To what am I comparing student responses? It could be:

1. Performance of classmates
2. The teacher's or expert's model answer, such as a rubric

Even with qualitative analysis we often summarize student evidence into quantitative data (some simple numbers) for ease of analysis. For quantitative analysis we tally the evidence or calculate the percentage correct against a predetermined standard (e.g., test answers). This book is intended for the novice, so we are not going to get into more complicated descriptions of statistical analyses. We strongly recommend Suskie's (2009) *Assessing Student Learning: A Common Sense Guide* for those who want to delve further into assessment analysis. Angelo and Cross (1993) also suggest procedures for analysis for each of the 50 CATs in *Classroom Assessment Techniques.*

This section will show how we can still keep an eye on the bottlenecks and mental actions as we analyze the learning assessments and discuss three approaches:

1. Sorting into piles—a comparison to peers
2. Comparison with a model answer
3. Counts and other quantitative analyses

Sorting Into Piles—A Comparison to Peers

The qualitative "sorting-into-piles" approach, based on comparing student responses to each other, is a simple way to assemble student evidence. We often use this method with exploratory assessment or when we are trying to understand the possible ways students perform the mental action. We may use this with Visual CATs when we cannot predict the student results in advance.

In sorting, while we can set criteria first based on an expert's model answer, we can also do the reverse—sort student responses into piles (very good, acceptable, unacceptable or stuck in the bottleneck, at a way station, and expert) and then give each pile a descriptive name, thereby letting the categories of performance emerge from the student evidence. Then the number in each stack is tabulated. For example, the teacher with the hundreds of tweets can simply print out the tweets and sort them into piles, tabulate them, and name each category. The sorting-into-piles method is relatively simple and provides insights into students' preconceptions and emotional bottlenecks.

Comparison Responses With a Model Answer (Including Rubrics)

In this method, the teacher creates a model answer or rubric (attributes of the mental action and their calibration—see chapter 2), including the elements and relationships expected (Concept Map CAT) and then applies it to the student assessments. For the model answer approach, you should decide what the characteristics of high-level, midlevel, and low-level responses would be and what words might be expected in each category in advance of looking at student responses. Then sort students' verbal responses into these categories. We can further sort responses by the quality of their explanations. We then categorize the kinds of explanations and decide at what levels they occur. The main point with this method is to compare students' responses with the expert's answer. Although this method may seem laborious at first, this method gets easier over time. Having collected such evidence more than once, the teacher is more likely to know what categories to anticipate and can better prepare for future groups of students.

The results of learning assessments can be processed in many ways. For example, Word Journal CAT results can be processed either by letting the categories emerge with the sorting-into-piles method from the previous section or by starting from model answers to which student responses will be compared.

Counts and Other Quantitative Analyses

Simple counts of the data can be used for such CATs as Focused Listing and Memory Matrix at lower levels of Bloom's typology. Student results can be sorted and then counted based on criteria or according to degree of relationship to the targeted topic: Do they show primary, secondary, and tertiary relationships? You will notice that the rubric in Figure 6.9 can easily be turned into a count (and was). But any rubric that lists student errors, such as the rubric in Figure 2.4, could be the basis of a count.

There are several ways to summarize evidence of student learning from assessments, but this is an essential step. The data are simply not very useful without such a summary. Summaries allow others to get the main point or "big picture" at a glance from an image or quickly by reading a few sentences; they also guard the instructor against taking a too anecdotal approach to the data. We often turn these summaries into numbers or a few comparative items. With the assessment results summarized, we are in a better position to improve learning next time. Teaching is not as effective without the feedback loop of assessment, where teachers realize something they need to adjust in their teaching (Hattie & Timperley, 2007) and learners can see areas they need to adjust in their learning. Assessment is like regularly checking the heading of an ocean liner to make sure the ship is not drifting off course and to apply a correction when it does. That way the ship is more likely to make its proper port of call.

Figure 6.9. A simple sorting rubric in history.

Leah Shopkow and Arlene Díaz asked their preservice history students to answer the following question as a pre- and posttest: "What do good historians do?" Using a rubric, student answers were sorted into low (history as facts), medium (historians process evidence), and high (history as interpretation) categories and assigned a numeric value between 1 and 3, with half-point increments. In this approach, the qualitative data were roughly quantified to find a pattern in the answers and show the shift in understanding from the beginning to the end of the semester.

Results showed that nearly all of the students improved. The most frequent change was a significant drop in the number of students operating at the most novice-like epistemological level. Many students landed at a midway position, which was very stable—not likely to change easily or slip back to the more novice position. Chapter 7 describes further theorizing that grew out of this initial assemblage of the data.

Low (1)	Medium (2)	High (3)
• Collect facts or investigate. • Find unbiased "truth" and be accurate. • Describe the past. • Write historical narratives or tell stories about the past from pieces of evidence.	• Connect past to present and find historical themes across time. • Understand historical causality. • Collect data comprehensively • History that includes multiple perspectives or historical context (without clear indication of what that means). • Evaluate sources for validity. • Historical empathy (putting oneself in someone's shoes without acknowledgment of the intellectual moves involved). • Consider historical context (when it is considered as a given).	• Use evidence to interpret the past. • Evaluate historical sources. • Construct histories (using evidence and making claims). • Use primary and/ or secondary sources that reflect different perspectives. • Historical empathy (with indication of intellectual moves involved). • Be aware of own positionality and those of authors used. • Consider historical context as something the historian constructs or as an interpretive framework.

With data, the teacher sees the extent of student success on the mental action, as well as detailed information about where students are still struggling. We almost never find that students as a group got as far as we hoped, and we frequently find that one large bottleneck is actually comprised of several sub-bottlenecks. The following are three questions teachers can reflect on when drawing conclusions about their data:

1. What did you learn about student performance on the bottlenecks or mental actions?
2. Do you plan to make any changes to the modeling, practice, or motivation steps in your bottleneck lesson in light of these data?
3. Were the data from this assessment useful? What changes, if any, will you make to the assessment/CAT you used?

Assessment Principle 6: Track the Mental Actions in Assessments for Grading—The Final Course Products

Once teachers have learned to assess student performance on one specific bottleneck and mental action, they can begin to track those even in their global assessments for grading. Assessments for grading measure a lot of things at once (some of them the same as with CATs, some of them not). Even when we have combined the component skills into a synthetic final course product such as an essay exam or a team project, we can still track the mental actions, as long as we can separately score the parts. In the example in Figure 6.10, a bottleneck was identified and lessons were developed so students could perform better on it. By comparing items on course exams specifically related to this bottleneck prior to implementing the Decoding the Disciplines approach with after implementing decoding (not just the overall exam scores), the results showed significant improvements on the mental action; the number of students who did not master the concept decreased, and the number of students who performed well on it increased.

The decoding perspective can improve assessments for grading, by scoring components so the bottlenecks and the mental action can be tracked. Rubrics can be used to track bottlenecks and mental actions in papers and essays, but only if they explicitly describe what students should do. Even in graded assessments the mental actions and bottlenecks can be spelled out to guide student efforts so students know what is expected and are shown explicitly what to do (or what *not* to do).

Figure 6.10. Use of existing data in a computer science course.

Recursion is a bottleneck in computing. The mental action consists of repeating items in a program in a self-similar way, like Alice in *Through the Looking Glass*, when two mirrors are placed exactly opposite each other and the nested images continue into infinity. The recursive program is repeated until the program tells it to stop. Suzanne Menzel's students have written programs for list recursion and tree recursion as part of exams for many years. Results were compared with exam items prior to the implementation of Decoding the Disciplines and checked for difference in academic preparation (as measured by the SAT) in the pre- and postgroups. The posttest group performed significantly better in both the list and tree recursion items. (German et al., 2015)

Throughout this chapter we have urged you not to confuse assessment with grading, and we have pointed out the different functions of these two approaches to evaluating student work. The one (grading) tends to assess complex student performances, while the CATs we have recommended tend to focus on one aspect of student learning, the bottleneck. As we have said, we have found it possible, through the use of subtractive rubrics or ungraded focused assessments, to isolate student success in negotiating the bottleneck even in complex projects. It is an excellent step, however, to compare student performance on bottleneck assessments with student overall performance to see whether there is a correlation. If the bottleneck is truly well connected to the epistemic moves expected of students in your class and discipline, there should be a correlation. That correlation will probably not be perfect, because we grade students on a number of criteria, not just one criterion. However, if there is no correlation, one of two things is the case. Either the bottleneck you have chosen isn't really central to your discipline or it isn't really central to your course.

Summary

By assessing mastery of a specific mental action, teachers create a feedback loop that empowers teachers and learners. Step 6 Assessment involves learning to collect learning data *beyond* graded assignments (and sometimes through graded assignments) through a variety of assessment techniques, and matching the assessment technique to the mental action. There are relatively simple methods to assemble and interpret the evidence. By knowing through evidence rather than by making assumptions where our students stand on a specific mental action, we can help more students perform the mental action.

Even in final course exams and projects, mental actions can be tracked and scored. In fact, it is highly worthwhile to look in final projects and global assessments for places where students should be making mental moves. If these places do not exist, there is a mismatch between what you are trying to teach in the course and what you are asking students to do. Furthermore, if the grades on the final global assignments do not correlate at least loosely with your findings on the smaller assessments, it is highly probable that such a mismatch has occurred. In that case you have chosen a bottleneck that is not critical to understanding in your discipline or you have given a global assignment that does not call for this form of critical thinking. Either way, adjustment is in order!

In Appendix A, you can see how a biologist and a musicologist have addressed Step 6 in the decoding process.

CHAPTER 6 EXERCISES

Exercise 6.1: Shopping for CATs

For individuals

1. Reread the section of this chapter on Assessment Principle 2 (pp. 141–148) as you "shop" for two CATs to assess student learning on your bottleneck/ mental action. What are two CATs that could check student competency on the targeted mental action of your students using a different mode than your grading assessments?

_____

_____

_____

_____

2. What is the difference between the kinds of feedback these two CATs will provide?

_____

_____

_____

_____

For ongoing teams

1. With your teammates' bottlenecks in mind, reread the section on Assessment Principle 2 (pp. 141–148).
2. Become familiar with a variety of learning assessment techniques as you "shop" for two CATs to assess the target mental action for each teammate's bottleneck (4 minutes × 2 teammates).
   - Write your suggestions on a sheet of paper.
   - Pass it to that person and repeat for next teammate.
   - Have a team discussion: What is your reaction to the CATs you received? Which ones do you think you might use? (3 minutes each)
3. Report out through a Reflection and Gallery Walk.
   - Write in large letters on a large sheet of newsprint paper your (a) bottleneck, (b) analogy, (c) mental action, and (d) CAT.

- Post newsprint papers along the wall.
- The whole group reads all the newsprint papers and places sticky notes to add clarifications and variations to the CATs.

Exercise 6.2: Matching Mental Action to Bloom's Type

What type of thinking is your mental action? (See Table 6.3.) What CATs would you select to check student performance on that type of thinking?

_____

_____

_____

_____

Exercise 6.3: CATs Data Analysis

For individuals

How will you analyze your CATs data? Summarize any results briefly on the lines provided. What have you learned from these results?

_____

_____

_____

_____

For teams

A Structured Conversation: Making Sense of Data From CATs

Each person gets a chance to show his or her data and get ideas for analyzing them. (There are three rounds of this structured conversation.) This works best across *new* teams, rather than in ongoing teams, for the fresh ideas from those who are unfamiliar with your bottlenecks (new teams of three). In a structured conversation participants are timed and required to talk and to listen, which promotes equitable team conversations (Curry, 2008).

Who	Discussion	Time
Presenter	Share course students' CATs results.	2 minutes
Interlocuters	Ask clarifying questions to the presenter.	1 minutes
Interlocuters	Discuss these clarifying questions: What are possible ways to analyze and organize this data? What do the data show?	3 minutes
Presenter	Respond to interlocutors: "Here is what I heard you saying . . ."	1 minutes

Debriefing questions for the whole group:

1. Were your data similar to or different from one another?
2. What did you learn about your own analysis from looking at each other's data?
3. What will you do differently next time you collect learning assessments?

7

STEP 7

Sharing

When Joan and David Pace developed Decoding the Disciplines in the Freshman Learning Project, they asked the faculty fellows to share what they had learned with others. The fellows could share in whatever manner they chose: take colleagues to lunch, report at a departmental meeting, present at campus workshops, or deliver papers at disciplinary conferences. The fellows did all of those things—and more, including winning over $3.5 million in outside grants in the first few years! This chapter will describe why and how sharing became a part of Decoding the Disciplines.

By the time a teacher has followed the first six steps of Decoding the Disciplines, Step 7 Sharing can follow naturally and comfortably. With a theoretical framework guiding the process that includes collecting evidence of student performance, it is not a big leap from looking at one's own data to presenting the findings to others. Many faculty are eager to share what they've discovered from their decoding efforts. Scholarly teachers may want to end the decoding process with a few of the summarizing activities described early in this chapter. For those who want to go on—and we urge you to do so— Step 7 Sharing encourages community, reflection, analysis, and reform of teaching.

The first part of this chapter describes the value of and ways to collaborate in decoding and go public with the results of your decoding. Individual faculty may choose to teach in community for the support and insights it provides. Or they may decide to research teaching and learning in community, typically in small, focused teams. Some faculty will take their insights further, into SoTL. We see all of these forms of sharing as valid and valuable. The second part of this chapter provides guidance for the creation and facilitation of faculty groups, including pedagogy courses, but equally important, we see this as a crucial step in changing the culture of teaching in educational institutions generally. To think about how we might foster these kinds of changes, we borrowed from systems thinking and planned change frameworks. In previous chapters, we have spoken of "principles" guiding our work, but in this chapter, we speak rather of stages, because each of these steps, from informal comparison of results to change at the organizational level, represents a different stage of applying Decoding the Disciplines.

Following are the Stages of Step 7 Sharing:

Sharing Stage 1: Individual completion of the decoding cycle
Sharing Stage 2: Teaching in community
Sharing Stage 3: Sharing through SoTL
Sharing Stage 4: Systems thinking and strategic decoding to introduce planned change

Sharing Stage 1: Individual Completion of the Decoding Cycle

Many faculty use Decoding the Disciplines as a theoretical framework to guide their classroom teaching efforts, using the bottlenecks as a signal for when their tacit mental actions need to be made explicit and the basis for modeling, practice, and assessment. For faculty who do not desire to share their results, we suggest completing the decoding cycle by filling out a bottleneck lesson plan worksheet (Exercise 7.1). This exercise compiles the total bottleneck lesson, bringing together exercises from chapters 1 through 6 in preparation for teaching your lesson. The bottleneck lesson plan worksheet will keep your efforts focused and help you determine what you learn from your lesson. Even if you do choose to share, the bottleneck lesson plan is a good place to start. Remember that sharing does not need to be formal or high stakes. It might be as simple as joining a faculty learning community (FLC), posting to a website, or contributing to a departmental teaching forum.

Sharing Stage 2: Teaching in Community

Although faculty are members of a community by virtue of being teachers, it often doesn't feel like a community, given all of the other responsibilities they often face. At research-intensive universities, a concern with teaching may also be deprecated. And although colleges and universities are, by definition, teaching institutions, the teaching mission is not always well supported. Faculty are often left to seek out information themselves and without a place to share their findings. The examination of classroom practice is often viewed as a form of remediation rather than a tool for creating new knowledge or improving the quality of instruction at the institution as a whole. Therefore, we advocate creating teaching communities, where working on one's teaching is not taken as a sign that one is not a competent teacher or that one is shirking more highly valued research.

We use the Decoding the Disciplines process to structure a teaching-positive culture (Condon, Iverson, Manduca, Rutz, & Willett, 2016), gathering faculty together in working groups, such as a departmental collegium or a cross-disciplinary FLC. These are often internally focused teaching communities committed for a set period of time. Teaching in this kind of community works off the synergy of the group; the combined efforts are greater than the parts and provide specific benefits: feedback, conceptual frames, and support and accountability.

Everything in the Decoding FLC builds up to the moment when the participants collect evidence of mastery of a specific mental task by their students. The community helps interpret each other's learning assessments, which is particularly important because in community faculty see that it is common for Step 6 learning assessments to provide disappointing results at first and that even with repeated refinement perfection is elusive.

As faculty prepare to share, their analysis and reflection on their assessments send them back through the Decoding the Disciplines cycle. Were there sub-bottlenecks in the original bottleneck? Which part will they focus on? Did they successfully tackle one bottleneck and now there is another one to go after, maybe in another class? Do they need to do more decoding of the expert? Do they need to improve the bottleneck lesson at the modeling and practice steps? Having addressed the cognitive part of the bottleneck, are there emotional bottlenecks blocking student success? Do they need to collect further learning assessments to use as evidence? Is it time to move from the individual classroom to the curricular level?

Because sharing induces faculty to analyze and reflect on their results, we often require a final product at Step 7, some real-world task such as the ones suggested in Exercise 7.2. The more publicly members of the teaching community share what they have learned, the greater the potential for culture change and the more widely teaching innovations spread. Some faculty will share the results of bottleneck lessons with colleagues only within their teaching communities. Some will share more widely in campus and national presentations. For many, reflection on their results and sharing the data may be transformative.

Sharing Stage 3: Sharing Through SoTL

As faculty apply what they understand about doing scholarly work to their teaching efforts, some faculty become serious about wanting to publish their decoding research on teaching and learning. The CATs, data, or other insights they have collected through Decoding the Disciplines provide evidence for SoTL publications. Much disciplinary publication about teaching has consisted of "teaching tips" and has offered no more evidence than "Here's what I did in my class and my students liked it." The gathering of evidence positions decoders to move beyond anecdote to the presentation and analysis of data—the standard to which we are held for our disciplinary work. Exercise 7.3 explores various SoTL venues for sharing results.

Although we think sharing one's findings is an important step in owning them, the goal of decoding is not to turn every teacher into an SoTL researcher. Sue Clegg (2008) has cogently warned of the dangers of making SoTL more like the scholarship of discovery without a close examination of the suppositions of the scholarship of discovery. We don't want to reproduce the sometimes spurious work done in the scholarship of discovery nor do we want to shift attention away from the application of what we learn to the classroom.

But even if faculty members don't want to become scholars of teaching and learning, it may be easier and more comfortable for some faculty members to engage in this sort of work if they are able to relate it to the scholarly world of which they are already a part. We found that college teachers were more engaged in considerations of teaching when we set up structures that resembled what happens in doing research. Bottlenecks serve as specific, visible points of entry to inquiry about student learning (Middendorf & Pace, 2007). At research-oriented institutions, this sort of inquiry feels familiar. Like other good research questions, this inquiry originates in the faculty member's own specific concerns. But even at teaching-oriented institutions there are increasing pressures to do research. One of us was approached after a workshop at such an institution by a faculty member, who explained that his institution couldn't really support disciplinary research in his field (which was highly technical and required a lot of equipment the school couldn't afford), but that research into teaching and learning was something he could do with the available resources.

While decoding can help one teacher at a time, with such great need for systemic educational reform, we want to take aim at large numbers of faculty (and the students they teach), departments, curricula, and institutions. The second part of this chapter explains the principles from systems thinking and planned change that we incorporated into our process in order to bring about broader transformations.

Sharing Stage 4: Systems Thinking and Strategic Decoding to Introduce Planned Change

Strategic Decoding to Identify Systemic Patterns

Strategic decoding entails careful planning for educational reform beyond the individual teacher or classroom, using the decoding process along with principles of change and systems thinking. Implementing Decoding the Disciplines has the potential to revolutionize and streamline the process of teaching and learning. But without the broader systemic changes that decoding is uniquely positioned to achieve, teaching will continue to rely on traditional methods that are long on coverage and short on student engagement and critical thinking. Whether on an individual basis or in broader discipline- and community-wide change, decoding can help make the critical thinking that experts perform explicit, unlocking the door to success for faculty and students. But when we are talking about broader changes, there are limits to what individuals can accomplish through changing their own teaching practices. More significant kinds of changes *require* collaboration, generally of a more formal kind, whether through FLCs, pedagogy courses, or curriculum reform. All of these efforts can be rendered more effective and coherent, however, if we keep the disciplinary mental actions students need in our sights.

Decoding the Disciplines facilitates consideration of the big picture through systemic analysis (Sterman, 1994). What are the large components of the teaching and learning system? What are the places where many faculty get stuck in helping students learn? Exercise 7.4 uses the decoding framework to contemplate bottlenecks in your teaching–learning system. Contemplating the parts from 30,000 feet above (metaphorically speaking) helps faculty, administrators, and especially funders with the vision and resources to take a nonlinear view and reinvent the teaching and learning system. Systems analyses examine the parts as well as their interactions. Bottlenecks, mental actions, and assessment are useful ways to view the parts and their interactions.

We are not claiming that Decoding the Disciplines is a panacea for everything in teaching and learning. It isn't the only framework available, but it is a powerful one, precisely because it fits a variety of educational methods and techniques into one coherent framework. When, for example, some faculty from underrepresented groups who have worked hard on their teaching receive dismal teacher ratings year after year, it can give us the strategic viewpoint about just what the bottleneck is. Is it the actions of the individual teacher? Or is it something structural such as implicit bias in student ratings (Nilson, 2012)? The systemic view of decoding helps us see patterns and relationships within the system and with other systems, rather than a lot of separate parts.

The Decoding the Disciplines process can be used to plan carefully for improving teaching and learning beyond the individual lesson or classroom. As a strategy, it can help programs and schools develop a learning- and assessment-centered culture. Through the bottleneck perspective, it can diminish "student bashing" and develop respect for the real difficulties students encounter.

Decoding Curricula and Program Review

The systemic analysis will reveal some learning problems that are not due to the individual course or instructors. For example, when a transdisciplinary program in sustainability had not decoded its curriculum, some faculty were unsure of what to emphasize in their courses that crossed departmental lines. We decoded the curriculum, establishing goals for disciplinary expertise, interdisciplinary fluency, systems thinking, justice and culture, and sustainability practice. Having negotiated a common set of program goals and student learning outcomes (SLOs), it was much easier to work together toward a shared vision.

Curriculum design is commonly associated with subject content (Carter, 2007). Curricula that start with what is being taught by certain teachers or a list of already existing courses is like trying to build a house starting from several prebuilt rooms: We have a nice blue bedroom, a long dining room, plus a big room with lots of windows (maybe that could be the living room?). A house patched together in this way may be chaotic. What we really need when designing a house is to have a vision for what we want the house to "do" in our life or on this site and after that to determine what the parts will be. Similarly, a curriculum should have a guiding vision so that all the parts of the curriculum can work toward it and all the stakeholders—the teachers, administrators, students, and prospective students—pull in the same direction.

We first realized the power of decoding for curricula after we conducted interviews with 24 professors as part of the History Learning Project (Díaz, Middendorf, Pace, & Shopkow, 2008). The bottlenecks and mental actions allowed us to describe conceptual goals and scaffold a set of competencies over the four years of college to arrive at a developmental curriculum. At a departmental retreat, we assigned teams of history professors to crucial bottlenecks and asked them to describe the competencies students would need to develop to overcome the bottlenecks over their four years (History Learning Project Curriculum Overview, 2011). This process provides a basis for assessment and program review that is grounded in the disciplines.

Since then we have further developed a process for curriculum design and revision (Metzler, Rehrey, Kurz, & Middendorf, 2017), as well as for overall program assessment, which led to assessment of disciplinary critical thinking (see Appendix E). The process starts backward (Wiggins & McTighe, 2005) with teams of teachers writing four to eight program goals in answer to the question, "What do we want students to be able to do when they graduate from our program?" Program goals are conceptually large, such as "think quantitatively," "develop sociological imagination," or "acquire a body of astronomical knowledge." If there are vague program goals such as "critical thinking," they can be made more specific by asking the teachers where students get stuck when doing that kind of thinking. Establishing overall program goals can uncover the ways of knowing in one's field (see the comments in chapter 8 on epistemology).

Next, SLOs are written by taking each program goal and spelling out what it entails. Asking, "What are the bottlenecks in reaching this goal?" helps to define the component mental actions/competencies. The cross-disciplinary collaboration that Decoding the Disciplines is based on helps programs better uncover their own ways of knowing. With feedback from other departments in a gallery walk format, we can make our program goals and SLOs more specific. It can be difficult to see our own field's critical thinking, but by comparing ours to that of other disciplines, the ways of knowing in our field become clearer.

Next in the process is to "map" the curriculum. Eric Metzler of Indiana University showed us an approach by which teachers analyze a completed curriculum map, but one that intentionally includes problematic gaps and redundancies. (For Table 7.1 we "broke" Indiana University Latino Studies department's decoded curriculum map [Martinez & Díaz, 2015].) After analyzing the problematic curriculum map, the teachers load curriculum templates with their own program goals, SLOs, and courses, indicating the level at which student learning will be assessed (novice, intermediate, or advanced). When they review their own curriculum maps, their attention is drawn to the holes and repetitions where mental actions are not properly scaffolded. The curriculum design process can end with curriculum revision, but if program review is the goal, then efforts turn to assessment and documentation of student learning.

While getting faculty to buy into assessment can be difficult, those who become comfortable with it through the decoding process can readily take on the challenge of analyzing and assessing student learning for program assessment. We use Step 6 Assessment to show faculty how to assess student performance on specific mental actions. Faculty who start from their own bottlenecks feel more in control of assessment, because it is driven by their classroom priorities and concerns and not by administrative fiat. Together, decoding the curriculum and Step 6 Assessment can provide authentic evidence of student learning for purposes of program review. To begin assessment for program review (Kurz, Kearns, Middendorf, Metzler, & Rehrey, 2015) the department or faculty committee selects a goal or an SLO to assess so that everyone is working in concert. Faculty who are familiar with Step 6 Assessment can readily choose how they will provide evidence for that goal. Once the evidence has been collected, someone (an assessment specialist, an administrator, or a committee member) needs to analyze the results and provide a report of the findings. Finally, the department or committee will study the extent to which students are achieving the goals/SLOs and what further steps need to be taken—such as making changes to the curriculum or changes to the assessment process.

TABLE 7.1
Sample Curriculum Map (Deliberately "Broken")

No. & Goal	Student Learning Outcome (SLO)	L100	L103	B105	B239	A329
1. Perspectives and Points of View	1.1. Describe/recognize their own positionalities.	N	N, I		N, I, A	A
	1.2. Articulate different points of view.	N	I, A		N, I	I
	1.3. Contextualize new knowledge to better understand Latino/a peoples and cultures.	N	I		N, I	N, I
	1.4. Empathize with people from the past in their own terms and historical context.	N	A		N, I, A	I, A
	1.5. Switch perspectives.		N, I			
2. History and Diversity of the Latino/a Communities	2.1. Recognize critical concepts such as Latino/a, Chicano, Hispanic, ethnicity, race, culture, and Latinidad.		I, A		I	

(*Continues*)

TABLE 7.1 (*Continued*)

	2.2. Understand how and why Latinas/os are part of U.S. history.	N	I, A			
	2.3. Associate with the humanity of Latinos, not stereotypes.		I, A			
	2.4. Apply critical themes of Latino/a experience: immigration, culture, identity, family, race, language, and social movements.			N, I, A		
	2.5. Identify the complexities of the Latino/a experience.		A	A		
3. Political Conscious- ness	3.1. Identify barriers leading to economic and social inequalities.	N	A			
	3.2. Recognize the varied ways Latinos/as organize and articulate claims to promote change.	N	A			A
	3.3. Bridge the university– community gap by engaging with issues affecting Latino communities.					I, A
	2 SLOs under Goal 3 (Political Consciousness) and program Goal 4 (Critical and Analytical Skills) and its SLOs were deleted for the sake of space.					

Note. N = Novice Level; I = Intermediate Level; A = Advanced Level

Decoding the Disciplines is a powerful tool for strategic curriculum design and review, and no small reason for its effectiveness in these processes is the collaboration and reflection that decoding provides. Faculty resist compliance-based curriculum efforts, but may even enjoy negotiating their goals in common. They certainly prefer this to having heavy-handed administrations hand down generic learning goals. We make no secret of our desire to change the culture of higher education to one that values evidence-based teaching methods and coherent curriculum design, and we want to see the next generation of teachers well trained to advance in this direction. The next part describes some strategies for applying decoding to this end.

Planned Change: FLC and Pedagogy Courses

When we invite faculty to participate in an FLC to work with decoding (Middendorf, 2004), we are asking them to rethink the way they approach teaching; thus, we are asking them to change. From the inception of Decoding the Disciplines we have applied principles of planned change (Dormant, 2011; Kotter, 1996; Middendorf, 1999; Schein, 1996) to spread innovation in teaching. This section describes how we have combined principles of planned change and Decoding the Disciplines to transform traditional teaching culture. The power of Decoding the Disciplines is that it provides a common language for faculty to speak about bottlenecks and the epistemology of their field and offers a way to assess specific mental moves. These together support a teaching-positive culture for an entire institution (Condon et al., 2016).

Select Opinion Leaders

Being strategic in the selection of FLC members begins by identifying faculty whom others will want to follow. The literature on the spread of innovations (Rogers, 2010) helped us understand that about half of the spread of new ideas takes place from "copying" admired colleagues. While we can't change faculty who do not want to change, we can reach into the cohorts outside of the "usual" teaching center collaborators through peer networks. The usual collaborators are great for trying out and modeling new teaching approaches, as they already know or have sources for new teaching ideas and are ready to take risks in their teaching, but they are not likely to be copied by their colleagues in the department. Faculty with the characteristics of "opinion leaders" can be most helpful in leading their colleagues to accept new approaches. Opinion leaders are natural "missionaries" for influencing others outside the FLC to accept new approaches to teaching (Middendorf, 1999). From the outside looking in, it can be difficult to identify such opinion leaders. We use social network analysis (J. Scott, 2012) to gauge relationships inside the department. In discreet discussions, we ask a few faculty members for whom we are known entities if they can suggest faculty for our FLC who meet the following criteria:

- The faculty member is influential within the department. That is, the faculty member is listened to when speaking up at departmental meetings and is central in departmental decision-making. This criterion is straight out of the planned change literature and is critical.
- The faculty member teaches well (does not have problems with teaching), and yet is, for the most part, unfamiliar with the literature on teaching and learning. Someone who has a problem with teaching

might have been "sent" to the FLC, feel punished, and resist change rather than view the FLC as an honor or intellectually of interest.

- The person plays well with others—one unpleasant personality can interfere with the social cohesion of the FLC.
- The faculty member teaches—not all faculty at large research universities teach undergrads or teach the students your program intends to help.

By comparing the suggestions from several departmental insiders, we generate overlapping lists of names, and these tend to be the reliable opinion leaders. Faculty who meet the previous criteria are most likely to be transformed by Decoding the Disciplines, are happy with the result, and thus are more likely to spread the bottleneck- and learning-centered perspective on teaching. Over time, even if all the people are not individually influential in the department, but are interested in transforming their teaching, the department comes to have a language and shared values for working together on their teaching. In a world in which departments may be quite individualistic and fragmented, a small group of individuals who work collaboratively can be quite persuasive.

Identify Concerns

One of the principles of planned change prescribes that before we try to change people's approach to the innovation (in this case, new ways of teaching), we should try to understand their concerns regarding it (Dormant, 2011; see Figure 7.1). Personal concerns are especially important, because people tend to start with personal concerns before accepting a new idea or method. We elicit concerns throughout the process, with different concerns arising at different parts. Eliciting the specific concerns of faculty about decoding is not unlike identifying bottlenecks: Where do teachers get stuck in trying to decode? Some may want to know how decoding will make things better for them. They may fear that changing their teaching will require them to do everything at once, which may seem overwhelming and impossible. Lack of time to make changes may be a concern. They may need supportive colleagues when faced with assessments that turn out worse than they expected. Different faculty will have different concerns as they begin to use decoding and change their teaching, but if we do not find out what their concerns are, we can't address them.

Besides being a principle of planned change, assessment of concerns has the added benefit of modeling how frequent, small-scale assessments work in the classroom. Assessment is vital for bringing about the deep change that allows faculty to become learning centered.

Figure 7.1. Assessing faculty concerns about themselves and the process.

Pre- and posttest questions for FLC members focused on getting faculty to adopt evidence-based teaching methods:

- What makes it difficult for students to learn?
- What can faculty do to help students learn better? Why do you say that?

When decoding is used in a curriculum process:

- What concerns do you have about the curriculum process? Why do you say that?

At the end of this chapter, we provide a reflective exercise (Exercise 7.5), but some traditional CATs, such as the Minute Paper, Word Journal, Simile, and Directed Paraphrasing, can also be used to check on faculty concerns as they complete the different decoding steps.

Seek Administrative Champions
Successful projects need the help of key administrators to link our efforts to campus priorities, help us understand the decision-making system, provide resources for our efforts, and help facilitate them. Maintaining good working relationships for project sponsors is strategically important for visibility and credibility (Middendorf, 2001). None of our efforts would have been possible without a series of supportive administrators, who always appreciated the evidence of faculty change and student learning the decoding process generates. One supporter, W. Ray Smith, encouraged us to focus on planned change to spread the ideas more widely throughout the university. A current administrator, Dennis Groth, has supported our use of Decoding the Disciplines for Indiana University's approach to a nine-university, evidence-based teaching transformation for STEM departments.

Establish Cohesive, Long-Term Communities
Whatever they are called, FLCs are organized around a bottleneck of each member's choice and follow the Decoding the Disciplines process. Occasionally they employ the Decoding the Disciplines model to address thematic issues, such as large classes, sustainability, or inclusion and diverse viewpoints. Some begin with an intensive (half days for a week) seminar followed by monthly meetings to share CATs results and explore emotional bottlenecks; others are spread across a year. Though intensive seminars are especially good for building community and establishing the basic

concepts, we have led faculty groups in many formats, including some that were held biweekly for an hour over a year's time, or had one-and-a-half to two-hour monthly meetings. We typically ask for a one-year commitment. After experiencing an FLC, many group members remain involved with FLC colleagues, get involved in campus or disciplinary leadership efforts to affect teaching on a broader scale, or teach pedagogy classes. Inviting faculty to join in a community is more likely to provide structure and support over the long term as they learn new approaches to teaching and the bottleneck perspective.

Work Across Disciplines
From early on we organized decoding processes to take place in cross-disciplinary teams (mostly three-member teams) to minimize the likelihood of shared assumptions about what students "should" know. In doing so we worked against the notion that groups of experts from the same field, along with educational specialists with backgrounds in the same field, know everything there is to know about their field and should work with their discipline-only group to advance teaching and learning. While they certainly do know everything they need to know to practice in their fields, as we have argued repeatedly in this book, the revolutionary kernel of decoding is that the tacit knowledge of experts is often not available to themselves but can be elicited by those who do not share their disciplinary knowledge. Thus, rather than have a group of only psychologists, for instance, guided by an educational developer with a psychology background—the way many teaching development endeavors are organized—we work across fields. In addition, by putting faculty in cross-disciplinary groups, we draw them outside the culture of their departments where traditional approaches to teaching (often lecturing) continue to dominate. Exercise 7.6 prompts you to reflect on the basis for which you would want to join or form a teaching community of practice.

Use the Decoding the Disciplines Process
We typically address one decoding step per session, using many of the exercises in this book. Faculty choose their bottlenecks, decode experts' way of operating, and plan analogies and practice for the mental actions. There is not a lot of lecturing by the decoding facilitators, but a great deal of the effort is in teams working through decoding exercises.

Following the discussed principles of planned change along with the decoding process influenced key leaders across the faculty to shift away from standard teaching perspectives.

This approach can be applied in the future to the most pressing teaching problems in American education. For example, STEM fields are desperate to find a way for more students to experience success.

Mimi Zolan, a biology professor at Indiana University, wrote about her experience in the Freshman Learning Project:

> My undergraduate teaching style has changed dramatically, most obviously in my extensive and always growing use of formative assessments (CATS) that help the students understand the material, help them see what they do and do not understand, and help me see what they do and do not understand. I am also much more aware of preexisting misconceptions about what I teach, and I take active steps to address these. (Middendorf & Pace, 2009, p. 6)

Another area where Decoding the Disciplines can be applied strategically is K–12 education. Many primary and secondary school teachers tend to think in terms of teaching prepackaged "lessons," which can make it difficult for them to see bottlenecks and to design new lessons to get students through them. They have a daunting job just with classroom management and holding students accountable. There may well need to be a special project to design lessons based on bottlenecks and mental actions for primary and secondary education.

Summary

Step 7 Sharing turns out to have a surprising effect: Faculty are transformed when they work together in a community to teach to the bottlenecks and share their results. This book aims to put the theory and practice of Decoding the Disciplines in the hands of any teacher or educational developer who is interested in knowing more. Perhaps you are interested in developing as a scholarly teacher. Perhaps you want to do classroom research without having to become an educational measurement expert (Middendorf & Pace, 2007). Decoding can play all of these roles. We invite you to join us in this work.

In Appendix A, you can see how a biologist and a musicologist have addressed Step 7 in the decoding process.

CHAPTER 7 EXERCISES

Exercise 7.1: Bottleneck Lesson Plan Worksheet (See Appendix B for a Blank Template)

For individuals
Briefly outline your answers to the following:

1. The bottleneck—What are students unable to do?
2. Mental action—What mental actions does the expert perform to get past the bottleneck?
3. Model the thinking—What analogy will you use to model these mental actions?
4. Practice and feedback—How will the students practice these mental actions? How will they receive feedback to make improvements?
5. Motivation—What will I do to hold students accountable and disrupt ritual ways of learning?
6. Assessment—How will I assess student mastery of the mental actions? Prepare a brief summary of the results of the pre- and post-CATs—including, if possible, some quantities. What inferences can you draw from the data? It can be as simple as "On the pretest, 33% were able to do XXX, while on the posttest, 57% did XXX and 22% still could not. These results show a 24% improvement, although about one-fifth of the class are still struggling with XXX." Or "The majority of students correctly answered five of the eight test questions on the bottleneck concept."
7. Sharing—Do I want to share my results? If so, what kind of sharing will I do?

For teams: Team Send-A-Problem exercise (teams of three)

1. Swap your teams' completed bottleneck worksheets with another team.
2. As teams review and provide written feedback on each bottleneck lesson worksheet from the other team.
   a. What are some of the strengths of this bottleneck lesson?
   b. What suggestions do you have for improving it? Was the problem clearly formulated? Does the CAT focus on the mental action?
3. Debrief the question for the whole group:
   a. Were your bottleneck lessons similar to or different from one another?
   b. What did you learn about your bottleneck lesson from reviewing other bottleneck lessons?
4. Revise your own bottleneck lesson based on the comments you receive.

Exercise 7.2: Step 7: Final, Real-World Products for Your Decoding Work

For individuals

What will you produce as a result of your Decoding the Disciplines work? Choose from the following list of possible Step 7 final products—or generate your own:

- Share your bottleneck lesson from Exercise 7.1 (which can consist of teaching it to a campus audience or posting it to the decodingthedisciplines.org).
- Facilitate a campus workshop about your bottleneck assessment results.
- Do a lesson study of your bottleneck lesson (see Fernandez & Yoshida, 2012). This will require working with at least one other person who teaches the same or a similar class.
- Redesign first-year courses to address bottlenecks.
- Share and get feedback on pre- and post-CATs results.
- Create models for the way different fields consider a problem, such as a coal ash pile on campus. Consider the knowledge claims made, and ways to assess students' ability to build such models (Sorenson et al., 2015).
- Post your assessment results to decodingthedisciplines.org or https://groups.google.com/group/decoding-the-disciplines

_____

_____

_____

_____

Once you have selected your desired outcome, discuss your choice with a colleague for the feedback he or she can provide. It may be helpful to find a partner to produce this final product—another faculty member with similar interests or staff at the campus teaching center.

For teams

1. Silently write your ideas to the prompt for 3 minutes.
2. Discuss in a team of three people for 12 minutes (4 minutes per person).
3. Prepare to report out to the whole group.
4. Whole-group debrief: Share your plans for future efforts.

Exercise 7.3: Step 7: Sharing Your SoTL Results

For individuals

What will you produce as a result of your Decoding the Disciplines research on teaching and learning? Choose from the following list of possible Step 7 final products or events or generate your own:

- Design a research project on teaching and learning to be conducted over the next year.
- Submit a conference proposal about your bottleneck study.
- Publish a list of bottlenecks in your field.
- Publish decoding interviews.
- Publish an epistemological chart of your field.
- Apply for a grant to fund the continuation of your efforts on decoding.

_____

_____

_____

_____

Once you have set the goal for your research on teaching and learning, discuss your choice with a colleague for the feedback he or she can provide. It may be helpful to find a partner to produce this final product—another faculty member with similar interests or staff at the campus teaching center.

For teams

1. Silently write your ideas to the preceding prompt for 3 minutes.
2. Discuss in teams of three for 12 minutes (4 minutes per person).
3. Prepare to report out to the whole group.
4. Whole-group debrief: Share your plans for future efforts.

Exercise 7.4 Reflection: Decoding Your Teaching System

Consider the system in which your teaching takes place. What size chunk will it be useful to review—one program, several departments, or other groupings? What are the one or two most pressing learner-related problems they face? (Try to focus on something that is in the control of the faculty, not out of their control, such as a new building.) Where can Decoding the Disciplines help address the problem?

Bottleneck/Problem	Decoding Action

Having analyzed the teaching system, what decoding actions will you and your program take?

_____

_____

_____

_____

Exercise 7.5 Reflection: Assessment of Teacher Concerns

Write a prompt to assess faculty concerns about engaging in the decoding process. (Feel free to adapt one from Figure 7.1.) Why do you think this prompt will be useful? Where in the process would you use it?

_____

_____

_____

_____

Exercise 7.6 Reflection: Basis for Forming an FLC

Would you like to join or form a decoding community of practice to transform teaching and help faculty become aware of their tacit knowledge and assumptions in teaching? What are your reasons for this? Would it be best for it to be cross-disciplinary? Or would it be best to be intradisciplinary? (You may want to look back at your reflection on Exercise 7.4 where you identified some of the broad problems with teaching in your area.) Who are likely collaborators or supporters for such an effort?

_____

_____

_____

_____

8

DECODING AT THE INTERSECTION OF OTHER THEORIES

I n our previous chapters, we have given an extensive overview of Decoding the Disciplines as a methodology and as a comprehensive theory of pedagogy. The methodology is the seven-step process; the theory of pedagogy is that when we have isolated significant bottlenecks and taught students to negotiate their way through them we have also been teaching important moves in the epistemic protocols that constitute the academic disciplines. It will be clear to readers who know some of the theoretical literature on thinking in the disciplines that decoding offers parallels to some theories, while it draws on others and advances them. The shift from seeing teaching as the conveyance of content or just being "active" in the classroom to seeing it as helping students master disciplinary mental actions is a powerful framework. Furthermore, there are many worthwhile theories of general application. Vygotsky's (1978) "zone of proximal development" helps teachers gauge the appropriate level of challenge for students. In addition, Zimmerman's (2000) self-regulation theory explains the developmental tasks students undertake to become responsible for their own learning. There are also theories about classroom management and classroom authority, and theories about how race and gender shape the classroom. But when learning is the focus, Decoding the Disciplines can serve as an effective framework for understanding pedagogy.

The purpose of this chapter, therefore, is twofold: to give some account of the development of Decoding the Disciplines and to position Decoding the Disciplines among current research and educational theories, including cognitive science, threshold concepts, backward course design, signature pedagogies, SoTL, and teacher preparation.

Theoretical Underpinnings

Cognitive Science

When Joan and David created the Decoding the Disciplines model, they included some ideas from cognitive science: bottlenecks, misconceptions, and analogies. They first encountered the term *bottlenecks* at a talk by James A. Anderson (1996), a psychologist by training. When they asked faculty to identify bottlenecks in their classes, the faculty became engaged like never before. Yet Joan and David wanted faculty to do more than just identify the bottlenecks; they wanted the faculty to teach their students to move through the bottlenecks. So, bit by bit, they developed a process to teach faculty to do just that, with further refinements to decoding emerging through collaborative work.

Another area where decoding theory has drawn from cognitive science is in dealing with emotional bottlenecks, which are especially difficult to address (see chapter 5). Michelene Chi's (2008) work on persistent misconceptions in science provided key insights. Her work shows that misconceptions often arise when students are using the wrong category—one different from the one experts use—to understand a particular phenomenon. However, her examples tend to be free of strong emotional charge. While students may be frustrated when they try to understand diffusion, an indirect and emergent process, with thinking more appropriate to direct processes, they don't get angry about the difference. But the notion that students might be applying criteria and thinking that come from one epistemic community to work performed in an academic context was a very useful one. The emotional charge comes from the feeling students have that they are being asked to reject these communities, for instance, when a student feels that to recognize the unique disabilities under which African Americans functioned in American society is to devalue his or her European immigrant family's struggles. In other words, while not all category error produces an emotional bottleneck, emotional bottlenecks are symptoms that indicate students are using a nondisciplinary category to accomplish disciplinary mental tasks. Chi's work showed us how to assess and teach to emotional bottlenecks.

Cognitive theory also helped us to understand effective modeling, particularly our use of analogies (see chapter 3). According to cognitive theory, analogies work because they are mental simulations (Shanton & Goldman, 2010): One mental event, state, or process is the reexperience of another. Analogies can be used to explain an unfamiliar domain in terms of a familiar one, importing the familiar domain's relational structure (Lakoff & Johnson, 2008; Savion & Middendorf, 1994). Although we use analogies for more than modeling concepts, analogies do demonstrate to students which "mental muscles" to use from all the possible mental actions people regularly use.

Troublesome Knowledge

Decoding the Disciplines has also played very well with theory about troublesome knowledge, particularly tacit knowledge (Perkins, 2007). Decoding works from the premise that the troublesome knowledge is actually that of the teachers rather than that of the students, and that the reason it is troublesome is that the teachers cannot articulate what they know, leaving students to attempt to intuit the proper mode of thought (see chapter 2). In addition, we have found the concept of alien knowledge helpful as well, because it contributes to emotional bottlenecks. The procedures we have developed for category comparison work to the degree that they can familiarize students with academic epistemologies so that they may see them as less threatening and alien (see chapter 5).

Epistemology and Decoding the Disciplines

Another breakthrough was when we realized that the bottlenecks we were seeing were individual manifestations of places where faculty and students were playing different games based on different rules. This is not unrelated to the kinds of category error Chi (2008) describes, but on a grander scale. If we see each of the disciplines as following a set of procedures or rules to produce knowledge—which Collins and Ferguson (1993) label epistemic games—each bottleneck represents a violation of one or more of the rules of the game. In other words, bottlenecks reveal naïve (or sometimes alternative) ways of operating and point to what is not understood about the ways of operating in the discipline. For example, science students may reason that seasons are due to warmth and are caused by Earth's orbit getting closer to and farther from the sun, because this is their experience in their daily lives with sources of heat, whereas astrophysicists explain the seasons as being caused by the tilt of the Earth, as more solar radiation hits the hemisphere of the Earth tilted toward the sun. History students may think their goal is to remember the facts and events of *what* happened in the past, based on their prior school experience, while for historians it is about interpreting *why* things happened (Shopkow, Díaz, Middendorf, & Pace, 2013a, p. 26).

The rules, however, are interconnected. So, for instance, when students confuse the magnitude of an earthquake with its intensity, they are ignoring a set of procedures about how each of these is measured (a single data point versus multiple data points), what each describes (energy release versus effects), and what factors influence intensity (e.g., the composition of the ground in the affected region). In other words, students do not understand some basic features of how seismologists go about their work. But we might expect that if student understanding improved in one of these areas—for instance, if they gained a better understanding of how seismologists gathered data or if they studied the behavior of waves in different sorts of terrain—their overall ability to distinguish between intensity and magnitude would improve more than if they simply memorized the definitions. In other words, epistemologies are systems and altering some parts of the system will have an effect on other parts.

The disciplines (whether they are called transdisciplines or fields) have gotten very sophisticated at producing knowledge, but practitioners in general are not conscious of these systems as a whole, because they operate tacitly (and here we once again invoke the tacit form of troublesome knowledge). They are often (but not always) good at telling students what to do, but not so good at telling students why they should do it. To give a perhaps trivial example, many faculty members find student unwillingness to learn proper citation very frustrating, but they almost never articulate why it is important. Students may think that citation is either busywork or needed so faculty can check for plagiarism. The latter may be true, but few faculty explain to students that citation allows readers to know what conversations an author is partaking in and that this is a fundamental aspect of knowledge creation in many fields. There is no guarantee that if students know *why* faculty demand this they will be more responsive, but faculty insistence alone does not seem to do the trick.

Through our work on the History Learning Project, we realized that by starting with the categories of bottlenecks we could map the epistemology of history (Shopkow et al., 2013a), that is, the ways of knowing in the discipline—how one knows what one knows, the knowing that permits the creation of knowledge. The epistemology of a discipline shows the mechanisms of thought that produce the characteristic knowledge and meaning within that field. It would include the assumptions of the discipline and its notions of what constitutes evidence. Shopkow and Díaz laid out the epistemology of the field of history by listing student bottlenecks to learning, how the bottlenecks appeared in student work, and the implicit disciplinary way of operating (see Table 8.1). Defining the epistemology can keep instructors focused on the most essential learning in a field, and we found it can increase student learning (Shopkow et al., 2013a).

Furthermore, by practicing Decoding the Disciplines in cross-disciplinary groupings, we can make comparisons that facilitate seeing the epistemology of different fields. Because expertise is tacit, we can't readily describe the kinds of knowing in our own field, but when we compare yours—a very

TABLE 8.1

Mapping Bottlenecks in History to Epistemology

Example of a Bottleneck	How it Appears in Student Work	Student Conception	Implicit Epistemological Issue
Difficulty developing a historical argument (Interpretation)	A student essay without any argument. The essay may be a simple narrative that tells "what happened" or may be a list of factual material.	The job of a historian is to tell stories about the past, and the student is unaware that historians make arguments through scholarly writing.	While historians sometimes tell "what happened," they do so in aid of advancing a particular argument about the meaning of the past, and they recognize that they must explain the meaning of the evidence as well as present it. Far from speaking for itself, the past needs historians to reconstruct it and speak about its meaning.
Not taking the perspective of people in the past (Presentism)	A student presents people in the past as "stupid" or "primitive" or "immoral" for not acting in particular ways. A student makes assumptions in writing about the past based on his or her own experiences and ideas.	People in the past basically thought about things as modern people do. When they don't behave like modern people, there must be something wrong with them. Past conduct is judged by current culture.	Historians recognize that most people's ideas are constrained by positionality (their culture, education, social position). Historians know that people in the past lived in cultures quite different from modern culture and that these cultures need to be reconstructed to the degree this is possible. The historian is committed to reconstructing why a historical actor might have thought or spoken as he or she did, while also recognizing the ways in which the culture being examined is different from the historian's own.

(*Continues*)

TABLE 8.1 (*Continued*)

Example of a Bottleneck	How it Appears in Student Work	Student Conception	Implicit Epistemological Issue
Ignoring significance	A student provides a narrative or a long list of facts but doesn't explain why the narrative or facts are important or presents a trivial argument.	The student is not aware or doesn't care what, if anything, is at stake in the story he or she is telling.	While historians do provide abundant factual information and also tell stories, most historians would argue that what separates historians from antiquarians is that historians should answer the "so what?" question, that they should explain why a particular subject is worth investigating and present the meaning they see lying in the material.
Intolerance for ambiguity	A student makes a seemingly arbitrary choice about what argument to make or cannot decide between two scholarly arguments and resolves the difference by taking from both.	Students are challenged by situations where scholars aren't fully sure of what happened or argue over what it means, because students don't see history as probabilistic or contested.	Much evidence from the past is fragmentary and historians do not necessarily agree on its meaning. Historians do not expect history to be a zone of undeniable truth, even though they are committed to their own ideas. They are aware not only that other historians may demolish their arguments and that they themselves may come to think they were in error, but also that in many cases there may be no grounds from within the discipline of history to determine which interpretations are correct.
Difficulty maintaining appropriate emotional distance	A student rants in an assignment rather than providing evidence or making an intellectual argument or omits information or parrots what the teacher has said.	The student wants to be "fair" or identifies only with one side and assumes that all knowledge about the past is equal.	Historians cannot let their passions run before the evidence. Even when evidence is upsetting, historians are expected to police their own emotions and to take the perspectives of even repugnant actors. Historians interrogate vernacular history and discard it if it can't be sustained by academic history methods.

different field—to ours, we may find some similar reasoning or maybe the same, or reasoning very different from ours. This comparison makes our own ways of operating and the epistemology of our field clearer to us.

Middendorf, Shopkow, and Pace (2014) also used bottlenecks to begin to define the epistemology of geoscience and tax accounting. We found that there are some common mental actions across the three very different fields of history, geology, and tax accounting. While there were distinctive ways of thinking in each field, there were also some surprising similarities. All of them consider aspects of the past, whether this is taking the perspective of people in the past (history), interpreting a past tax situation (accounting), or imagining the forces over time in the past that brought about a current outcropping (geology). There is perspective-taking in each, and there is also an aspect of extrapolating into the future (except that historians are careful to argue the meaning something has for today and not to make hard predictions for the future, because humans are so unpredictable).

More generally, some metaepistemologies cross many fields. For example, the generation of arguments, theses, or hypotheses appears in many fields' analysis of evidence or data. Visualization, along with symbolic representation, appears in fields as varied as art and nanochemistry. Systemic thinking appears in health sciences, law, and sustainability studies—to name a few.

To make the critical reasoning of every field clearer, it would be useful for every field to flesh out their epistemologies as Raab and Frodeman (2002) did for geology and Shopkow and Díaz did for history (see Table 8.1). The exercise at the end of this chapter follows the process we have used several times to uncover epistemology.

Decoding the Disciplines and Other Theories

Threshold Concepts

We have been asked many times the difference between Decoding the Disciplines and threshold concepts, but, in fact, the two parallel concepts are actually *bottlenecks* and *threshold concepts*: two metaphors for identifying where students get stuck when trying to learn. Bottlenecks/thresholds both occur at Step 1 in the Decoding the Disciplines model (see Figure 8.1).

Threshold concepts are often conglomerations of bottlenecks and represent complex performances that may be paradigm shifting (Meyer & Land, 2006). Perspective-taking in the field of history, for example, is a threshold concept involving a large number of separate bottlenecks: Awareness of one's own positionality, the historical context (itself another whole complex

Figure 8.1. Diagram of bottlenecks and threshold concepts at Step 1 of decoding model.

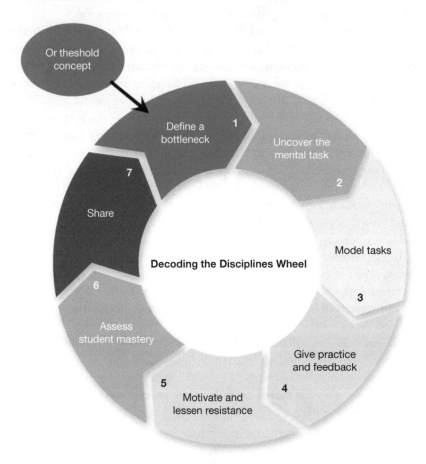

of issues), contingency (not knowing what will happen in the future), and empathy with others on their own terms are parts of perspective-taking in this one field (Shopkow & Díaz, forthcoming; Shopkow, Middendorf, Díaz, & Pace, 2012). This distinction is not always completely correct, as some of the initial threshold concepts, such as opportunity cost, are not so complex. What is true, however, is that ways of thinking within a discipline are at stake in both. The way of thinking that underlies opportunity cost or replacement cost, for instance, is the notion that all human relationships and choices can be effectively monetized and that the purpose of economic activity is to maximize one's economic benefit (according to the field of economics).

Both bottlenecks and threshold concepts are useful frames for analyzing what trips students up and the nature of the difficulty. Adherents of threshold concepts are currently developing ways to address them, the purpose for which Decoding the Disciplines was invented.

Backward Course Design

Backward design is one of the most powerful ideas in education and it can play well with Decoding the Disciplines, but the two approaches actually start from different places, so using backward design in a decoding context requires some careful preparation (see Figure 8.2). Starting with bottlenecks to design a course is a "frontward design" process. We think about the places where students get stuck, planning the course to prioritize getting students through these bottlenecks. The bottlenecks mark the critical thinking of the expert that will be the focus of the course. Once we have identified the bottlenecks, we decode what the expert would do to avoid getting stuck in the bottlenecks. Uncovering the expert mental action allows us to design lessons to get through the bottlenecks and assess student performance in doing so (see Figure 5.10).

With backward course design, in contrast, we think about what we want students to be able to *do* by the end of a course, how we will assess performance on the end-of-course skills, and the subassessments to check competency along the way. To make this work, however, we first need to decode the mental tasks involved in completing the major assignment, including its component tasks. Thus, Step 2 Decoding Mental Actions is necessary for both approaches. And both frontward design (bottlenecks) and backward design keep us away from content coverage approaches to course design.

Signature Pedagogies

While there is no necessary relationship between Decoding the Disciplines and signature pedagogies, decoding can certainly help decide on an appropriate set of pedagogies for teaching in a discipline. *Signature pedagogies* as defined by Shulman (2005) are "the forms of instruction that leap to mind when we first think about the preparation of members of particular professions" (p. 52). The problem with this definition is that faculty may use certain methods because that was the way they were taught, rather than because they are the best ones for developing the critical reasoning in that field. Bruner (1999) calls these inherited, but not evidence-based, methods "folk pedagogies." As Jeffrey Bernstein (2012) points out, just because the lecture is ubiquitous in political science does not mean it *should* be the signature pedagogy for the field. He identifies several core mental actions in political science: to strategize as political actors would; to predict actions taken that

Figure 8.2. Decoding the Disciplines and backward design.

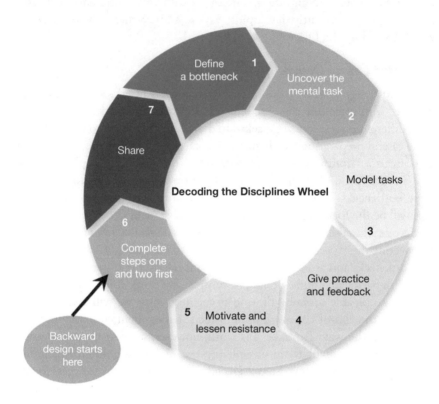

can constrain other actions; and to view a situation from the perspective of interested parties, not just one's own. He proposes role-playing simulations and service-learning for political science's signature pedagogies, because they foster these kinds of mental actions. Though they do not currently predominate, their wider adoption could be useful to the field.

If we use Decoding the Disciplines to uncover the epistemologies of a field, we may be in a better position to designate the pedagogies that would develop the mental actions from that field. With the epistemology laid out, the signature pedagogies can be selected to address the bottlenecks of a field in order to bring students into the epistemology, rather than continue with received folk pedagogies.

Decoding the Disciplines can uncover disciplinary epistemologies in order to more readily bring students into our disciplinary ways of creating knowledge. One of the reasons for founding SoTL was to serve as a base in the disciplines and to bridge the gap between teaching and research (Boyer, 1997).

Decoding and SoTL

It should be clear by now that decoding is deeply connected to current theoretical approaches to higher education and that it has contributed to those approaches by generating a significant body of SoTL. In the previous chapter, we described how some individuals can begin with decoding and end up as SoTL scholars. There is, however, still plenty of room for others to get involved in this scholarship. The epistemology needs to be laid out in many fields, and the work we have initiated needs verification. Not everyone has to do this work, but fields in which someone does it will benefit because then not everyone will have to re-create the wheel as he or she approaches teaching.

Decoding the Disciplines can serve as a strategic and natural partner for SoTL, starting from any of the steps. What are the bottlenecks in our field? What is the tacit knowledge underlying disciplinary expertise in our field? What analogies can help model critical disciplinary mental actions? What is the epistemology of our field and what teaching methods support these kinds of reasoning? Decoding the Disciplines is one approach to frame studies of what is, what works, and what might be (Hutchings, 2000). With sharing as the final step of the model, going public with what we have learned from decoding in our field is straightforward and eases entry to SoTL. Early in the development of the decoding model, Joan and David were able to publish a book with coauthors who had never published about teaching and learning before (Middendorf & Pace, 2004). (For a list of SoTL research using the Decoding Framework, see Appendix F.) Our point is only that decoding can open a door to SoTL if an individual is interested.

Decoding Innovations in Teaching and Learning

We have repeatedly stressed (at least, we hope we have made it *very* clear!) that it is not our goal that every teacher (or even most teachers) who uses decoding become a scholar of teaching and learning. However, anyone who uses this book will be a teacher, perhaps a teacher of undergraduate students or a teacher of teachers. Decoding can be very helpful in helping teachers sort through the stream of new teaching ideas and technologies, which can seem incessant and which would overwhelm us if we tried to accept every one. How can we judge if they are worth our consideration? Decoding can make the deluge more manageable. Keeping the desired mental action in mind, we can determine the unique capabilities of an innovative tool or method to see which mental action it matches. Recent innovations include flipped classes, podcasts, learning spaces designed for active learning, and learning management systems (see Table 8.2). With decoding we can think strategically about the innovation and its purpose by asking ourselves what mental action it produces and seeing whether this is, in fact, the effect we want in our classroom.

The really important question is whether innovative techniques actually advance student learning. The assessment process (Step 6) is crucial to moving our understanding of teaching and learning ahead. However, even today, some teaching publications still report student satisfaction rather than evidence of student learning, even though we know that student satisfaction does not necessarily mean that an approach is effective. For instance, data studies showed that "learning styles" were mythic, a matter of student preference rather than effectiveness (Riener & Willingham, 2010). In the future we may have data to evaluate the usefulness of innovations and which are most successful in teaching mental actions. In the meantime, checking the

TABLE 8.2
Assessing Teaching Innovations With Decoding Theory

Innovation	Relevant Decoding Step
Flipped classes—concept exposition outside of class	Step 3 shows how to demonstrate the mental action.
Flipped classes—in-class time used for practice	Step 4 shows how to match the mental action to teaching methods for student practice.
Active learning spaces (adaptable physical classroom spaces)	Usually based on flipped classroom; see previous entry for flipped classes.
Podcasts	Ways to use this technology: as disruptive final projects for students (Step 5) or to convey course concepts (Step 3).
Learning management systems	Can manage content (Step 3) or course administration (which may not be related to student learning and thus is outside the realm of the decoding framework); track practice (Step 4); record, score, and summarize assessments (Step 6); prepare reports for sharing (Step 7).

innovation in light of intended mental actions helps us gauge its effectiveness in light of our purposes.

Teacher Preparation: Pedagogy Courses

While experienced teachers may be using decoding to sort through various teaching innovations and theories to find the ones that will improve the learning of their students, what about beginning teachers? Most people beginning teaching careers have overwhelmingly experienced only two styles of teaching: large lecture classes and small discussion-based seminars. A 2012 survey (Hurtado, Eagan, Pryor, Whang, & Tran, 2012) revealed that 53% of faculty across disciplines still primarily use lecture as their main teaching method. Given our tendencies to teach the way we were taught, to rely on our "folk pedagogies" (Bruner, 1999), changing the culture of teaching can seem like an insurmountable task.

Teachers often take generic pedagogy courses in order to accumulate teaching methods for leading discussions and active learning. In disciplinary pedagogy courses, they may want to be instructed about "what to cover" in foundational areas. But the entire teaching and learning enterprise makes more sense when we operate with an underlying theory. Decoding the Disciplines can serve as a strong foundation for teaching methods and setting disciplinary priorities.

We have used Decoding the Disciplines strategically in pedagogy courses for over 10 years to provide a theoretical basis for teaching and learning. Theories are explanations of ways the world works. In education, they are about the way teaching and learning work. From educational theories, we derive models—testable ideas that predict how people learn in the real world. Decoding the Disciplines is both a theory and a model. The theory says that there is a gap between the way experts and novices think in any discipline (or across fields). That gap shows us where we need to uncover the thinking of experts to make it more available to students. The decoding model is implemented strategically to help teachers gain the bottleneck perspective, uncover tacit mental moves, and collect evidence about student performance to iteratively improve it. Using this theory and model in pedagogy classes helps new instructors start out using evidence-based teaching methods that may not be prevalent in their disciplines. What's more, students of the pedagogy course have a firm grasp of bottlenecks and ways to address them.

In Joan's graduate pedagogy course, she has found four main bottlenecks:

1. Lack of confidence in the role as teacher
2. Lack of a model for lesson design
3. Lack of a model for course and curriculum design
4. Lack of familiarity with the literature on teaching and learning related to their own discipline

Joan's students, who come from a variety of disciplines, uncover and teach to a bottleneck in their own disciplines, practicing with feedback from peers to build confidence before they teach the lesson to an actual undergraduate class. They can use the resulting lesson and its assessments as part of a teaching portfolio that includes a course they construct through backward design (Wiggins & McTighe, 2005) or frontward design (bottleneck theory). Along the way they learn the value of assessing student efforts on the mental actions that underlie all of their teaching efforts. They write feedback such as, "I struggled with one of my new classes this year and had to go back to material from your class to get back on track. Please know that even years later, it still helps me in the classroom!"

To familiarize them with the specific literature in their field and in future inquiry in teaching and learning, each member creates a synthesis of the state of SoTL in their fields, which can take the form of a poster, an epistemological map of their field, a review of the literature (in writing or presented on VoiceThread)—whatever form will make for the best communication in their field. More than a few have gone on to publish this work (French & Westler, submitted 2016; Junisbai, 2014; Sturts & Mowatt, 2012).

In Leah's history pedagogy course, students have conducted SoTL inquiry into students' grasp of some of the basic epistemic underpinnings of history, such as what professional historians do and the purpose and use of primary sources. In effect, the students do research on the major bottlenecks in the field of history (Barrett, Kirven, & Leach, 2015; Blizard, 2014; Hengtgen, Leach, Szostało, & Kim, 2015).

Pedagogy courses can use the Decoding the Disciplines framework to explore where students get stuck in their learning, dissect the issues that trip them up, and assess the teacher and their students' efforts. It serves as a basis for course design and acquaints them with SoTL and the mental actions in their fields. In all, decoding offers a comprehensive approach to theory and a practical process to guide pedagogical preparation.

Summary

Decoding the Disciplines developed out of an awareness of disciplinary differences and their implications for learning: Where students got stuck and how to get them unstuck was clearly different in different fields. Likewise, one of the primary motivations in the development of SoTL was a concern with the disciplinary nature of learning. Decoding the Disciplines is connected to current theoretical approaches in higher education and contributes to these approaches. It can be used to spell out the disciplines' ways of knowing or specific "critical thinking." By laying out the epistemologies, each field will be able to describe the nature of the endeavor and help students avoid mistaken notions and perform the mental actions of the field. Decoding can be used to analyze the worth of teaching innovations and provides a practical and theoretically sound approach to teacher preparation.

CHAPTER 8 EXERCISE

Worksheet: Compile the Epistemology of Your Field

For individuals

First, give the *name* of the bottleneck or threshold concept. Second, describe how it appears in *student work* (what the students do). Third, define the student misconception (what they get wrong). Fourth, explain the implicit epistemological issue—that is, how *experts* reason to avoid getting stuck in the bottleneck; this involves some decoding. It's important on this fourth one to leave the student thinking *out* of the picture and concentrate on what the expert does. Repeat these steps for the main bottlenecks in your discipline.

1.1. Name of bottleneck #1	
1.2. Appears in student work as	
1.3. Student misconception	
1.4. Implicit epistemological issue/what expert does to avoid bottleneck	
2.1. Name of bottleneck #2	
2.2. And so on.	

After completing your epistemology chart, ask for feedback on it from colleagues within and outside your field to see what you may have missed.

For teams

Teams from similar fields can create an epistemology chart. After completion compare the epistemology charts of different fields, providing feedback about clarity and thoroughness for other teams. Seeing other charts can make your own ways of creating knowledge clearer.

Using bottlenecks as the starting place to map out the disciplinary ways of operating provides a starting place to discuss what comprises a discipline and its subfields. The conversation can then consider implications for teaching the mental actions laid out in the epistemology, including implications for curricular matters and assessment. We have some evidence from the History Learning Project that showing students just one part of how a discipline operates can help them move forward in the discipline as a whole (Shopkow et al., 2013a).

Two Bottleneck Lesson Plans

	Biology Bottleneck Lesson **Mimi Zolan (Biology)**
Context	Biology L112, Foundations of Biology: Biological Mechanisms, is one of two foundational courses students take if they are planning on careers in one of the health professions or graduate studies. This course is taught in a flipped format with 60 students enrolled.
Step 1: The Bottleneck. What are students unable to do?	Memorization versus visualization. Students can memorize the components of particular biological processes, but no matter which mechanism is involved, students do not know how to visualize biological processes. Visualizing a three-dimensional process such as translation of RNA is difficult, and if you can't visualize it, you can't make predictions.
Step 2: The Mental Action. What mental actions does the expert perform to get past the bottleneck?	I visualize the components of processes—I do this all the time. To watch the process in my mind, I have to first know the components and their functions, and then go back and forth between what happens to the process and what happens to the components, which is iterative. This is a mechanistic visualization. [She starts sketching chromosomes and chromosome pairs on a sheet of paper, using arrows, bars, and boxes to indicate the process going forward, being interrupted. This shows another part of visualization—turning the objects and processes into symbols in order to symbolically manipulate them.] In my work, there's a process and the chromosomes and the different stages that the process is in. If it arrests at a certain phase, in my head I'm watching the chromosomes go through their movements and seeing the effects of them *freeze* at a certain stage or if they switch from one process to another. I'm visualizing whether a protein makes something happen or stops it. I have the chromosome behavior so firmly in mind, I can apply the effects of other things on this process. (And you can say this for every process I visualize.)

Step 3: Model the Thinking. What analogy will you use to model these mental actions?	Translating RNA to a protein is like building a car out of LEGO starting from the written instructions. This analogy works because the LEGO car has an active function along with being three-dimensional—colors and shapes that make up the parts that move.
Step 4: Practice and Feedback. How will the students practice these mental actions? How will they receive feedback to make improvements?	• At Week 2 in the semester students draw the course vocabulary words instead of memorizing them (as in concept maps or process maps). • At Week 3, students draw pictures of movements across the membrane. • At Week 4, students practice visualizing in their learning groups using the Human Tableau CAT that I learned from my colleague Roger Innes (Zolan, Strome, & Innes, 2004) (though this CAT is NOT for assessment but for practice). Students act out the process of RNA translation with their bodies so they have to know what the components are and what they do; plus—it's iterative. • Afterward, the teams reflect on the human tableau scenes in writing to reinforce their understanding of the process.
Step 5: Motivation. What will I do to hold students accountable and disrupt ritual ways of learning?	• I use some mnemonic phrases, repeating them for emphasis: "Close your eyes and visualize," and "Less memorize, more visualize." • I have "flipped" the class so there is less of a tendency for passive memorization and more active explanation and visualization by students. While there are prerecorded lectures, students spend most of their in-class time in learning groups facilitated by teaching assistants. The once-weekly whole-group meetings are teacher explanations interspersed with clicker questions. Students constantly seek out someone they don't agree with on the clicker questions to explain their understanding to and listen to the explanations of others.

(Continues)

Biology Bottleneck Lesson *(Continued)*

Step 6: Assessment. How will you assess student mastery of the mental action?	Students (*n* = 54) scored 89% correct on an item on the final exam that assessed students' ability to visualize by drawing and explaining transport in plant cells. By the time we realized it would have been good to collect a pretest, it was too late in this course. But the next semester, we "pretested" the students in an even larger section of the same course (300 students, with *n* = 124 signing IRB permissions to participate in study) on a similar task (drawing and explaining the process of transport). While this was not the same class, it did give us an idea of what the typical class can do in regard to visualizing a biological process prior to it being taught explicitly—24% answered it correctly. The students who could not answer correctly went wrong in interesting ways: Some students could draw the visualization but could not explain it (8%). Some students could explain it (were they just parroting words?) but could not draw it (7%). The incorrect responses gave us ideas for further study, as we try to better understand how to help students develop visualization and the skills to represent their mental processes. (Thanks to Professor Megan Dunn for the pretest study and Natalie Christian for data analysis.)
Step 7: Sharing. How will you share what you learned?	I teach a pedagogy course for biology graduate students based on Decoding the Disciplines—every student develops a bottleneck lesson and teaches it with feedback. I occasionally present to faculty groups about how decoding affected my teaching (Zolan, Strome, & Innes, 2004).

Music Bottleneck Lesson

Kate Altizer (Musicology)

Context	Music Z315, Music for Film, is a 36-student class for non-majors in the IU Jacobs School of Music with which STEM students can meet an arts and humanities requirement. One-third of the students are from the Media School, and the rest come from a wide variety of other departments.
Step 1: The Bottleneck. What are students unable to do?	Students have difficulty identifying what to listen for in a particular genre and communicating what they hear verbally. Underlying this is the emotional bottleneck that they struggle to articulate their felt knowledge of music. Despite the fact that students spend a lot of time with music, they commonly say, "I don't know anything about music." It is a message they give themselves, not unlike "I'm no good at math" or "I'm no good at writing." There is also an aspect of "Music is to be enjoyed, not studied" too.
Step 2: The Mental Action. What mental actions does the expert perform to get past the bottleneck?	Trying to translate the sounds we hear into meanings we can communicate begins with listening very closely, something we don't always do. Sometimes we listen to music as merely background, or just feel it communicate an idea or image. To listen for the various aspects of music and how they come together to create a musical piece, we can listen for instrumentation, melody, rhythm, or form. To listen and describe music in this way requires focus on how music exists in time, and the quality of the sound, no matter the genre. I will focus in on three parameters that make up time in Western music: rhythm (durations), meter (patterns/regularity), and tempo (speed). Students readily understand tempo (speed), so rhythm and meter are the bottlenecks. Meter is the pulse of the music, a regular, organized pattern of strong or weak beats. In Western music, meter is usually structured in some variation of twos—such as in a march or a gallop (weak-strong)—or threes—such as in waltzes (strong-weak-weak). On the other hand, rhythm refers to the specific length or duration of notes. When a note is played, it can hit on the metric pulse, last longer than the pulse, or hit in between the pulse. In some pieces the pulse is articulated by instruments and in others, it is implicit.

(Continues)

Music Bottleneck Lesson *(Continued)*

	I can experience the meter and rhythm with my senses—hear with my ears, watch the sway of the instruments being played, and feel as the notes strike my body—maybe even as I tap my toes to the music, the meter, or the rhythm. As a music expert, I can tap my toes to the meter and maybe even clap the rhythm with my hands. Once I know how to observe meter and rhythm, then I am better able to describe them.
Step 3: Model the Thinking. What analogy will you use to model these mental actions?	Listening to meter and rhythm is like feeling the regular clickety-clack pattern of a train moving along a track (meter) and rocking along with it or doing something against the pattern, such as texting on a phone or talking loudly to someone (either of which could match the regularity or deviate from it). For the within-the-discipline example, I clap the rhythm of the *Star Wars* main title, exaggerating the clapping motion to help them find it. I highlight my actions with these questions: Can I feel it in my body? Regular, irregular? Striking or unobtrusive?
Step 4: Practice and Feedback. How will the students practice these mental actions? How will they receive feedback to make improvements?	Then it's the students' turn: Half of the students clap meter, half clap rhythm. For more practice, students reverse roles, with the half that clapped meter clapping rhythm, and vice versa as we work with different pieces of music as well as duple and triple. (And we note another bottleneck: Students may feel awkward about playing the beat in "public.")
Step 5: Motivation. What will I do to hold students accountable and disrupt ritual ways of learning?	As usual with emotional bottlenecks, we have to help students become aware of their preconception—I don't know anything about music—and then they can more readily learn the cognitive mental action—how to listen for the meter and rhythm, and differentiate between that part of the musical piece as it plays across time. Also, metaphors are a powerful way to help their understanding.

Step 6: Assessment. How will you assess student mastery of the mental action?	Students were asked before and after the rhythm lesson: Explain to a friend who missed class today how to find rhythm and meter in music. Of the 28 students who took both pre- and posttests, 7% gave a competent explanation on the pretest and 57% on the posttest. (To meet the criteria for competence, students had to do more than parrot the definition; they had to differentiate between meter and rhythm in their own words and some even explained how it feels or invented an analogy.)
Step 7: Sharing. How will you share what you learned?	I have taught this model lesson to pedagogy classes and for campus workshops several times.

Bottleneck Lesson Plan Template

Describe your course and context.	
Step 1: The Bottleneck. What are students unable to do?	
Step 2: The Mental Action. What mental actions does the expert perform to get past the bottleneck?	
Step 3: Model the Thinking. What analogy will you use to model these mental actions?	
Step 4: Practice and Feedback. How will the students practice these mental actions? How will they receive feedback to make improvements?	
Step 5: Motivation. What will I do to hold students accountable and disrupt ritual ways of learning?	

Step 6: Assessment. How will you assess student mastery of the mental action?	
Step 7: Sharing. How will you share what you learned?	

"Decoding the Disciplines" Course Planning Template

Your Name ⸻⸻⸻⸻⸻⸻⸻⸻⸻⸻

Expand the template as needed. Note that you will not necessarily fill in all the boxes for each week. You may not be modeling in a given week or doing an assessment or even working specifically on the bottleneck (you may be giving attention to other course topics).

	Noncontent Objectives of the Week (Mental Action)	Readings	Modeling (What analogy will be used?)	Practice (What form will practice take?)	Assessment (What is being assessed? What method is used?)
Week 1					
Week 2					
Week 3					
Week 4					

Matching Mental Actions to Teaching Methods Based on Bloom

Teaching Methods for Remembering

Verbs: Recognize, state, define, list

Metaphor: Remembering the hospital's address

Face-to-Face Methods	Online Methods
Flash cards	Quizzes (includes surveys)
Mnemonics	Collaborations (Google Docs) for focused listing
Jeopardy! game	
Quiz bowls	Pages (wiki)—memory matrixes
Question and answer with clickers	Piktochart (create infographics)
	Lucidchart (flowchart creator)

Teaching Methods for Understanding

Verbs: Explain, paraphrase, summarize

Metaphor: Giving directions to the hospital

Face-to-Face Methods	Online Methods
Paraphrasing activities	Discussions
Concept mapping (or "mind maps")	VoiceThread (media-based discussions)
Create an analogy	Graphics (canva.com)
Save the Last Word for Me	Animoto (create a video using your photos)
Jigsaw exercises	
	Prezi presentation

Note. Adapted from Hines, 2015. See also Bloom & Krathwohl, 1984.

Teaching Methods for Applying

Verbs: Solve, employ, demonstrate

Metaphor: Employing procedures for blood draws at the hospital

Face-to-Face Methods	Online Methods
Worked out problems	Discussions for critiquing video exemplars
Represent concepts through art (drawings, Play-Doh)	Discussions with assigned roles
Prediction exercises	Fishbowls using VoiceThread
Role playing	Group projects supported through course management software
In-box exercise	Blogger
Case studies	

Teaching Methods for Analyzing

Verbs: Divide, visualize, classify

Metaphor: Investigating charges on a hospital bill

Face-to-Face Methods	Online Methods
Interpret a data set (graph, chart, etc.)	Data interpretation using Microsoft Excel, Word Databases (discuss using the Canvas Discussions tool, VoiceThread, or CN Post)
Diagnose a problem	
Compare and contrast various approaches/theories/processes/products	Interview analysis of audio or video recordings (assignments, pages, discussions, VoiceThread, or CN Post)
Ranking/prioritizing alternatives	
Pattern finding	Data collection/analysis: Survey Monkey, Google Forms, Google Earth, and post analysis to Canvas
	Relation concept, herring/fishbone mind maps
	Strengths, weaknesses, opportunities, threats (SWOT) analysis (from the Web, created in Word)

Teaching Methods for Evaluating

Verbs: Judge, critique, support

Metaphor: Gauging the quality of someone's care in the hospital

Face-to-Face Methods	Online Methods
Judge the quality of a product (based on criteria) Test/critique a product or process Create an editorial Create an assessment to evaluate a product, process, or outcome Peer reviewing	Judge videos of student-created examples or demonstrations (VoiceThread, CN Post, or discussions) Comparison of real-world products (video capture, photos)—discuss using CN Post or VoiceThread Self-assessment (assignments, pages tools, discussions) Peer reviewing (assignments, discussions) Live debates or trials (Adobe Connect or Zoom)

Teaching Methods for Creating

Verbs: Produce, plan, reconstruct

Metaphor: Designing a new hospital

Face-to-Face Methods	Online Methods
Develop a game Invent a new product or process Create a proposal Compose a song, video, poem, artwork Redesign an existing model	Create a video or podcast (assignments, Pages tools) Create a webpage (Pages) Compose a poem or song (Google Docs, Word) Create an animation or cartoon Create a photostory (Animoto, Prezi, Storify)

Decoding Curriculum and Program Assessment

1. *Draft the Program Goals*
   - What are the six to eight types of knowledge, competencies, or attitudes students should have upon graduating from your program? (Think of the main places where the students get stuck.) Name each category using noun phrases.
   - Do a cross-disciplinary peer feedback session (Gallery Walk Exercise).
   - Share program goals across fields/departments. Mark comments on them: Are they comprehensive? Clear? Distinctive?
   - What changes will you make to your goals based on the feedback and viewing the goals of other fields?
2. *Identify Student Learning Outcomes (SLOs)*
   - Pick a program goal. What do you want students to be able to *do* to demonstrate competence with respect to this goal? To spell out SLOs it helps to
     o describe where students get stuck in reaching this goal (the bottlenecks), and
     o include four to six SLOs for each program goal.
   - Write these as verb phrases (e.g., Game Production: define tasks, derive tasks from designs, estimate time usage, form and lead teams, playtest).
3. *Compile the Curriculum Map*
   - Plot the program goals and SLOs on one side of a table.
   - Fill the other side with the courses in your department/program. This is your curriculum map (see Table 7.1).
   - Analyze it—look for gaps, redundancies, and disorganized sequencing. Look for courses that
     o do not address program goals and SLOs (gaps), and
     o claim to address too many goals and SLOs.

- Look for goals and SLOs that
  - o are poorly addressed in the curriculum, and
  - o do not ensure proper scaffolding (novice, intermediate, advanced).
- Review this curriculum map analysis among faculty and bring in the decision makers. What changes need to be made?

4. *Assess Student Learning*
   - Stage 1. Collect evidence of student learning.
     - a. Select a goal/SLO to assess based on the curriculum map findings. What do you want to know more about? (This may be a departmental decision. For example, "Everyone is going to assess goal 1.2, 'Articulate different points of view.'")
     - b. How will you provide evidence of student learning for this goal/SLO? What method will be used (quantitative, qualitative, pre-post, reflection)? Which assignments will be analyzed? On which bottlenecks/mental actions will we assess student performance?
     - c. What criteria or source will be used to compare results?
   - Stage 2. Reflect on evidence of student learning.
     - a. Analyze the evidence of student learning. What do the results show? (This might be done by individual instructors or the assessment results might be turned over to an assessment specialist who collects and synthesizes all the data.)
     - b. Synthesize the results across instructors or courses. To what extent are students achieving the SLOs? Which issues need to be discussed at a faculty meeting?

Report results to whomever is holding the group accountable. (This might be a departmental committee or an administrator.)

Decoding as the Basis for SoTL Research

Step 1 Bottleneck Studies

Analyses of bottlenecks provides insight into a discipline

- Gurung and Landrum (2013) attempted to uncover bottlenecks and define the concept of bottlenecks in psychology.
- Abbott (2015) analyzed student study logs to try to objectively identify bottlenecks in music therapy.

Step 2 Decoding Interviews Studies

Each one of the decoding steps can stand on its own in support of teaching and learning; but strategically, there is one powerful tool that is being used for a variety of purposes, Step 2 Decoding. The decoding step is a form of task analysis that is particularly good at uncovering the thinking of experts. A number of academics are using decoding interviews to uncover tacit knowledge and to conduct research in their academic fields. Others are developing new methods for decoding tacit knowledge.

Pettit and colleagues (2017) explored reciprocity, a threshold concept in service-learning as well as the value of self-study and ethnography that underlies the decoding interviews.

- Three undergraduate researchers used decoding interviews with college teachers and other undergraduates to determine the mental tasks and bottlenecks involved in writing a literature review for a political science course (Rouse, Phillips, Mehaffey, McGowan, & Felten, 2017). They identified differences in the ways faculty and students conduct literature reviews and insights into student-faculty partnerships.
- Decoding in disciplinary knowledge creation. Sargeant and Shang (2016) used the decoding interviews in the field of philanthropy, interviewing leading international foundations. From these decoding interviews, they were able to suggest ways foundations can optimize

their investment strategies. Before they published this work, their decoding effort resulted in a *New York Times* interview with Jen Shang, "Getting Into a Benefactor's Head" (Wallis, 2012).

- Lahm and Kaduk (2016) developed writing prompts to decode an expert's tacit mental actions.
- Hines (2015) developed a kinesthetic method for decoding with play-dough.

Steps 1 Through 6 Studies

These studies work through all of the steps of Decoding the Disciplines to enhance learning.

- Norton (2015) addressed a classical threshold concept in statistical inference (sampling distribution) by applying the Decoding the Disciplines model.
- Shopkow (2017) describes several bottlenecks that need to be dealt with to improve student history papers, including reading primary and secondary sources (see Figure 6.9).
- Pinnow (2016) conducted experiments in psychology classes. Students taught in decoded classes outperformed students in the traditional lecture format on three bottlenecks—hypothesis generation, creation of operational definitions, and identification of independent and dependent variables.

Decoding the Disciplines as the Basis for Theoretical Work

Some researchers used philosophical frameworks to understand how decoding makes disciplinary tacit ways of knowing conscious.

- MacDonald (2017) explored the use of decoding interviews to better understand the development of professional disciplinary identities.
- Currie (2017) used phenomenology to study how decoding uncovers and puts into words what teachers do when working with students.
- Yeo and colleagues (2017) used hermeneutics to describe how decoding interviews make the familiar strange.
- Middendorf, Shopkow, and Pace (2014) used bottlenecks as the starting point to theorize and uncover the epistemologies of three disciplines (accounting, geology, and history).

Decoding the Disciplines for Secondary Education

- Barbour and Streb (2014) developed a reader for high school government classes that uses a political science analysis model that they developed in the Freshman Learning Project.
- Lovin and Schultz (2012) employed a self-study method to better understand their own mathematical thinking and thus help prospective mathematics educators develop their own disciplinary thinking.

Decoding Service-Learning

- Miller-Young and colleagues (2015) posit from their decoding interviews about reciprocity in service-learning courses—colearning and the cogeneration of knowledge—that it may be a bottleneck both for the teachers and for their students.

ADDITIONAL RESOURCES

Decoding the Disciplines Website

http://decodingthedisciplines.org/

YouTube Channel

www.youtube.com/channel/UCqCaJ-dgBDqCD8WnAZmO4Nw/videos

Decoding the Disciplines and Threshold Concepts

www.youtube.com/watch?time_continue=3&v=Wqe_kKFoOq4

Electronic Mailing List

To join the Decoding the Disciplines electronic mailing list, please contact decodingthedisciplines1@gmail.com

Twitter

Follow us on Twitter @JoanMiddendorf

REFERENCES

Abbott, E. A. (2015). Characterizing objective observations in music therapy: A study of student practicum logs. *Music Therapy Perspectives, 35*(1), 71–78. doi:10.1093/mtp/miv037

Ambrose, S. A., Bridges, M. W., DiPietro, M., Lovett, M. C., & Norman, M. K. (2010). *How learning works: Seven research-based principles for smart teaching.* Hoboken, NJ: John Wiley & Sons.

Anderson, J. A. (1996, October). *Merging teaching effectiveness, learning outcomes, and curricular change with the diverse student needs of the 21st century.* Keynote talk presented at the 21st annual Conference of the Professional and Organizational Development Network, Salt Lake City, UT.

Anderson, P. (2013, July 29). *New research expands what we know about how to use writing to enhance student learning.* Retrieved from http://www.centerforengagedlearning.org/new-research-expands-what-we-know-about-how-to-use-writing-to-enhance-student-learning/

Andrade, H. G. (2005). Teaching with rubrics: The good, the bad, and the ugly. *College Teaching, 53*(1), 27–31.

Andrews, T. M., Leonard, M. J., Colgrove, C. A., & Kalinowski, S. T. (2011). Active learning not associated with student learning in a random sample of college biology courses. *CBE-Life Sciences Education, 10*(4), 394–405.

Angelo, T. A., & Cross, K. P. (1993). *Classroom assessment techniques: A handbook for college teachers.* San Francisco, CA: Jossey-Bass.

Ardizzone, T., Breithaupt, F., & Gutjahr, P. C. (2004). Decoding the humanities. *New Directions for Teaching and Learning, 2004*(98), 45–56.

Asai, R., Cook, A., Haynes, R. K., Kitzmiller, G., Linton, J., Sherwood-Laughlin, C., & Wang, R. (2013, April). *Mine the gap: Engaging differences across instructors and students.* Poster presented at Scholarship of Teaching and Learning Celebration, Indiana University, Bloomington.

Austin, D. E. (1994). Incorporating cognitive theory into environmental policymaking. *Environmental Professional, 16*, 262–274.

Bain, R. (2006). Rounding up unusual suspects: Facing the authority hidden in the history classroom. *Teachers College Record, 108*(10), 2080–2114.

Bao, L. (2006). Theoretical comparisons of average normalized gain calculations. *American Journal of Physics, 74*(10), 917–922.

Barbour, C., & Streb, M. (2014). *Clued in to politics: A critical thinking reader in American government* (4th ed.). Thousand Oaks, CA: Congressional Quarterly Press.

Barrett, R., Kirven, A., & Leach, J. (2015, January). *The perception of primary sources by college-level history students.* Paper presented at the American Historical Association Conference, New York, NY.

Barton, K. C., & Levstik, L. S. (2004). *Teaching history for the common good.* New York, NY: Routledge.

Bass, R., & Elmendorf, H. (2011). *Designing for difficulty: Social pedagogies as a framework for course design.* Teagle Foundation White Paper. New York, NY. Retrieved from https://blogs.commons.georgetown.edu/bassr/social-pedagogies/

Bean, J. C. (2011). *Engaging ideas: The professor's guide to integrating writing, critical thinking, and active learning in the classroom.* Hoboken, NJ: John Wiley & Sons.

Becher, T., & Trowler, P. R. (2001). *Academic tribes and territories.* London, England: Society for Research in Higher Education.

Bernstein, J. L. (2012). Signature pedagogies in political science. In N. L. Chick, A. Haynie, & R. A. R. Gurung (Eds.), *Exploring more signature pedagogies: Approaches to teaching disciplinary habits of mind* (pp. 85–96). Stirling, VA: Stylus.

Bernstein, J. L. (2013). Plowing through bottlenecks in political science: Experts and novices at work. In K. McKinney (Ed.), *The scholarship of teaching and learning in and across the disciplines* (pp. 74–92). Bloomington: Indiana University Press.

Black, P., & Wiliam, D. (1998). Assessment and classroom learning. *Assessment in Education, 5*(1), 7–74.

Blizard, M. (2014, January). *The scholarship of teaching and learning: Why should we engage?* Paper presented at the American Historical Association Conference, Washington, DC.

Bloom, B. S., & Krathwohl, D. R. (1984). *Taxonomy of educational objectives: The classification of educational goals: Handbook 1. Cognitive domain.* Boston, MA: Addison Wesley.

Boyer, E. L. (1997). *Scholarship reconsidered: Priorities of the professoriate.* San Francisco, CA: Jossey-Bass.

Brown, J. S., Collins, A., & Duguid, P. (1989). Situated cognition and the culture of learning. *Educational Researcher, 18*(1), 32–42.

Bruner, J. (1999). Folk pedagogies. In J. Leach & B. Moon (Eds.), *Learners and pedagogy* (pp. 4–20). London, England: Paul Chapman and the Open University.

Buchanan, K. (2015, July 22). What fitness bands can teach us about classroom assessment. *Faculty Focus.* Retrieved from http://www.facultyfocus.com/articles/educational-assessment/what-fitness-bands-can-teach-us-about-classroom-assessment/

Buckland, D. (2012, August 27). How physicians, engineers, and scientists approach problems differently. *Medgadget.* Retrieved from http://www.medgadget.com/2012/08/how-physicians-engineers-and-scientists-approach-problems-differently.html

Calder, L. (2006). Uncoverage: Toward a signature pedagogy for the history survey. *Journal of American History, 92*(4), 1358–1370.

Carter, M. (2007). Ways of knowing, doing, and writing in the disciplines. *College Composition and Communication, 58*(3), 385–418.

Chase, W. G., & Simon, H. A. (1973). Perception in chess. *Cognitive Psychology, 4*(1), 55–81.

Chi, M. T. (2005). Commonsense conceptions of emergent processes: Why some misconceptions are robust. *Journal of the Learning Sciences, 14*(2), 161–199.

Chi, M. T. (2008). Three types of conceptual change: Belief revision, mental model transformation, and categorical shift. In S. Vosniadou (Ed.), *International handbook of research on conceptual change* (pp. 61–82). New York, NY: Routledge.

Chi, M. T., Glaser, R., & Farr, M. J. (Eds.). (2014). *The nature of expertise.* New York, NY: Psychology Press.

Chi, M. T., Slotta, J. D., & De Leeuw, N. (1994). From things to processes: A theory of conceptual change for learning science concepts. *Learning and Instruction, 4*(1), 27–43.

Christodoulou, D. (2014). *Seven myths about education.* London & New York: Routledge.

Clayton, P. H., Hess, G., Hartman, E., Edwards, K. E., Shackford-Bradley, J., Harrison, B., & McLaughlin, K. (2014). Educating for democracy by walking the talk in experiential learning. *Journal of Applied Learning in Higher Education, 6,* 3–36.

Clegg, S. (2008, October). *The struggle for connections.* Keynote address presented at the International Scholarship of Teaching and Learning Conference in Edmonton, Canada. Retrieved from http://www.indiana.edu/~issotl/past_issotl/2008proceedings.html

Collins, A., & Ferguson, W. (1993). Epistemic forms and epistemic games: Structures and strategies to guide inquiry. *Educational Psychologist 28*(1), 25–42.

Condon, W., Iverson, E. R., Manduca, C. A., Rutz, C., & Willett, G. (2016). *Faculty development and student learning: Assessing the connections.* Bloomington: Indiana University Press.

Cook, C., & Kaplan, M. (2012). *Advancing the culture of teaching on campus: How a teaching center can make a difference.* Stirling, VA: Stylus.

Crisp, B. R. (2007). Is it worth the effort? How feedback influences students' subsequent submission of accessible work. *Assessment & Evaluation in Higher Education, 32*(5), 571–581.

Crowe, A., Dirks, C., & Wenderoth, M. P. (2008). Biology in bloom: Implementing Bloom's taxonomy to enhance student learning in biology. *CBE-Life Sciences Education, 7*(4), 368–381.

Crutchfield, T. N., & Klamon, K. (2014). Assessing the dimension and outcomes of an effective teammate. *Journal of Education for Business, 89*(6), 285–291.

Currie, G. (2017). Conscious connections: Phenomenology and decoding the disciplines. *New Directions for Teaching and Learning, 150,* 37–48.

Curry, M. (2008). Critical friends groups: The possibilities and limitations embedded in teacher professional communities aimed at instructional improvement and school reform. *Teachers College Record, 110*(4), 733–774.

Davies, P., & Mangan, J. (2007). Threshold concepts and the integration of understanding in economics. *Studies in Higher Education, 32*(6), 711–726.

De La Harpe, K., Terry, N., Novotny, S., & Novak, G. (2014, October). *The role of homework in a flipped classroom.* Paper presented at the International Scholarship of Teaching and Learning Conference, Quebec City, Quebec, Canada.

Díaz, A., Middendorf, J., Pace, D., & Shopkow, L. (2008). The History Learning Project: A department "decodes" its students. *Journal of American History, 94*(4), 1211–1224.

Dormant, D. (2011). *The chocolate model of change.* Raleigh, NC: Lulu.com.

Dragon, T., Arroyo, I., Woolf, B., Burleson, W., el Kaliouby, R., & Eydgahi, H. (2008). *Viewing student affect and learning through classroom observation and physical sensors.* Retrieved from http://centerforknowledgecommunication.com/publications/recentPubsandAwards/2008/DragonAffectITS08Final.pdf

Duffy, D. K., & Jones, J. W. (1995). *Teaching within the rhythms of the semester.* San Francisco, CA: Jossey-Bass.

Fernandez, C., & Yoshida, M. (2012). *Lesson study: A Japanese approach to improving mathematics teaching and learning.* New York, NY: Routledge.

Fisher, S. (2013, April). *Teaching evolution to nonmajors: Methods for increasing understanding and acceptance.* Paper presented at the 7th Annual Academy on Excellence in Teaching, Ohio State University, Columbus.

Freeman, S., Eddy, S. L., McDonough, M., Smith, M. K., Okoroafor, N., Jordt, H., & Wenderoth, M. P. (2014). Active learning increases student performance in science, engineering, and mathematics. *Proceedings of the National Academy of Sciences, 111*(23), 8410–8415.

French, E., & Westler, B. (2016). How to lose a class in ten days: The link between pedagogy and student retention. *Journal of Political Science Education.* Manuscript submitted for publication.

Gentner, D., Loewenstein, J., & Thompson, L. (2003). Learning and transfer: A general role for analogical encoding. *Journal of Educational Psychology, 95*(2), 393–408.

German, A., Middendorf, J., Pace, D., Erkan, A., Lee, E., Menzel, S., & Duncan, J. (2015, October). *Decoding in the STEM disciplines: From threshold concepts to bottlenecks.* Paper presented at the International Scholarship of Teaching and Learning Conference, Melbourne, Australia.

Gick, M. L., & Holyoak, K. J. (1983). Schema induction and analogical transfer. *Cognitive Psychology, 15*, 1–38.

Glaser, R., Chi, M. T., & Farr, M. J. (Eds.). (1988). *The nature of expertise.* Hillsdale, NJ: Lawrence Erlbaum Associates.

Gottlieb, E., & Wineburg, S. (2011). Between veritas and communitas: Epistemic switching in the reading of academic and sacred history. *Journal of the Learning Sciences, 21*(1), 84–129.

Graff, G., Birkenstein, C., & Durst, R. (2006). *They say, I say: The moves that matter in academic writing.* New York, NY: W. W. Norton.

Gurung, R. A., & Landrum, R. E. (2013). Bottleneck concepts in psychology: Exploratory first steps. *Psychology Learning & Teaching, 12*(3), 236–245.

Hake, R. R. (1998). Interactive-engagement versus traditional methods: A six-thousand-student survey of mechanics test data for introductory physics courses. *American Journal of Physics, 66*(1), 64–74.

Hattie, J., & Timperley, H. (2007). The power of feedback. *Review of Educational Research, 77*(1), 81–112.

Hengtgen, K., Leach, J., Szostało, M., & Kim, G. (2015, May). *Teaching with primary sources: University students' perspective on their high school experience.* Paper presented at Teaching History: Fostering Historical Thinking Across the K–16 Continuum, University of California, Berkeley.

Hines, S. (2015, September). *Motivate learning: Step four of the decoding model.* Workshop presented at Fall Faculty Conference, Twin Cities, MN.

History Learning Project Curriculum Overview. (2011). Retrieved from http://www.iub.edu/~hlp/curoverview.html

Hoellwarth, C., & Moelter, M. J. (2011). The implications of a robust curriculum in introductory mechanics. *American Journal of Physics, 79*(5), 540–545.

Hurtado, S., Eagan, K., Pryor, J. H., Whang, H., & Tran, S. (2012). *Undergraduate teaching faculty: The 2010–2011 HERI faculty survey* (Published Report). Los Angeles, CA: Higher Education Research Institute at UCLA.

Hutchings, P. (2000). Approaching the scholarship of teaching and learning. Introduction in P. Hutchings (Ed.), *Opening lines: Approaches to the scholarship of teaching and learning* (pp. 1–10). Menlo Park, CA: The Carnegie Foundation for the Advancement of Teaching. Retrieved from http://files.eric.ed.gov/fulltext/ED449157.pdf

Immordino-Yang, M. H. (2011). Implications of affective and social neuroscience for educational theory. *Educational Philosophy and Theory, 43*(1), 98–103.

Johnstone, A. H. (2009). You can't get there from here. *Journal of Chemical Education, 87*(1), 22–29.

Jones, N. A., Ross, H., Lynam, T., Perez, P., & Leitch, A. (2011). Mental models: An interdisciplinary synthesis of theory and methods. *Ecology and Society, 16*(1). doi:10.5751/es-03802-160146

Junisbai, B. (2014). The promise and potential pitfalls of a "learning-centered" approach to creative social inquiry: Lessons learned from an undergraduate seminar on authoritarianism through literature and film. *Journal of Political Science Education, 10*(3), 331–351.

Kotter, J. P. (1996). *Leading change.* Cambridge, MA: Harvard Business Press.

Kuh, G. D., Kinzie, J., Buckley, J. A., Bridges, B. K., & Hayek, J. C. (2006, July). *What matters to student success: A review of the literature.* Commissioned report for the National Symposium on Postsecondary Student Success: Spearheading a dialog on student success. National Post-Secondary Educational Cooperative. Retrieved from https://nces.ed.gov/npec/pdf/kuh_team_report.pdf

Kurz, L., Kearns, K., Middendorf, J., Metzler, E., & Rehrey, G. (2015, March). Program review. Workshops facilitated for the College of Arts and Sciences of Indiana University, Bloomington.

Lahm, S., & Kaduk, S. (2016). Essay on Decoding the Disciplines as a starting point for research-based teaching and learning. In H. A. Mieg & J. Lehmann (Eds.), *Forschendes Lernen: Ein Praxisbuch* [Undergraduate research: A practical guide]. Potsdam, Germany: FHP Verlag.

Lakoff, G., & Johnson, M. (2008). *Analogies we live by.* Chicago: University of Chicago Press.

Lave, J. W., & Wenger, E. E. (1991). *Situated learning: Legitimate peripheral participation.* Cambridge: Cambridge University Press.

Lovin, L., & Schultz, K. (2012). Illuminating mathematics teacher education through decoding disciplinary thinking: Unpacking mathematical knowledge for teaching. *Extending inquiry communities: Illuminating Teacher Education Through Self Study* (pp. 183–186).

MacDonald, R. (2017). Intuitions and instincts: Considerations for decoding disciplinary identities. *New Directions for Teaching and Learning, 150,* 63–74.

Martinez, S., & Díaz, A. (2015, November 14). Borderlands and Latino/a studies teaching symposium [Workshop]. Newberry Independent Research Library Seminar in Borderlands and Latino/a Studies, Chicago, IL.

Metzler, E., Rehrey, G., Kurz, E., & Middendorf, J. (2017). The aspirational curriculum map: A diagnostic model for action-oriented program review. In *To improve the Academy: Resources for faculty, instructional, and organizational development.* Manuscript submitted for publication.

Meyer, J., & Land, R. (Eds.). (2006). *Overcoming barriers to student understanding: Threshold concepts and troublesome knowledge.* London, England: Routledge.

Michaelsen, L. K., Knight, A. B., & Fink, L. D. (Eds.). (2004). *Team-based learning: A transformative use of small groups in college teaching.* Sterling, VA: Stylus Publishing.

Middendorf, J. (1999). Finding key faculty to influence change. *To Improve the Academy: Resources for Faculty, Instructional, and Organizational Development, 18,* 83–93.

Middendorf, J. (2001). Getting administrative support for your project. *To Improve the Academy: Resources for Faculty, Instructional, and Organizational Development, 19,* 346–359.

Middendorf, J. (2004). Facilitating a faculty learning community using the Decoding the Disciplines model. *To Improve the Academy: Resources for Faculty, Instructional, and Organizational Development, 98,* 95–107.

Middendorf, J., Mickutė, J., Saunders, T., Najar, J., Clark-Huckstep, A. E., & Pace, D. (2015). What's feeling got to do with it? Decoding emotional bottlenecks in the history classroom. *Arts and Humanities in Higher Education, 14*(2), 166–180.

Middendorf, J., & Pace, D. (2004). Decoding the disciplines: A model for helping students learn disciplinary ways of thinking. *New Directions for Teaching and Learning, 2004*(98), 1–12.

Middendorf, J., & Pace, D. (2007). Easing entry into the scholarship of teaching and learning through focused assessments: The "Decoding the Disciplines" approach. *To Improve the Academy: Resources for Faculty, Instructional, and Organizational Development, 26,* 53–67.

Middendorf, J., & Pace, D. (2009). *Freshman Learning Project review.* Unpublished manuscript, Campus Instructional Consulting, Indiana University, Bloomington.

Middendorf, J., Pace, D., Shopkow, L., & Díaz, A. (2007). Making thinking explicit: Decoding history teaching. *National Teaching and Learning Forum, 16*(2), 1–4.

Middendorf, J., Shopkow, L., & Pace, D. (2014, October). *Decoding disciplinary epistemologies.* Paper presented at the International Scholarship of Teaching and Learning Conference, Quebec City, Quebec, Canada.

Miller-Young, J., Dean, Y., Rathburn, M., Pettit, J., Underwood, M., Gleeson, J., . . . Clayton, P. (2015, Fall). Decoding ourselves: An inquiry into faculty learning about reciprocity in service learning. *Michigan Journal of Community Service Learning, 22*(1), 32–47.

Moura, I. C. (2012). Worked-out examples in a computer science module. *Proceedings of the World Congress on Engineering, 2,* 4–6.

Nathan, M. J., & Petrosino, A. (2003). Expert blind spot among preservice teachers. *American Educational Research Journal, 40*(4), 905–928.

Nilson, L. B. (2012). Time to raise questions about student ratings. *To Improve the Academy: Resources for Faculty, Instructional, and Organizational Development, 31,* 213–228.

Nilson, L. B. (2013). Measuring student learning to document teaching effectiveness. *To Improve the Academy: Resources for Faculty, Instructional, and Organizational Development, 32,* 287–300.

Norton, S. (2015, May). Sampling distribution as a threshold concept in learning classical statistical inference: An evaluative case study report. *Higher Education Research Network Journal, 10,* 58–71.

Novak, G. M. (2011). Just-in-time teaching. *New Directions for Teaching and Learning, 128,* 63–73.

Novak, G., Pace, D., & Novotny, S. (2010, October). *Just-in-time teaching and decoding the disciplines.* Paper presented at the International Scholarship of Teaching and Learning Conference, Liverpool, England.

Oblinger, D., & Hawkins, B. (2006). The myth about no significant difference: Using technology produces no significant difference. *Educause Review, 41*(6), 14–15.

Ohland, M. W., Loughry, M. L., Woehr, D. J., Bullard, L. G., Felder, R. M., Finelli, C. J., . . . Schmucker, D. G. (2012). The comprehensive assessment of team member effectiveness: Development of a behaviorally anchored rating scale for self- and peer evaluation. *Academy of Management Learning & Education, 11*(4), 609–630.

Osborn, A. F. (1963). *Applied imagination: Principles and procedures of creative problem-solving.* New York, NY: Scribner.

Paul, R. W., & Binker, A. J. A. (1990). *Critical thinking: What every person needs to survive in a rapidly changing world.* Rohnert Park, CA: Center for Critical Thinking and Moral Critique.

Perkins, D. (2007). Theories of difficulty. In N. Entwistle & P. Tomlinson (Eds.), *Student learning and university teaching* (pp. 31–48). Leicester, England: British Psychological Society.

Perkins, D. (2010). *Making learning whole: How seven principles of teaching can transform education.* Hoboken, NJ: John Wiley & Sons.

Perry, W. G. (1999). *Forms of ethical and intellectual development in the college years: A scheme.* San Francisco, CA: Jossey-Bass.

Pettit, J., Calvert, V., Dean, Y., Gleeson, J., Lexier, R., Rathburn, M., & Underwood, M. (2017). Building bridges from the decoding interview to teaching practice. *New Directions for Teaching and Learning, 150,* 75–86.

Pilgreen, J. (July 6, 2012). *Simplified Bloom's taxonomy visual.* Retrieved from: http://pilgreenenglish.blogspot.com/2015/05/blooms-inverted-taxonomy-on-my-me-and.html

Pinnow, E. (2016, March). Decoding the disciplines: An approach to scientific thinking. *Psychology Learning and Teaching, 15*(1), 94–101.

Quintanilla, V., Middendorf, J., & Kile, E. (2017, February). *The interplay of design thinking, legal education, and technology.* Presentation at the Indiana Journal of Law and Social Equality; The Center for Law, Society, and Culture; and The Milt and Judi Stewart Center on the Global Legal Profession Symposium, Maurer Law School, Indiana University, Bloomington.

Raab, T., & Frodeman, R. (2002). What is it like to be a geologist? A phenomenology of geology and its epistemological implications. *Philosophy & Geography, 5*(1), 69–81.

Redlawsk, D. P., Civettini, A. J. W., & Emmerson, K. M. (2010). The affective tipping point: Do motivated reasoners ever "get it"? *Political Psychology, 31*(4), 563–593.

Reynolds, J., Smith, R., Moskovitz, C., & Sayle, A. (2009). BioTAP: A systematic approach to teaching scientific writing and evaluating undergraduate theses. *Bioscience, 59*(10), 896–903.

Riegler, P. (2016). Fostering literacy in and via mathematics. *Zeitschrift für Hochschulentwicklung, 11*(2), 163–174. Retrieved from http://www.zfhe.at/index.php/zfhe/article/view/946/729

Riener, C., & Willingham, D. (2010). The myth of learning styles. *Change: The Magazine of Higher Learning, 42*(5), 32–35.

Rosch, E., & Lloyd, B. B. (Eds.). (1978). *Cognition and categorization* (Vol. 1). Hillsdale, NJ: Lawrence Erlbaum Associates.

Rogers, E. M. (2010). *Diffusion of innovations.* New York, NY: Simon & Schuster.

Rohrer, D., & Pashler, H. (2010). Recent research on human learning challenges conventional instructional strategies. *Educational Researcher, 39*(5), 406–412.

Ross, P. M., Taylor, C. E., Hughes, C., Whitaker, N., Lutze-Mann, L., Kofod, M., & Tzioumis, V. (2010). Threshold concepts in learning biology and evolution. *Biology International, 47*, 47–54.

Rouse, M., Phillips, J., Mehaffey, R., McGowan, S., & Felten, F. (2017). Decoding and disclosure in students-as-partners research: A case study of the political science literature review. *International Journal for Students as Partners, 1*(1), 1–14. Retrieved from https://mulpress.mcmaster.ca/ijsap/article/view/3061/2769

Sargeant, A., & Shang, J. (2016). Risk perception and management in development philanthropy. *Voluntary Sector Review, 7*(3), 251–267.

Savion, L., & Middendorf, J. (1994). Enhancing concept comprehension and retention. *National Teaching & Learning Forum, 3*(4), 6–8.

Scheinberg, C. (2003). Conversacolor: A metacognitive discussion tool. *National Teaching & Learning Forum, 12*(6), 1–3.

Schein, E. H. (1996). Kurt Lewin's change theory in the field and in the classroom: Notes toward a model of managed learning. *Systems Practice, 9*(1), 27–47.

Scott, E. (2004). The creation-evolution continuum: How to avoid classroom conflicts. *Skeptic, 10*(4), 50–55.

Scott, J. (2012). *Social network analysis.* Thousand Oaks, CA: Sage.

Shanton, K., & Goldman, A. (2010). Simulation theory. *Wiley Interdisciplinary Reviews: Cognitive Science, 1*(4), 527–538.

Shopkow, L. (2010). "What 'Decoding the Disciplines' has to offer 'Threshold Concepts.'" In J. H. F. Meyer, R. Land, & C. Baillie (Eds.), *Threshold concepts and transformational learning* (pp. 317–332). Rotterdam, The Netherlands: Sense Publications.

Shopkow, L. (2017). How many sources do I need? *History Teacher, 50*(2), 169–200.

Shopkow, L., & Díaz, A. (forthcoming). On thresholds, bottlenecks, and waystations. *Teaching and Learning Inquiry Journal.*

Shopkow, L., with Díaz, A., Middendorf, J., & Pace, D. (2013a). From bottlenecks to epistemology: Changing the conversation about the teaching of history in colleges and universities. In R. Thompson (Ed.), *Changing the conversation about higher education* (pp. 15–38). New York, NY: Rowman & Littlefield.

Shopkow, L., Díaz, A., Middendorf, J., & Pace, D. (2013b). The History Learning Project "decodes" a discipline: The union of teaching and epistemology. In K. McKinney (Ed.), *Scholarship of teaching and learning in and across the disciplines* (pp. 93–113). Bloomington: Indiana University Press.

Shopkow, L., Middendorf, J., Díaz, A., & Pace, D. (2012, October). *We have found the threshold and it is us: "Decoding" the disconnect between disciplinary thinking and teaching practice.* Paper presented at the International Scholarship of Teaching and Learning Conference, Ontario, Canada.

Shulman, L. S. (2005). Signature pedagogies in the professions. *Daedalus, 134*(3), 52–59.

Smith, G. (2017, February). *Moving beyond misconceptions: The influence of motivated reasoning on learning.* Invited talk at Indiana University in the Scholarship of Teaching and Learning Series, Bloomington.

Sorensen, A. E., Jordan, R. C., Shwom, R., Ebert-May, D., Isenhour, C., McCright, A. M., & Robinson, J. M. (2015). Model-based reasoning to foster environmental and socio-scientific literacy in higher education. *Journal of Environmental Studies and Sciences, 6*(2), 287–294.

Sterman, J. D. (1994). Learning in and about complex systems. *System Dynamics Review, 10*(2–3), 291–330.

Sturts, J. R., & Mowatt, R. A. (2012). Understanding and overcoming "bottlenecks" in student learning. *Schole: A Journal of Leisure Studies and Recreation Education, 27*(1), 39–45.

Sundberg, M. D., & Dini, M. L. (1993). Science majors vs nonmajors: Is there a difference? *Journal of College Science Teaching, 22*(5), 299–304.

Suskie, L. (2009). *Assessing student learning: A common sense guide.* New York, NY: John Wiley & Sons.

Thibodeau, P. H., Winneg, A., Frantz, C. M., & Flusberg, S. J. (2015). Systemic metaphors promote systems thinking. In *Proceedings of the 37th Annual Meeting of the Cognitive Science Society,* Pasadena, CA.

Thiede, K. W., Anderson, M., & Therriault, D. (2003). Accuracy of metacognitive monitoring affects learning of texts. *Journal of Educational Psychology, 95*(1), 66–73.

Timmermans, J. (2010). Changing our minds: The developmental potential of threshold concepts. In J. Meyer, R. Land, & C. Baillie (Eds.), *Threshold concepts and transformational learning* (pp. 3–20). Rotterdam, The Netherlands: Sense Publishers.

Ubuz, B., Eryilmaz, A., Aydin, U., Bayazit, I., Universitesi, E., & Kayseri, T. R. (2009, February). Pre-service teacher-generated analogies for function concepts. *CERME 6–Working Group, 10,* 1871–1879. Retrieved from http://fractus.uson.mx/Papers/CERME6/wg10.pdf#page=187

Vygotsky, L. S. (1978). *Mind in society: The development of higher psychological processes* (Rev. ed.). Cambridge, MA: Harvard University Press.

Wallis, D. (2012, November 8). Getting into a benefactor's head. *New York Times.* Retrieved from http://www.nytimes.com/2012/11/09/giving/understanding-donor-behavior-to-increase-contributions.html?mcubz=1

Walvoord, B. E., & Anderson, V. J. (2011). *Effective grading: A tool for learning and assessment in college.* New York, NY: John Wiley & Sons.

Weimer, M. (2012, March 5). Getting students to act on our feedback. *Faculty Focus.* Retrieved from http://www.facultyfocus.com/articles/teaching-professor-blog/getting-students-to-act-on-our-feedback/

Weimer, M. (2015, February 4). Group work: What do students want from their teammates? *Faculty Focus.* Retrieved from http://www.facultyfocus.com/articles/teaching-professor-blog/group-work-students-want-teammates/

Weiss, R. A. (1971). *Protein synthesis: An epic on the cellular level* [Video]. Stanford University. Retrieved from https://www.youtube.com/watch?v=u9dhO0iCLww

Wentworth, M. (2009, July). *Continuum dialogue.* Retrieved from http://schoolreforminitiative.org/doc/continuum_dialogue.pdf

Wiggins, G. P., & McTighe, J. (2005). *Understanding by design.* Alexandria, VA: Association for Supervision and Curriculum Development.

Wood, G. (2014, April 14). The future of college. *Atlantic.* Retrieved from http://www.theatlantic.com/features/archive/2014/08/the-future-of-college/375071/

Wood, D., Bruner, J. S., & Ross, G. (1976). The role of tutoring in problem solving. *Journal of Child Psychology and Psychiatry, 17*(2), 89–100.

Yeo, M., Lafave, M., Westbrook, K., McAllister, J., Valdez, D., & Eubank, B. (2017). Impact of Decoding work within a professional program. *New Directions for Teaching and Learning, 150,* 87–96.

Zhou, G. (2012). A cultural perspective of conceptual change: Re-examining the goal of science education. *McGill Journal of Education/Revue des sciences de l'éducation de McGill, 47*(1), 109–129.

Zimmerman, B. J. (2000). Attaining self-regulation: A social cognitive perspective. In M. Boekarts, P. R. Pintrich, & M. Zeidner (Eds.), *Handbook of self-regulation* (pp. 13–39). San Diego, CA: Academic Press.

Zolan, M., Strome, S., & Innes, R. (2004). Decoding genetics and molecular biology: Sharing the movies in our heads. *New Directions for Teaching and Learning, 98,* 23–32.

INDEX OF DISCIPLINARY EXAMPLES

This index contains more extensive examples, whether they appear in text boxes or in the text itself. For every reference to a particular discipline, see the main index.

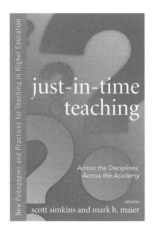

Just in Time Teaching

Across the Disciplines, and Across the Academy

Edited by Scott Simkins and Mark Maier

Foreword by James Rhem

"*Just in Time Teaching* commendably promotes the pedagogical procedure that bears its name. The book is an excellent resource for professors who are serious pursuers of improving students' learning. . . . The text is adeptly compiled and skillfully written."

—*Teaching Theology and Religion*

Just-in-Time Teaching (JiTT) is a pedagogical approach that requires students to answer questions related to an upcoming class a few hours beforehand by using an online course management system. While the phrase "just in time" may evoke shades of slap-dash work and cut corners, JiTT pedagogy is just the opposite. It helps students to view learning as a process that takes time, introspection, and persistence.

Sty/us

22883 Quicksilver Drive
Sterling, VA 20166-2102

Subscribe to our e-mail alerts: www.Styluspub.com

Also available from Stylus

Flipped Learning
A Guide for Higher Education Faculty
Robert Talbert

Foreword by Jon Bergmann

"Think you know what flipped learning is? Think again. I had to. It's not about technology, recording your lectures, or physical classrooms. This is why you have to read Robert Talbert's *Flipped Learning*. It's the definitive book on the pedagogy, with a new and refreshing perspective. Talbert relates flipped learning to theories of motivation, cognitive load, and self-regulated learning and gives step-by-step directions for flipping your course, along with plenty of examples, answers to typical questions, and variations for hybrid and online courses."—*Linda B. Nilson, Director Emeritus, Office of Teaching Effectiveness and Innovation , Clemson University*

"Robert Talbert's *Flipped Learning* challenges us to think about this approach as much more than just putting videos online, diving into the real story of how and why flipping works. The models, examples, and detailed explanations presented in this book will inspire faculty to try flipping if they haven't already and for those who have, will show them how to make the approach work even better."—*Michelle Miller, Director, First Year Learning Initiative and Professor, Department of Psychological Sciences, Northern Arizona University*

Getting Started With Team-Based Learning
Jim Sibley and Pete Ostafichuk
With Bill Roberson, Billie Franchini, and Karla Kubitz

Foreword by Larry K. Michaelsen

"The book does a terrific job of covering all the basics, but it also does much more. On almost every page, it sprinkles in amazingly helpful tidbits. The icing on the cake are the quotes and vignettes that make the ideas come to life. In every chapter, I found a number of ideas that I will be using to improve my own teaching—and so will you."

—*Larry K. Michaelsen*

Team-Based Learning (TBL) is a uniquely powerful form of small-group learning. It harnesses the power of teams and social learning with accountability structures and instructional sequences. This book provides the guidance, from first principles to examples of practice, together with concrete advice, suggestions, and tips to help you succeed in the TBL classroom. This book will help you understand what TBL is and why it is so powerful. You will find what you need to plan, build, implement, and use TBL effectively. This book will appeal to both the novice and the expert TBL teacher.

(Continued on preceding page)